LEGACY, VISION, AND IMPACT

We all need compelling reasons to invest our time and money in a book or in an organization. The author of *Four Percent*, Michael Malone, presents the amazing legacy of over 100 years of Eagle Scouts by bringing individual Eagle Scouts to life on every page. From the early days of Scouting when the design of the Eagle badge had to be created in a hurry after the first Eagle Scout rank was earned, to the impact the Knights of Dunamis organization had on generations of Eagle Scouts, to the vision that is being carried forward by the National Eagle Scout Association (NESA) are all interwoven on the pages of this book.

The vision of NESA goes well beyond the role of steward of all things Eagle Scout. We are focused on supporting Boy Scout Councils, where the important work of helping Scouting units be successful and grow, takes place. To accomplish this objective we have created new and exciting adventures for Eagle Scouts-Argonauts traveling the planet with Dr. Bob Ballard the discoverer of the *Titanic;* astronomers attending the firing of the largest telescope mirrors ever created by human kind; Eagle Scout adventurers of all persuasions are finding opportunities to be exceptional in the legacy of great Eagle Scout explorers of previous generations like Neil Armstrong, the first man to walk on the moon, and Dr. Paul Siple, who as a young Eagle Scout of 21, explored Antarctica with Admiral Richard E. Byrd in 1928 and went on to invent the term "wind chill factor" after a life-long career of exploring places where no humans had gone before.

NESA is very proud of its accomplishments through its forty plus years of existence, but especially over the past few years. It's reached a much higher level of service and benefit to its constituency, the highest achievers of the BSA program, Eagle Scouts.

Some examples of recent successful projects include the first nationwide searches ever completed of where Eagle Scouts are now. Conducted in 2008 and again in 2010, well over half of the over 2 million Eagle Scouts since the first one in 1912 have been located and are being welcomed back.

And college scholarships: NESA awards over 200 college scholarships annually valued at nearly $600,000, an increase of almost 300% in six years. The largest of these scholarships is the NESA STEM Scholarship, a $50,000 scholarship awarded annually to an Eagle Scout who plans to study and have a career in a STEM subject within science, technology, engineering, or math.

A requirement for earning the Eagle Scout rank is to plan and give leadership to a project benefitting the community. NESA has established the Glenn A. and Melinda W. Adams National Eagle Scout Service Project of the Year Award to recognize the most outstanding Eagle Scout projects at the council, regional, and national levels. The national-level winner is considered to be the best Eagle Scout project in the USA out of over 50,000 annually.

Nearly everyone believes that being an Eagle Scout means something. It makes a big difference in a person's life. But has it ever been studied by academics? In the results from the 2010 Baylor University study titled, *Eagle Scouts: Merit Beyond the Badge,* conducted by the university's Program for Pro-Social Behavior, the researchers found statistically significant differences between Eagle Scouts, and men that were never in Scouting. Eagle Scouts:

- Establish greater lifelong connections to family, friends, and neighbors
- Exhibit a higher sense of responsibility to give back through volunteering and donating
- Gain a greater connection and concern for their community
- Exercise more self-discipline to plan ahead and set and achieve goals
- Hold higher self-expectations
- Demonstrate greater appreciation and concern for the environment
- Display increased respect for religion and religious diversity
- Enjoy an increased variety of hobbies and interests
- Develop greater commitment to lifelong learning

Now we know for sure.

Yours in Scouting,

Glenn A. Adams
NESA President

C. William Steele
NESA Director

THE STORY OF UNCOMMON YOUTH
IN A CENTURY OF AMERICAN LIFE

FOUR
PERCENT

MICHAEL S. MALONE

WindRush
PUBLISHERS

Published by WindRush Publishers.

First Edition 2012

WindRush
PUBLISHERS
WindRush Publishers
PO Box 670324
Dallas, Texas 75367

Book design and layout by Publications Development Co.
Cover design by LandMarc Design www.landmarcdesign.com
Cover image copyright John K. Shipes 2012

www.4percentbook.com

ISBN-13: 978-0-9859097-1-0

10 9 8 7 6 5

To those who wear the Eagle medal—
and to all who helped them earn it.

THE STORY OF UNCOMMON YOUTH
IN A CENTURY OF AMERICAN LIFE

FOUR
PERCENT

Being an Eagle, and having now mentored nearly fifty Scouts on their Trail to Eagle, I can say with certainty that no boy ever gets to Eagle easily. Most Scouts, of course, don't make it at all – and of those who do, some stall at the lower ranks, others in merit badges, and nearly all with the service project. And even if you do get through the long, arduous process quickly and earn your Eagle young (as I did), you will still find yourself learning about what it means to be an Eagle for many years to come.

And along the way, both before and after you earn your Eagle, there will be scores, even hundreds, of people who will help you along the way – some for hours and some for decades, and you will never be able to thank them all for what they did for you. But, thanks to this book, I'm at least getting this chance to try.

It always begins with your parents. My father had a terrible, Depression-era childhood. Boy (and Sea) Scouting gave him just about the only structure in his life. He was also one of those '30s Scouts who never got his Eagle because of the Bird Study merit badge. When I joined Scouting in 1965, he rejoined as well, becoming Assistant Scoutmaster and mentor the troop's future Eagles – exactly the leadership path that I have followed. Meanwhile, my mother sewed my patches and washed my filthy clothes after my camping trips – often getting poison oak in the process.

Scouting is also about your fellow Scouts. You learn something important from each of them; from the boy who stays in the troop for a few weeks; to the ones you know the rest of your life. My fellow Troop 480 Eagles, as you might expect, have all gone on to successful careers and Impressive lives – and they stand in perpetual reminder to me of what it means to be an Eagle.

Then there are the Scoutmasters. I had four as a Boy Scout – Mr. Thompson, Mr. Habermeyer, Mr. Rinfret and Mr. Henderson. Each showed me what it means to be a man, to be a leader, and to be a teacher. Each took on the enormous responsibility and time commitment of being a Scoutmaster – and though each approached it differently, each did the role great honor.

The second phase of being an Eagle begins when you leave Boy Scouting and continues until you die. I am now well along that path. And over the years I have met thousands of my fellow Eagles, usually serendipitously – and they too have all taught me about what it means to be an Eagle. The fact that these lessons have been almost universally positive is yet more evidence that America's Eagles are an extraordinary group and a national treasure. And it was that realization that both impelled me to write this book and to pull no punches on the story. I believe Eagle Scouting can withstand any level of scrutiny.

Finally, more than a decade ago, and like many middle-aged Eagles, I returned to Scouting when my oldest son turned 11. He earned his Eagle – and far more impressively than I did – and is now being followed along that path by his younger brother, 16 years old as I write this, who is about to embark on his own Eagle service project. My wife has been involved with their Scouting careers from their very first troop meeting – these days she sits on the Eagle Board of Review, an experience that, she says, gives her hope for the future.

We joined Troop 466 in Sunnyvale, California because of remarkable figure, Norm Ehmann, who had served as the troop's Scoutmaster for more than 30 years (I had even earned a merit badge from him as a teenager). Ehmann called our troop "the Eagle Makers", and 200 Eagles later we continue to live up to that name. And along the way, I have been honored to serve a number of terrific Scoutmasters: John Rugo, Chris Early and Dave Holt. Seeing them close-up I am only more in awe of what it takes to be a Scoutmaster. They are remarkable men, indeed.

As assistant Scoutmaster in charge of the troop's older Scouts, I've had the honor of mentoring almost 50 new Eagles. Each one is different, and each is a kind of miracle. And each is also a chance – one largely lost on your younger, dazed self – to experience with a clear eye what it is like to take the Trail to Eagle. What I've learned, all of the myths aside, is that this generation of Eagles may be the most impressive of all. I am honored, and more than a little intimidated to serve them. And I have been inspired by their parents to try to be a better parent myself.

There were a number of individuals who helped with the production of this book, most notably David Scott, a fellow Eagle. Given all of the vicissitudes of the last two years within Scouting and without, he has shown tremendous courage in taking on the project. I would also like to thank BSA counsel Richard Mathews for convincing me of the need to publish this book. Rich Goldman, Silicon Valley Executive, Eagle Scout and fellow Scout parent, did superhuman work to connect me with Dr. Neil Armstrong to assure the accuracy of his biography. And Jason Stein, Ron Schoenmehl and Jake Carlson of the Santa Clara County Council (on whose board I serve), John Richers of the Fresno Council and Matt Myers of the National Office, remind me every day of the great calling of being a professional Scouter.

Finally, to all of America's Eagle Scouts, past and present, I hope that this book captures at least a part of the story of Eagle Scouting's first century – and does so in a way that honors your medal. I'm humbled to be counted among your ranks.

Michael S. Malone
ASM, Troop 466
Sunnyvale, California

CONTENTS

CHAPTER ONE

THE PhD
of BOYHOOD

*It is a ceremony that takes place
more than 50,000 times each year.*

SOME OF THEM ARE AS SIMPLE AS A MEDAL pinned on the pocket of a young man's uniform, followed by a firm handshake; others are as elaborate as a stage show and feature VIP guests. But most are comparatively intimate: a few dozen people including close and distant relations, a grandparent or two, schoolmates, a group of other Boy Scouts in uniform, often a religious leader or favorite teacher and, despite the stereotype of the awkward Scout, usually a girlfriend sitting with the recipient's family. In the past, the ceremony typically took place at a school or public building . . . but, thanks to the cultural debates of the last half-century, it now almost always takes place at a church, temple, or mosque.

But for all of the variations in style, the substance of the Eagle Scout Court of Honor is almost always the same. There is an opening invocation, a welcome, a flag ceremony, and the recitation of the core texts of Scouting—the Scout Oath and Law—often with some form of candle lighting ceremony. The Eagle usually stands at center stage, joined by his parents, flanked by an

"Eagle Court" of other, older Eagles—often quite elderly—who announce the date and location of their own Courts of Honor.

At some point, many of these ceremonies step away from the formalities. The lights dim, and a movie or slide show runs that presents the Scout's "Trail to Eagle," beginning with baby photos, but mostly focusing on the boy's Scouting career. Given that the honoree is usually 16 or 17 years old, and may have joined Scouting as a seven-year-old Tiger Cub, that trail is pretty long for such a short life. Indeed, there may not be much of the young man's life that he can remember when he *wasn't* a Scout.

The images are usually pretty standard and predictable: baby pictures to elicit oohs from the audience, first day of school, family vacations, a class pageant, perhaps a first communion or bar mitzvah, and then a run of Scouting photos. If the honoree was a Cub Scout, there are the inevitable Pinewood Derby and Webelos bridging ceremony (the transition to Boy Scouts) images.

The 11-year-old Tenderfoot Scout who appears in the next few images—frightened, excited, and overwhelmed by the new world in which he finds himself—seems impossibly small in light of the full-grown young man who now sits confidently in the front row.

The next few images are of the Scout's career: troop campouts, district-wide camporees, 50-mile hikes, summer camp, and perhaps even a jamboree. Through it all, the Scout continues to grow—not only physically, but through taking on ever-greater responsibilities—and, as he advances through the ranks and earns more than a score of merit badges, one of them perhaps giving him the first glimpse of an adult career, his competence increases as well.

But the veteran viewer knows to look for something else. It is the moment when the Scout—whether he is 15 or just short of his 18th birthday—makes the decision to pursue his Eagle community service project; not just to formulate the idea of the project—but to *accept* it as his own. At that moment, he takes full responsibility for the biggest project of his young life; and, in relation to his skills, perhaps in his whole life. He will have to learn time management to organize the project; create a list of materials, and either purchase them or solicit businesses for donations; manage a small army of fellow Scouts, classmates, and friends; deal with adults in positions of power; and most of all, complete the project on time to the satisfaction of the nonprofit organization that is its recipient.

In doing so, the prospective Eagle will be making his own contribution to the largest youth service program in American history. In the last 50 years, since the service project has taken its place as the signature requirement of the Eagle rank, it is estimated that these projects have contributed as much as 100 *million* hours of targeted service, changing the face of America in the process.[1]

Challenging as the project will be—and *all* Eagle projects are challenging, whether they involve painting benches at a local school or devoting thousands of hours to an international initiative that wins the Adams award for best Eagle project of the year—the single most difficult moment comes with the acceptance of that responsibility. There is no going back, and with that understanding comes the beginning of maturity.

That decisive moment is never captured on film—but its consequences are there to see for anyone who knows to look. The goofy teenager of a few images before metamorphoses into the grave and serious young adult leading his team through the project. You don't so much earn the Eagle rank as you *become* an Eagle—a fact only the Eagles in the audience, and the Scout's parents, fully appreciate. And in becoming an Eagle, you are changed forever.

When the lights go back up, and the Scout takes the stage, it is this transformed young man who accepts the Eagle medal from his mother and the patch from his father. Because many Scouts take right up until the last moment to earn their Eagle before the official cutoff of their 18th birthday—and thus, their Court of Honor is held after they "age out," sometimes just days before they leave for college—the odds are about even that the honoree will never actually wear his Eagle patch.

But he will wear his Eagle medal again; perhaps soon, as a member of a fellow Scout's Eagle Court just a few weeks hence, or 40 years distant, at his own son's Eagle ceremony. As he has been reminded throughout the ceremony—and will continue to be reminded in the years ahead—"once an Eagle, always an Eagle." You were a Boy Scout, but you are, and will always be, an Eagle Scout.

It is a message that will continue to resonate in the decades ahead, long after the new Eagle's memories of details about his Scouting career, even of this ceremony, begin to fade. And its impact starts now, as the new Eagle steps up to the podium to thank all the people who helped him reach this moment. The young man who now speaks with such assurance and command is the transformed boy of those last few images on the Trail to Eagle. For good reason, the Eagle award has been called the "PhD of Boyhood"; and this is a graduation ceremony in which recipient—with a hard-earned new perspective on life and achievement—gives his own final address.

Then, after *Taps* or some other official adjournment of the Court of Honor, it is time for cake and punch, handshakes, and a visit to the table that holds the congratulatory letters from national figures and the display of all the honoree's other awards. Soon, the younger Scouts will fold the flags and chairs and the ladies will pack up and hand out the remaining food. And the honoree, as he prepares to leave with his family and friends, will put the patch in his pocket, and the medal in its box. He has already begun to experience what it is like to be an Eagle Scout. He will spend the rest of his life learning the rest.

ANTECEDENTS

Founded in 1910, the Boy Scouts of America (BSA) is the largest, and most enduring, training and development organization for young men in the United States.

Created during the Progressive Era, it was born largely out of the perception that, with the end of the frontier and the rise of industrial cities, something profound in the American character was being lost, especially among youth. The Scouting movement itself was founded in the United Kingdom in 1907 by a retired Lt. General, Lord Robert Baden-Powell, who feared the same forces at work on British life.

Casting about for an operating philosophy for his nascent movement, Baden-Powell settled on a hybrid between his own experiences working with young messengers (Scouts) during the Siege of Mafeking in the Boer War, and the work being done in the United States—the Woodcraft Indians—by naturalist and author Ernest Thompson Seton.

Thus, even though Scouting began as a British institution, its philosophical roots were equally American. And that may be the reason, when Scouting was brought to the States in 1909 by Chicago publisher and promoter W.D. Boyce after his fateful (and perhaps apocryphal) encounter with the helpful "unknown Scout" in the London fog—the BSA's founding myth—it met with an immediate and strong response from American boys. Indeed, numerous independent Scouting organizations had spontaneously sprung up throughout the country—creating something of an identity crisis for the U.S. movement in its first decade until the BSA emerged as the dominant organization.

Two additional factors were crucial to the triumph of the BSA. The first was the incorporation of a second, older, domestic boys' outdoor group—the Sons of Daniel Boone—created by Dan Beard, who would go on to become the most famous of all Scout leaders. Beard brought a patriotic (jingoistic, some complained) attitude to Scouting that not only nicely balanced Seton's pacifism and anti-Americanism, but also distinguished BSA from the international Scouting movement as a uniquely American institution.

The second factor was the appointment, in early 1911, of businessman James E. West as the first chief Scout executive. West, a comparatively bloodless bureaucrat, brilliantly navigated between these various passionate and self-promoting advocates, all while placing the BSA on a stable financial footing, backed by both the nation's leading industrialists and the United States Congress. The Boy Scouts of America was on its way.

In the century since the organization's founding, more than 110 million American boys (and girls as well, beginning in 1969 with the Exploring— now Venturing and Learning for Life—programs) have passed through Scouting. There are 2.6 million Scouts today, with another 1 million adults in 125,000 packs, troops, and crews.[2]

The impact of these tens of millions of Scouts over the last century on American life and culture is all but immeasurable. Scouts served on the home front in both World Wars, selling millions of dollars in war bonds and assisting in war rationing programs. Scouts have also devoted millions of hours to the preservation of the nation's national parks, to collecting food for the indigent, and assisting in disaster relief. Former Scouts can be found in the top leadership positions in American industry, government, academics, the military, and nonprofit institutions.

So deep and profound has been the impact of Scouting on American life in the twentieth, and now in the twenty-first, century that it is hard to imagine the United States without Boy Scouts. The image of the Boy Scout—especially as rendered by a half-century of Norman Rockwell paintings—has become as much an American icon as Uncle Sam. And, like most icons, it has also been a ripe target for cartoonists, satirists, and social activists. The earnest young man in puttees and campaign hat (or later, the baggy uniform and baseball cap) quickly became a symbol not only of resourcefulness and integrity, but also of wide-eyed innocence and tiresome earnestness. The noble Scout heroically saving a life through skill and resourcefulness has long lived alongside the wide-eyed and ardent Scout dragging an unwilling old lady across the street as his daily "good deed." And thus, even before it was a half-century old, to be a "real Boy Scout" had entered the language as both a compliment and a pejorative.

ALWAYS AN EAGLE

But there is one part of Scouting that has always stood apart from the rest, largely immune from the various cultural winds that have swept back and forth across the rest of the organization—Eagle Scouts.

If, in everyday parlance, "Boy Scout" is, for good or bad, a description, then "Eagle Scout" is almost always an explanation. "Well, he's an Eagle Scout" has become shorthand for an entire body of skills that has enabled a man, young or old, to accomplish something—build a fire, lash down a roof load, splint a broken arm, organize and lead a group—that surprises his peers.

Even in the tumultuous years of social upheaval in the late 1960s when every American institution, not least the Boy Scouts, was under assault, Eagle Scouts were somehow immune. Scouts, with their gaudy patriotism and uniforms, might have been decried as a paramilitary organization—but

Eagles, after all, were college professors and forest rangers, scientists and social workers.

They were also (ironically, because of their roots in Scouting) seen as the nation's premiere environmentalists. When the hippies went back to the land at the end of the decade, many, as with generations of reconstructed naturalists before them, depended on people who knew how to build and cook on fires, lash together wooden structures, and provide first aid for injuries. Eagle Scouts, some with ponytails and tie-dyed shirts led the way— and it was with good reason that the *Whole Earth Catalog* listed the *Boy Scout Handbook* as its outdoor guide.

Forty years later, at the height of the national debate over the refusal of Scouting to accept homosexuals in adult leadership roles, when municipalities were throwing Scout troops out of public facilities those same Scouts had built decades before, Americans momentarily paused to honor the passing of the nation's only Eagle-president, Gerald Ford. Not only did the encomiums from both sides of the political divide mention Ford's Eagle Scout award, but they also noted its central role in his life and in the creation of his character. And when the Ford family asked 200 young Eagles in the region to serve as the honor guard to the former president's casket, not only did no one object, it was praised as being perfectly appropriate.

Every Eagle Scout during the course of his life experiences this exceptionalism. Colleges and universities, to one degree or another, are known to give the Eagle applicant the advantage over an equal contender— largely (and probably accurately) based on the perception that, with the service project, the Eagle has already shown the discipline to successfully manage a complex project and see it through. Join the military as an enlisted man, and the Eagle rank usually confers an instant rank advancement and a leadership position.

College Eagles quickly discover, once the word gets out, that they are expected to take over every time a barbecue or bonfire needs to be built, whenever anyone in the dorm is injured, or when a team needs to be formed and led.

Adult Eagles come to appreciate the full implications of the phrase "always an Eagle." It is the only childhood award that appears on your resume—and will likely be included in your obituary. You become accustomed to the flicker of respect in the eyes of others when they learn you are an Eagle—suggesting as it does unseen skills and strength of character; and the quick affirmation from others you heretofore never suspected of being in the brotherhood.

It also means a lifetime of assumed responsibility and the perpetual risk of failure and humiliation. When the luggage needs to be lashed to the car roof, the wood chopped, the accident victim's bleeding stopped, or when the group is lost in the woods, everyone looks to the Eagle Scout to fix the problem, tend the wound, or save them. Any failure is not just your own, but of Eagle Scouting itself. They don't mention this at your Eagle Scout Court of Honor.

Not surprisingly, given what it once took to earn the award, most Eagles step up to this added responsibility. Eagles are disproportionately represented in the high-responsibility professions of modern American life, including the military, universities, politics, and senior management at Fortune 500 companies, law, and medicine. A midshipman or cadet at one of the service academies, or a White House Fellow candidate, will find him- or herself surrounded by Eagles.

Hollywood, while it may not employ many Eagles, hasn't hesitated over the last century to use the Eagle rank as quick shorthand to confer added ability or integrity to its characters. It's not surprising, then, that Steven Spielberg put the badge of the penultimate Scouting rank (Life) on the most iconic modern cinematic hero, Indiana Jones, in *The Last Crusade*, implicitly suggesting that the adult Indy is an Eagle—just like Spielberg himself.

Real heroes, especially when their achievements are a matter of daring, often turn out to be Eagles as well. No one was surprised to learn that Neil Armstrong was an Eagle Scout, along with least a dozen other astronauts. Nor were they surprised to learn that aerial adventurer Steve Fossett considered earning his Eagle equal to all his round-the-world balloon and small plane records, or that six of the nation's Medal of Honor recipients were Eagles.

By the same token, Eagles, young and old, are also disproportionately represented in the relief efforts of every major U.S. disaster. If they aren't leading the Scout troops that are providing assistance, then they are leading the nonprofit organizations that are managing the relief, are officers in the National Guard or Army units providing help and order on the scene, are covering the event for the national media, or advising the president of the United States as he flies over the destruction.

It can truly be said that in good times and bad, more than any other discernible category of citizens, Eagle Scouts lead America. And, consciously or not, their fellow citizens recognize that fact and honor it.

PATTERN IN THE FABRIC

To merely list the extraordinary achievements of a century of Eagle Scouts is to at least partially confuse cause and effect. It only proves the obvious fact that young people of achievement gravitate toward the opportunity for achievement.

What hasn't yet been explained is why this particular award has come to assume a place so honored in American life that it alone, of all childhood achievements, follows its recipients throughout their lives; why it remains important as a résumé highlight decades after the honoree has aged out of the program; why newspapers still devote precious editorial space to coverage of Eagle service projects and Courts of Honor; and why at a man's funeral, three score or more years after he earned the award, his eulogy will likely include the fact that he was an Eagle Scout.

SUPREMACY

The Eagle Scout award is, of course, the highest rank in Boy Scouting. Everything beyond (bronze, gold, and silver palms for earning additional groups of merit badges; the Distinguished Eagle Scout Award for life achievements as an adult Eagle) is merely gilding on the award itself. But Scouting has other supreme awards: the Silver Award in Venturing, the Quartermaster Award in Sea Scouts, the Hornaday Medal for Conservation, the Honor Medal for saving a life . . . but none have caught the public's imagination in the same way. The Gold Award in Girl Scouting is at least the equivalent of the Eagle (and some say it is even harder to earn), but few outside of the Girl Scouts of America (GSA) have ever heard of it. The Little League, American Youth Soccer Organization (AYSO), and other youth sport organizations have their MVPs and All-Stars, but those honors are all but forgotten by the time the next season begins.

Only the Eagle stands apart. Young Scouts are constantly reminded of the sheer rarity of its achievement. They are told that in the history of Scouting, only 2 percent of all Scouts have ever earned their Eagle. And though that ratio today may be two or three times that, it remains reserved for only a tiny fraction of the millions of boys who join Scouting. And for that little 11-year-old, looking ahead at the prospect of seven ranks, 21 merit badges, and hundreds of requirements, that Trail to Eagle can look very, very long. Six or seven years later, as that same boy stands on stage, having completed that climb, the notion of having reached a pinnacle of childhood is no longer an alien concept.

VENERABILITY

Not only is the Eagle medal the most famous award in American childhood, it is also the oldest. As has often been noted, childhood as we know it was a Victorian invention, the product of reduced infant mortality, greater leisure time, and the need to spend more years educating young people and preparing them for the complexities of an industrial world.

But the increasingly attenuated childhoods that resulted provoked their own backlash toward a greater structure and a more empirical approach to self-improvement, skill development, and good citizenship in children's upbringing. The first such institution dedicated to keeping the young from going astray was the Young Men's Christian Association (YMCA), brought to the United States in 1851. Its primary focus was on saving young men's souls.

The turn of the twentieth century saw numerous movements arise through the industrialized world, all designed to both avert the perceived impending catastrophe from a generation of "soft" young people (a widespread belief that disappeared overnight in August 1914 as World War I began), as well as to apply to youth the same empirical "scientific" principles then in vogue everywhere from factories (Taylorism) to sociology (Social Darwinism) to population management (eugenics). Fredrick Jackson Turner's famous 1893 paper "The Significance of the Frontier in American History" on the closing of the American frontier had stunned intellectuals, politicians, and industrialists. America, they realized, was changing rapidly—and the new century would be very different from the last. Were America's young people, the leaders of this new century, prepared for this emerging new world? Were their characters strong enough? Did they have the requisite skills to make it America's century?

The answer, many concluded, was that America's youth needed a new kind of training; that had one foot in the traditional values that had built the country—skill in the outdoors, resourcefulness, leadership, and independence—and the other in the new world of the industrial nation-state—patriotism, organizational management, skill with technology, and community service. Just how all of these components were to be mixed and matched was the subject of considerable dispute.

Scouting, as much through the clash of competing visions as conscious design, stumbled on the right mix for the American zeitgeist of the early years of the twentieth century—and it became as synonymous to that era as President Theodore Roosevelt. The result was explosive growth—there were already 182,303 Boy Scouts by 1915, and that number climbed to 541,000 by 1925.[3]

With the support of the nation's leaders, Scouting also became quickly embedded into the fabric of American life. It was Scouting that was enlisted to help with the war effort on the home front. Congress formally chartered the BSA in 1916, giving it special rights and privileges unavailable to other youth organizations for many years (such as the right to retire flags and to serve as the honor guard at inaugurations, national funerals, party conventions, and so on). And, during the depths of the Great Depression, Franklin Roosevelt—who had been a major supporter of Scouting since 1915 when he was a young assistant secretary of the navy—turned to Scouting as a way to bolster the spirit of American youth, ultimately playing a key role in the creation and production of the first BSA national jamboree in 1937.

As the "best" of Scouting, Eagle Scouts were at the heart of all these events. Indeed, in one of the most noted events of that first jamboree, FDR awarded the Eagle medal to one Scout and then invited a dozen other Eagles to join him at the major league baseball All-Star game at nearby Griffith Stadium.

Scouting earned its chapter in the American national identity, and Eagle Scouting embedded itself into that chapter as the exemplar of the movement—the apparent hero of the narrative.

By comparison, most of the other youth movements in the United States got their start two generations later, powered by the demographic engine of the baby boom. As large as many of them became, they were in a sense too late for history. Even Girl Scouts, almost as old Boy Scouting, didn't settle on its Gold Award until 1980—meaning its story, however memorable, has comparatively just begun.

PROMOTION

It would be wrong to credit the success of Eagle Scouting to successful public relations and advertising over the course of the decades by the Boy Scouts of America, but it would also be a mistake to assume that it had no part.

Scouting has always tried to push its Eagles front and center. And, of course, why not? Every institution wants to put its most successful members on display—not just to honor them, and to use them in recruiting new members—but also just to *keep* them from leaving to pursue other achievements.

That's why, since the mid-1920s, Scouting has always had a separate organization for Eagles: first the Knights of Dunamis and then the National Eagle Scout Association. It is also why almost every major Scouting event, especially national jamborees, has separate events for Eagles. One reason Eagle Courts of Honor stories are so popular in community newspapers is precisely because local troops, districts, and councils promote those stories. And, on the big-ticket events—such as presenting the annual report on Scouting to the president of the United States—it is almost always an Eagle Scout being tapped for the job.

It is amazing, given the enormous amount of attention Eagle Scouting receives, just how *little* the BSA spends promoting it. For example, Scouting almost never contacts the media about an individual Eagle project—rather, that is usually done ad hoc by the Scout's family, a troop leader, or often by the recipient institution. News coverage of Eagles helping in disaster areas, or of adult Eagles earning high honors, are typically just sidebars to a larger story. It can be said that beyond some pro forma press releases from Scouting headquarters, almost all of the attention given to the nation's Eagle Scout is organic and grassroots in origin. Eagle Scouting is its own promotion.

In fact, so effective is this marketing that it regularly spills over its own boundaries. For example, Wikipedia has compiled a list of famous individuals who are assumed to be Eagle Scouts but who are not: Henry Fonda (Scout and Scoutmaster), Walter Cronkite, Bill Gates (Life Scout), Jimmy Stewart (2nd Class Scout), Hank Aaron, and Harrison Ford (Life Scout). Some of the confusion comes from these individuals having earned other Scouting honors (such as the Silver Buffalo) or from doing Scouting advertisements—but most of all it is because they are such quintessentially American characters that it is assumed if they are in any way connected with Scouting then they must be Eagles.

Meanwhile, in the fictional world, as in the real one, while Boy Scouts have made thousands of appearances in books, television shows, and movies over the last century, the Eagle is usually reserved for the smartest, most accomplished, or noblest characters—not just Indiana Jones, but everyone from the Doctor on Gilligan's Island to Will Smith's character in *Men in Black* to Snoopy ("Beagle Scout").

ACHIEVEMENT

In the end, what really keeps Eagle Scouting in an honored, almost-impregnable position in American culture, are the achievements of the Eagles themselves. If the Eagle rank was only the highest achievement in Boy Scouting, its reputation would still be strong, but far more circumscribed—and it would wax and wane with Scouting's own reputation.

But as we've already shown, it is all but immune to such cycles. No, there is something larger at work.

Eagles have always made news, but most of that news was made by adult Eagles for whom this childhood achievement was just the first step to eventual fame. But beginning in the 1960s, with the ascendance of the service project over the simple accumulation of merit badges as the key requirement of the Eagle rank, the actual achievement of the Eagle rank not only came to be seen as a peerless achievement of childhood, but also as a major news event in its own right.

From that moment on, while there was (and would always be) the story of the new Nobel Prize winner who was also an Eagle Scout, those comparatively rare stories were now joined by a steady drumbeat of stories of teenagers accomplishing amazing, even landmark, things in every corner of the country.

In the last half-century, those stories have only increased in number and quality as something of an arms race has emerged among the most ambitious young Eagle candidates—and Scouting itself has begun to recognize the best of those projects with awards and scholarships. It is now easy to imagine a Scout earning national attention at age 17 for his Eagle project, local coverage six months later for his Eagle award; then 30 years later entering the public again with a major career achievement (an Oscar, a Nobel Prize, election to national office, ascending to the CEO job at a major corporation, or becoming the president of a university)—and then, after another decade, being recognized as the newest recipient of the Distinguished Eagle Scout Award.

That's a lot of attention, both for the Eagle and for Eagle Scouting. And it guarantees that the Eagle medal and the men who wear it will be a part of the nation's story for many years to come.

BADGE OF HONOR

There is no small irony to the fact that the Eagle Scout award, which began with a different name and was less a considered strategy than an institution's stopgap response to overachieving young members, has proven to be the most respected and best-known award for American youth. What began as a badge of honor for a small coterie of dedicated teenagers has become not only the most enduring award for youth in American life, but also the most consistently rewarding award in their own lives. And perhaps most amazing of all, what at first was considered just the next step in the accumulation of skill badges has, over the course of a century, generated the greatest outpouring of youthful community service in history.

In the pages that follow, we will look at the story of the Eagle Scout award. We will be on hand for its awkward beginnings in the general confusion of Scouting's early years. Then we will look at how it assumed the role of the Ambassador of Scouting during the Roaring Twenties—and its shift to becoming a beacon of hope for America's youth during the Great Depression.

After the Eagle goes to war for the second time, we will look at the 1950s and early 1960s and the golden age of American Scouting, and then at the chaos of the late 1960s and Scouting's greatest crisis—and the near-fatal mistake of trying to make the Eagle award "relevant." We'll then look at the slow renaissance of Scouting and the Eagle. And we'll end with the centennial—first of American Boy Scouting and then of the Eagle award—and at the growing professionalization of the Eagle rank and its service project as the value of the award becomes universally known.

Finally, we'll close with a look at Eagle Scouting as it enters its second century—and what roles it is likely to play in both Scouting and American life in the decades to come.

Along the way, we will meet some of the most remarkable Americans of the last 100 years and hear the stories of achievements that are touching, heroic, and in some cases almost superhuman. For some of these individuals, these successes represent the most important accomplishments of their lives; for others, it is the first glimpse of future fame.

The Eagle is ambitious, yet humbling; the height of achievement, yet devoid of competition; the ultimate challenge of childhood, yet accomplishable by anyone with the courage to pursue it, no matter what their physical or intellectual gifts. It is straightforward and plain in its requirements, but complex and subtle in their execution. The Eagle Scout award has taken its place at the heart of American life not only because it reflects what is best about the United States, but also because it captures some of the quixotic, even contradictory, nature of that life.

To understand how that came to be, we need to start at the beginning: with the very first Eagle Scout.

== CHAPTER TWO ==

PATHFINDER

*In April 1912, Arthur Rose Eldred of Troop 1 of Rockville Center,
Oceanside, Long Island, successfully completed his 21st merit badge .
. . and threw the Boy Scouts of America into a panic.*

Scouting in the United States was, at this point, just two years old—and
still more of a spontaneous movement revolving around a couple best-
selling books rather than a formal and cohesive organization.

In fact, the BSA was only one of a number of Scouting entities in the
United States competing for new members and the blessings of Baden-
Powell and UK Scouting. Besides the Boy Scouts of America, there was also
the more militaristic American Boy Scouts (the largest competitor to the
BSA), the Rhode Island Boy Scouts and Sea Scouts, the (Mormon) MIA
Scouts, the Boy Scouts of the United States, and the National Highway
Patrol Association Scouts—not to mention the Woodcraft Indians and Sons
of Daniel Boone that Seton and Beard, respectively, continued to operate in
case the BSA failed or didn't award them proper credit.

How the BSA emerged from this chaos as the sole winner is a long
and convoluted story. Ultimately, it was result of backing by the large and
established YMCA, recruitment of the biggest figures in the field (not just
Seton and Beard, but Baden-Powell himself), absorbing failing competitors,

and the superior diplomatic and financial skills of first Chief Scout Executive James E. West.

The initial shakeout in U.S. Scouting would continue until 1918. And so, in early 1912, as Arthur Eldred completed his final merit badge, it was no sure thing that the BSA would emerge victorious—or even survive.

In fact, Arthur himself almost didn't join the Boy Scouts of America. A tall, quiet boy with a thick shock of black hair, Eldred had been born in Brooklyn in 1895. After his father's death, the family moved to Oceanside. Arthur was raised by his mother and a brother, Hubert, who was a dozen years older.

In 1910, Hubert, the unsung hero of the story, joined thousands of other young Americans caught up in the new Scouting fad. An American Boy Scout (ABS) troop had been formed in Rockville Center—and Hubert resolved to join the ABS and bring along his baby brother—no doubt to give 15-year-old Arthur some structure and a greater male presence in his life.

But Hubert Eldred was a bit put off by all of the drilling, marching, and other martial activities that characterized the local ABS troop, so he decided to start a troop of his own—and set off for ABS headquarters in New York City to obtain a charter. Then while he was in Manhattan, Hubert decided to stop by the YMCA building and visit the offices of the Boy Scouts of America. In the end, he found the BSA's ideals a better fit to his own . . . and filed for a charter as BSA Troop 1 on Long Island, for which he would be the first Scoutmaster.

The story of Long Island Troop 1 captures something of the improvised, low-budget nature of Scouting itself in those early years. For example, the handful of boys who comprised the troop met in the loft of the Eldred barn—suggesting neither a lot of money or adult supervision. It also quickly became known as one of the few troops in the country in which every Scout owned a uniform. One story tells of a Scout in Troop 1 named Melvin Daly (we will meet him again) who came to a meeting in a snowstorm wearing shoes with just scraps of soles—having apparently spent his shoe money on his first Scout uniform.

To the children of today who can pass through an entire K–12 education without ever once having walked to school, this image of young Scouts tramping through snow to meet unsupervised in a barn, raising money for their own uniforms, and being led on camping trips by a post-adolescent may seem like life on another planet. But it was precisely this spirit of independence, self-sufficiency, and naturalism that Seton, Beard, and Baden-Powell espoused . . . and that struck such a powerful chord in young men of the era. Many of them were, after all, the sons and grandsons of Civil War veterans, pioneers, immigrants, cowboys, and Indian fighters—and the chance to experience that disappearing world must have exerted a powerful pull.

And no Scout in the troop thrived more in this world than Arthur Eldred. He had, after all, joined at 15, likely making him the senior Scout in the troop. And that fact, perhaps combined with an adult perspective that sometimes emerges at that age, made Arthur a classic young man in a hurry.

RANK AND FILE

In 1911–12, advancement in Scouting was just about as undefined as everything else in the movement. The first *Boy Scout Handbook*, written in 1910 by Seton, was essentially a reworking of Baden-Powell's seminal 1909 UK *Scouting for Boys*—which Seton (rightly) believed had borrowed extensively from Seton's own 1902 *Birch-Bark Roll*. This first official manual (nearly 29,000 copies were printed) was rushed out to give the Boy Scouts of America a clear and distinct identity.[1]

Not surprisingly, the result was a hodgepodge. Given Seton's reputation as a famous naturalist and writer, the manual worked best in establishing the philosophical foundation of American Scouting in the outdoors, woodcraft, Indian lore, camping, and natural science. It offered a vision of wildlife conservancy that wouldn't be seen in Scout handbooks (or American life) for another half-century. And it was also one of the best books of games for boys ever written.

But when it came to structure, organization, and advancement, Seton's notoriously unsystematic mind failed him. Ranks, such as they were, were divided into Red, White, and Blue classes, with honors and "high honors" levels. Many of these requirements were relatively straightforward—ride a horse, be trained in archery, or study geology—but others can only be described as romantic nonsense; notably, the high honor requirement to hunt a gorilla, grizzly bear, or elephant. As you might imagine, the first year of the BSA didn't see a lot of advancement.

The next year, the BSA tried again—with much greater success. *The Boy Scouts of America Handbook for Boys*, which would go through 37 printings and more than 3 million copies by mid-1927, was one of the most popular American children's books of all time. As a measure of Scouting's growing influence, the *Handbook* soon sported a cover, by leading illustrator J.C. Leyendecker, that had originally appeared on the cover of *Saturday Evening Post* (creating a precedent that would ultimately lead to Norman Rockwell). Showing why he was chief Scout executive, James West even sent out, with much fanfare, 4,500 reader's copies of the first printing to educators and civic leaders around the nation to solicit their suggestions—knowing full well that it was already too late to incorporate those suggestions in that edition.

Though no better organized than Seton's edition (and often more retrograde in its attitudes), the new *Handbook* was infinitely more structured in its message. For the first time, Scouting had its Oath, its multipart Law, and just as important, precise requirements for the Tenderfoot, Second Class, and First Class ranks—requirements that, in some form, largely survive today. And as soon as the book fell into the hands of enthusiastic young Scouts like Arthur Eldred, they set about tearing through those requirements as quickly as school and chores permitted.

Eldred may not have been the first Scout to earn his First Class badge, which he reached in March 1911, but he must have been very close. Indeed, since the *Handbook* wasn't even officially published until August of that year, Arthur must have learned about the requirements early, perhaps through a newspaper (*Boys' Life* magazine wouldn't begin publishing for another year) or Hubert's contacts at BSA headquarters.

But now, having reached the official pinnacle of Scouting, young Arthur Eldred found himself entering into unknown country. After First Class, where did a 16-year-old Boy Scout go next?

The answer was merit badges—awards for the mastery of a particular Scouting skill or for basic apprenticeship in a potential adult career. They were the crucial step in turning Scouting from being just an exciting adventure for 11-year-olds to being a life-enhancing experience for 17-year-olds. Baden-Powell had invented merit badges, and they had been a part of the British Scouting movement from the beginning. With its own founding, the Boy Scouts of America had imported the idea and had initially announced just 14 badges—none of which had yet been manufactured or awarded. With the new *Handbook*, the BSA announced a total of 57 merit badges and this time actually began to make them.

BADGES OF MERIT

Then as now, the BSA merit badges were an eclectic and intriguing bunch. Some of those original badges, in fact, still exist today—and even (in the case of architecture, art, athletics, bugling, chemistry, electricity, first aid, lifesaving, music, painting, public health, and scholarship) still look the same after a century. Other than a few badges that grew anachronistic in the modern world and were retired (e.g., taxidermy; stalking, not least because the meaning of the term changed; masonry; interpreting; pathfinding; blacksmithing; and bee farming), most still survive in some form under the same or slightly different name.

It is a measure of the thought that the BSA put into its merit badge program that there was only one real clunker—and only then because it was just too difficult. That was the Inventing merit badge, which required a Scout to not only invent a new device or mechanism but also to obtain a U.S. patent for it. Needless to say, not many Scouts ever attempted this badge during its four-year existence, and it is something of a miracle that nine Scouts actually managed to earn it. It remained so obscure that today we don't even know what the badge looked like.

But if the BSA merit badge program was a model of thoughtful planning, the new ranks these badges created were anything but. In the original *Handbook*, as is true today, the accumulation of earned merit badges created three special honors. But whereas those three ranks—Star, Life, and Eagle—today have very specific and distinct requirements, in 1912 they were little more than counters, a kind of super-merit badge designating a milestone in the total number of badges the Scout had earned. First Class, as the name suggested, was still considered the pinnacle rank of Scouting.

The original order of these "Merit Scout" honors was Life, Star, and Eagle, and they required 5, 10, and 21 merit badges respectively (Star and Life were reversed in the 1920s when it was determined that the five points of the Star insignia fit neatly with the five merit badge requirement.) The Life insignia, shaped like a heart, was chosen because the first cluster of required merit badges dealt with health and fitness (first aid, lifesaving, public health, personal health, and athletics). The Star rank had its own set of required merit badges and was likely designed to be like Polaris, the North Star, to guide the Scout to the zenith rank of Scouting: the Eagle.

This explanation sounds much more straightforward and logical than it really was. For one thing, because the merit badges for the first two ranks were so tightly specified and mutually exclusive, it was possible to earn either without earning the other. By the same token, it was also possible to work directly toward Eagle without earning the other two ranks in between.

And, in fact, that's what Arthur Eldred did: he went straight for Eagle—and soon discovered that Boy Scouts of America wasn't ready for him.

JUGGERNAUT

It's not as if Scouting didn't see Arthur coming. At the BSA's first great rally held at the 71st Regiment Armory in New York City in February 1911, Second Class Scout Arthur Eldred and Troop 1 wowed the crowd (and their fellow Scouts) by lashing together a 20-foot sapling tower, then climbing it, and putting on a semaphore demonstration. So impressed were the other troops at the event that the Scouts of Troop 1 spent the next few months following up on invitations to teach their skills to other troops around the region.

A month later, Arthur completed First Class, studied the requirements of those first 14 merit badges, and was on his way. By August, with the publication of the *Handbook,* Arthur's universe of merit badge opportunities nearly quadrupled. Now nothing would stop him. Because merit badge sashes were a sartorial innovation still more than a decade in the future—

and because the BSA assumed that most Scouts would never earn more than a couple merit badges—Eldred and his handful of peers in the vanguard of Scouting were required to sew their badges (embroidered circles on a square of khaki cloth) on the right forearm of their uniform. And by the end of 1911, Arthur's right sleeve was growing thick with merit badges.

Lord Baden-Powell was scheduled to visit American Scouting in late January 1912. Wanting to put on the best face to the founder of Scouting— the BSA was still, after all, competing against a half-dozen other pretenders for official International Scouting designation—Chief Scout Executive West and his staff remembered the troop with the full set of uniforms, the precise marching drills, and the impressive signaling tower. The invitation went out to Long Island Troop 1 to join a second area troop to serve as the honor guard for Baden-Powell's arrival.

It is telling about the precarious nature of most Scouting units of the era that Scoutmaster Hubert Eldred wrote back to West to politely decline the invitation because the troop could not afford to pay the train fare for the 21-mile trip to Manhattan. West quickly wrote back to say that the BSA would pick up the tab.

And so, on January 31, 1912, as Lord Baden-Powell stepped down the gangplank of the SS *Arcadian* to begin his multiple city tour, he was met by a contingent of 40 Scouts forming two ranks on each side of his path. Baden-Powell would tell Hubert "his finest memory of his entire trip around the world, was sailing up beautiful New York Harbor, and seeing the long line of erect uniformed Boy Scouts with the American flag on the right of the line and the British Cross of St. Andrew on the left of the line and the Boy Scout Flag in the center."[2]

As he passed through the ranks, the retired Lt. General, whose career had been built on being a quick judge of character, found his attention drawn to one particular Scout. This boy, older than the rest, stood a head taller than the others. His right arm bore an astonishing number of merit badges, and he wore a shiny First Class pin on his tunic. To the surprise of everyone, including the VIPs waiting at the end of the gangplank, Lord Baden-Powell reached out and gave Arthur Eldred the left-handed Scout handshake and quickly began peppering him with questions.

Eldred tried to answer the best he could, but the unexpected attention of the great man, along with his fear that he was screwing everything up in the eyes of the event organizers waiting at the end of the ranks, combined to make him both red faced and increasingly inarticulate. Finally, to his immense relief, Baden-Powell moved on. And rather than annoyed, it is easy to assume that West and the rest of the BSA leadership were positively thrilled that the founder had paused to meet and approve the flower of American Scouting.

After all this, the BSA must surely have seen Arthur Eldred heading its way, at the front of a cohort of Scouts all of whom had made the Eagle rank their ultimate target. And yet, Scouting still seemed oblivious.

THE SELECT FEW

Legendary business efficiency consultant Joseph M. Juran first proposed the "Pareto principle" (named after an Italian economist), popularly known as the 80–20 Rule. As most people know, and many have seen in practice in their daily life, this rule suggests that in most human organizations the minority accomplishes the majority of the work. That's the standard definition, but it also comes in many variations. Twenty percent of the members of a group represent 80 percent of the creativity, revenues, net worth, productivity, wealth, and achievement.

Scouting is not immune to this rule: a quick inspection shows that only about 20 percent of all Scouts stay in the organization and earn ranks beyond First Class. By the same token, 80 percent of all merit badges seem to be earned by about 20 percent of those who pursue them. Meanwhile, nearly all leadership positions in a troop are held by about one-fifth of the boys.

Looking at the early years of Scouting, it seems pretty obvious that by the time Lord Baden-Powell walked down that gangplank, this 20 percent cohort of achievers had already emerged in the BSA.

But it doesn't end there. As anyone who has ever been part of a major social movement or hugely popular technology start-up company knows, this emergent 20 percent begins to undergo its own 80–20. This "Pareto of Paretos"—an elite 4 percent—represents the superstars of any organization. They aren't just overachievers; they break through any boundary set for them, rewrite what it means to be successful in the organization, and very often establish legends and precedents that can last for generations. It is not a coincidence that the ratio of Eagles to total Boy Scouts has hovered around this same 4 percent over the last century.[3]

In retrospect, we can see in 1911 that the first 20 percent of successful Scouts emerged. But we can also recognize in 1912, especially after the widespread availability of the *Handbook*, this super-elite making its first appearance. The Boy Scouts of America, in creating the Merit Scout honors, thought it had shrewdly dealt with the challenge of overachieving Scouts for years to come. Within months, it had already fallen behind.

Arthur Eldred took Scouting to a whole new level in 1912. By April, eschewing both Life and Star (in fact, of the first nine Eagle Scouts, eight—including Arthur—did not earn either Life or Star Scout ranks as they were not required to do so before October 1914), Eldred had earned the 21 merit badges he needed for his Eagle rank. Arrayed in a three-by-seven grid on his sleeve, they began with Personal Health—then Plumbing, Gardening, Cooking, Painting, Swimming, Civics (symbolized by a fasces that would soon be abandoned), Lifesaving, Public Health, Cycling, Pathfinding, Interpreting (French), Electricity, Dairying, First Aid to Animals, Chemistry, Business, Handicraft, Firemanship, Horsemanship . . . and culminated in Poultry Farming. Six of Arthur's badges were from the original 14—suggesting that he, in a superhuman achievement, had earned the remaining 15 badges in less than six months.

But that doesn't capture the full magnitude of Arthur Eldred's achievement. In 1911 and early 1912, he was to Boy Scout merit badges what Babe Ruth was to home runs a dozen years hence. When he reached that 21st merit badge, a grand total of just 141 merit badges had been awarded to 50 Scouts in the *entire* BSA. Not only did Arthur Eldred at that moment own 15 percent of all of the awarded merit badges in Scouting, but he likely had more merit badges than all of the Scouts in entire Scout districts, councils, and perhaps even some regions. No Scout ever again would—or could—enjoy that kind of dominance.[4]

Arthur compiled affidavits from local city leaders confirming that the had been successfully tested for all of his merit badges . . . and sent the whole package off to BSA headquarters in New York City.

And there it sat for weeks, creating no little consternation. No one knew quite what to do about Arthur Eldred. Like many institutions, the BSA had, as a kind of theoretical exercise/membership motivator/publicity vehicle, established what it figured was an impossibly high achievement . . . and assumed it wouldn't have to sweat the details for many years, if ever. Instead, it had posed a challenge to every boy in Scouting—a challenge that had now been met in just seven months.

VALIDATION

What now? Was it enough that Arthur Eldred could prove that he had earned the requisite merit badges and had passed muster with some local committee? Or was some sort of national certification required—and if so, of what would it consist? Certainly by this point, James West and the rest of BSA leadership had come to the realization that there might be other near-Eagles queuing up out there across America, and that how they handled Arthur Eldred would set an important precedent for the approval of other new Eagles for years to come.

In the end, BSA decided on a "board of review"—the name would stick forever—during which young Eldred would be invited down to Manhattan and tested on his Scouting knowledge by learned adults in each field.

The exact date of this board of review was not recorded, but it was likely sometime in early summer, 1912. We also don't know whether the board met as a single gathering or was a series of individual interviews—that is, whether it more resembled a star chamber or a gauntlet. But one thing is certain: out of the more than 2 million Eagle Courts of Honor that have taken place, this was not only the first, but also easily the most intimidating.

Facing 17-year-old Arthur Eldred were the founding fathers of Scouting: Chief Scout Ernest Thompson Seton, National Scout Commissioner Daniel Carter Beard, Chief Scout Executive James E. West, and Wilbert E. Longfellow, who had drafted the swimming and lifesaving sections in the Scouting *Handbook*. Not only were Seton and Beard living legends, but also they and Longfellow were considered the leading experts in their fields. Worse, while Beard, West, and Seton held each other in enormous respect, they also mostly despised one another—in part because of their gigantic egos, but mainly because they held nearly antithetical views about the philosophy of Scouting.

Seton, with his floppy hat, walrus moustache, and poor hygiene, was not just a brilliant storyteller (he was in many ways the precursor of Jack London), but also one of those Edwardian man-children who served as a philosophical bridge between the Romantics and the Hippies. His Scouting was a kind of prelapsarian mash-up of personal freedom, adventure in the woods, Native American ceremonies, rites of manhood, and pacifist antigovernment (and anti-American) libertarianism. Beard's Scouting, by comparison, was structured, focused on woodcraft and other outdoor skills, and highly patriotic. Beard himself was crisp and neat, even when dressed in buckskins.

Tellingly, Seton had wanted to name the highest rank in Scouting the Silver Wolf, likely after his famous story about capturing Lobo the Wolf, the "King of Carrumpaw" Valley, New Mexico. It was not a title destined to sit well with Scoutmaster/Ranchers in rural America, who dealt daily with wolf predations. And when they complained, it was Beard who lobbied for, and won, the American eagle for the award.

For West, meanwhile, the Boy Scouts of America was a nonprofit institution that had enjoyed considerable initial success, but would soon fail unless it rationalized its operations, developed new sources of sponsorship from the wealthy and the powerful, continued its recruiting and marketing efforts, and beat the various contending Scouting organizations to official Congressional or White House certification. Even if it was about kids, West believed, it was time for Scouting as an institution to grow up. He had little time for the antics and self-aggrandizement of either of the other two men, and within three years, he had driven Seton out of the BSA and co-opted "Uncle Dan" Beard to serve for the next 40 years as the new unofficial Chief Scout.

Exactly how Arthur Eldred managed to navigate through the shoals of these competing interests may have been the biggest miracle of his miraculous year. The fact that each of these powerful men was looking for answers that were often the opposite of the one sought by the others—and each man presumably held a veto vote—would seem to make it impossible for Arthur to survive the process. And yet he did.

We can only speculate why. It may be that all four members of the board realized that BSA could use an Eagle Scout at this point in its development—and here they had before them not only a sterling example of American boyhood, but also someone who had already been singled out by the founder of Scouting himself. Arthur Eldred had earned his Eagle. He deserved it. And the feuding founding fathers of Scouting decided to put aside their differences and give it to him.

An exhausted Arthur Eldred went home to Long Island and awaited the board's decision.

HERO

You might think this would be enough of an accomplishment for one summer for this young man. But, incredibly, he had only begun. While he waited for news, Arthur Eldred went on a camping trip with his troop to Orange Lake, New York. At some point during the day, Melvin Daly, the Scout who'd walked through the snow to the meeting, decided to wade in the lake. But he went out too far, slipped off an underwater ledge and—being a nonswimmer—sank beneath the surface.

Arthur, realizing that Daly was drowning, dove in the lake, swam to the bottom and found the boy, and pulled him to the surface. He was quickly joined by another Scout, Merritt Cutler, who grabbed Daly to help pull him in. Unfortunately, at this point, Daly revived and panicked. He wrapped Cutler in a death grip and the two boys went under.

Arthur again dove. He managed to pull the two boys apart and then, using his lifesaving skills, dragged Daly to shore. He then swam back out and helped in the now-struggling Cutler. This feat of heroism had numerous witnesses—and thanks to their reports, Arthur Eldred was awarded one of Scouting's first Honor Medals, reportedly by Chief Scout Seton himself—who, if he'd had any doubts about the young man before, must have quickly retired them.

On August 21, 1912, a letter from Chief Scout Executive (CSE) James West formally informed Arthur Eldred, now five days past his 17th birthday that he had been awarded the first Eagle Scout rank of the Boy Scouts of America. It was a historic letter—diminished somewhat by the fact that, after he congratulated Arthur, West apologized that . . . well, his Eagle medal wasn't quite ready. It seemed that the dies for the top scroll and the Eagle dangle hadn't been fabricated yet.

This bit of news, had it been known, would have stunned thousands of Boy Scouts across America. They had assumed the Eagle medal was real. After all, they'd seen a drawing of it in the *Handbook*—a rectangular ribbon of solid-colored satin, suspended from an unmarked metal bar, culminating at the bottom with a metal Eagle, presumably gold, in flight from right to left.

No doubt that was what Arthur Eldred was expecting too. But that image had never been more than a preliminary artist's rendition. So Eldred was undoubtedly surprised, when the package finally arrived on Labor Day, 1912, to find a very different Eagle medal inside. This one, possibly manufactured by T.H. Foley Company, had a silver scroll at the top, bearing the Scout motto "Be Prepared," with a wire square knot (representing the Scout slogan "Do a Good Deed [later: Turn] Daily") dangling beneath— just like the bottom of the Scout insignia. Meanwhile, the satin ribbon suspended from the scroll was much more triangular, and red, white, and blue. Finally, at bottom, hanging from three interlinked rings (the largest one inside the ribbon) was a very different—and as many noted, scrawny— Eagle: rampant, wings outstretched, and apparently gripping a narrow segment of perch or a bundle of arrow shafts. Across the Eagle's narrow chest, in raised relief, were the letters "B S A."

Eldred was the first recipient to see the true Eagle medal. The design has changed slightly over the years—the square knot took different lengths, the BSA lettering disappeared in the mid-1950s and reappeared in 1969, and the Eagle itself mercifully grew more robust—but after more than a century it remains so similar to Eldred's medal that only a collector can quickly tell the difference. And, in fact, that comparison can be easily made: Arthur Eldred's Eagle medal still survives and is scrutinized by young Scouts each day in its display at the National Scouting Museum in Irving, Texas. Its satin ribbon has been partially reduced to threads and the Eagle itself has lost much of its silver plating to reveal the bronze beneath. But it is unmistakably what it is: both the prototype and the first awarded copy of the Eagle medal.

That September a proud, but obviously embarrassed, Arthur Eldred stood for a photographer (probably brother Hubert) in his full Boy Scout uniform—trousers and puttees, campaign hat tucked in his arm, and high-collared long tunic-jacket—with the 21 merit badges on the sleeve and his new Eagle Scout and Honor medals prominently displayed on his chest pocket. He posed (apparently in the yard in front of the screened porch of his house) for two photos: one facing forward, with his arms crossed and a confident look on his face; the other holding his hat and looking away with the beginning of a smile—as if he's about to answer a question from a curious onlooker.

And that was it. The only public notice of Arthur's achievement was his inclusion in a merit badge honor roll in the August 1912 issue of the new *Boys' Life* magazine and an article in the *Kingston* (NY) *Daily Freeman* that described him as a "sturdy, well-built, keen eyed little fellow" who was the first of 2 million Boy Scouts to earn the award.

And then Arthur Eldred disappeared from Scouting history.

AFTERMATH

He didn't disappear from the world, of course. But, like all Scouts, when he reached his 18th birthday in August 1913, Arthur Eldred officially "aged out" of Scouting. And like every Eagle after him, he packed away his medal and other Scouting mementos and got on with his life. Troop 1 faded away soon after as the other boys aged out—Scout troops in those days were often little more than a fraternity of schoolmates—and Hubert Eldred moved away from Rockville Centre.

Meanwhile, with a world war on the horizon, both Scouting and Scouts had much bigger concerns than preserving history.

Arthur Eldred attended Cornell University, ran on the cross-country team, and was president of the university's Agricultural Association. Graduating in 1916, he served in World War I as a Navy machinist on a submarine chaser based out of Corfu, Greece, patrolling the Strait of Otranto. He served honorably and saw combat on several occasions.

During the 1918 Spanish flu epidemic, Eldred became sick while still on Corfu and was hospitalized. So horrific were the conditions at the hospital that at one point a semidelirious Eldred had to crawl to a stream for water—permanently scarring his hip in the process. Eventually he was shipped home, a process that, after more than two months had only gotten Arthur as far as Gibraltar. There, he was given a choice of continuing the six-month long route home or taking his discharge on the spot and making his own way back.

The intrepid Eagle chose the latter. He was officially separated from the navy in March 1919. Luckily, soon after that, he met a group of U.S. Army soldiers who took a liking to him, put him in one of their uniforms, and sneaked him on as a stowaway on their troop ship. Eldred played soldier by day, and slept each night in a lifeboat, on the voyage home to the United States.

Life back stateside proved much less exciting for Arthur—and he seemed to welcome the peace and quiet. He went to work for a dairy, and by 1921 had worked his way up to become Agricultural Agent for New Jersey's Atlantic County. He served in that role for seven years, during which he was credited with creating the Atlantic City municipal farmer's market.

In 1928, Eldred joined the Reading Railroad as a specialist in promoting the railroad transportation of produce. In time, he was named manager of the Motor Carrier Committee of the Eastern Railroad Association. It was a position he would hold the rest of his life. In later years, Eldred also served on the Camden County Council and on the local school board.

Through the years, Arthur Eldred never forgot Scouting, nor ever really left it. As early as the 1920s, he served as a board of review examiner—no doubt for Eagle candidates who imagined that their experience was the toughest ever. Later, Eldred served as committee chairman for his son Willard's Troop 77 in Clementon, New Jersey. A photograph from 1944 shows Arthur, in a suit with thinning hair, looking on as an Eagle medal is pinned on Willard's uniform. Four generations of Eldreds have now earned their Eagles.

About this time, Eldred did something else that would prove crucial to Scouting's understanding of itself: he compiled his documents, including in the collection his brother's record of Baden-Powell's visit, his Honor Medal citation, James West's letter informing Arthur that he'd become an Eagle . . . and perhaps most important, a carbon copy of an account of his Scouting experiences that he'd written in 1940 and sent to his old high school principal.

Perhaps he'd had a premonition. Arthur Eldred, the first Eagle Scout, died of colon cancer on January 4, 1951. He was 55 years old. He had lived long enough to see nearly one-half million Eagle Scouts follow the path he'd cut, but not long enough to participate in his own rediscovery.

By the 1960s, as the first generation of Scouts began to fade away and a vast new generation of Scouts appeared on the scene, the Boy Scouts of America finally began to look back on its history, and its story. And it found Arthur Rose Eldred. Books about Scouting, many of them featuring brief mentions of Eldred and his achievement, were being published.

Unfortunately, and with the inexplicable confusion that always seemed to characterize Scouting's relationship with its first Eagle, the photo that accompanied these stories was of the wrong boy: Theodore Gaty Jr., the *38th* Eagle, whose good looks and square jaw were right out of a Leyendecker illustration. The puzzle was only solved in 2005 when Gary Twite, a commissioner in the Chief Seattle Council of the BSA purchased a pair of antique photographs—the two described earlier—and realized they had a much closer resemblance to the 1944 Eldred than the official photo. The truth was confirmed by Willard Eldred, now himself a senior citizen.

But if Gaty looked the part of the first Eagle, Arthur Eldred lived it. In his three short years in Boy Scouts, Eldred had transformed the Boy Scouts of America. He had set a shining example to Scouting's founder, earned the man's approval, and thus helped establish the primacy of the BSA over its rivals. He had saved the life of another Scout. He had permanently restructured Scouting's own operating philosophy to make the merit badge ranks the true second phase of the Scouting experience. And, by dint of his hard work and ambition, he had even forced Boy Scouts to make the Eagle Scout rank both real and the new pinnacle of Scouting. Most of all, quiet, serious Arthur Eldred had set a high standard for what a Boy Scout—an

CHAPTER THREE

SIR KNIGHT

RAYMOND O. HANSON WAS A HAUNTED MAN.

It was 1925, and the Boy Scouts of America had experienced profound changes in its first 15 years. For one thing, in the years since Arthur Eldred had earned his Eagle, the BSA had seen tremendous growth—its 62,000 members had exploded to 760,000, a twelvefold increase. The number of Eagle Scouts had seen a similar leap—Scouting had now produced a total of 10,746 Eagle Scouts, with many of them still active as Scoutmasters and Assistant Scoutmasters.[1]

The last figure was the one that had come to obsess Scout Executive Hanson for the San Francisco Council. What he, like many other professional Scouters around the country, saw was young men rising through the ranks of Scouting, and at last achieving not just the Eagle rank but the level of leadership and skill competence that came with being an Eagle . . . and then leaving Scouting.

Many of these Eagles left simply because they turned 18 and aged out— and, if Scouting was lucky, they might return a quarter-century later with an 11-year-old son. But others, perhaps even more, Eagles quit Scouting well before their 18th birthday simply because Scouting no longer appealed to them. They had earned all the merit badges that interested them, held all the leadership positions in the troop, and been to the same summer camp too many times. But most of all, they had found Scouting—enthralling when they were 11—now simply too *juvenile* in light of their growing adult interests.

And so they quit. So much talent and experience lost—a reality made even more painful by the recognition that even with its remarkable growth, Scouting could have grown even *more* had it been able to recruit more leaders. So why, Hanson asked himself, was Scouting consciously jettisoning the best of its newly trained young leaders simply because of an arbitrary retirement date? Why did Scouting devote so much time and energy bringing boys to a peak of competence and confidence . . . and then abandon them? Why couldn't this soon-to-be lost intellectual capital be retained and put to good use now—instead of waiting until, say, 1950?

Hanson asked himself, why had Scouting, which had proven itself so brilliant in creating a program that captured the imaginations of the nation's 11- to 15-year-old boys, not done the same for its 16- to 18-year-olds? Why did Eagle Scouts, the crowning achievement of the movement, young men who should have been savoring what they had accomplished, instead grow bored and walk away?

For Ray Hanson, each departing Eagle Scout in his council was like a body blow—an unrestorable waste of potential and a small betrayal to the Eagle himself. And sitting in his office in San Francisco, he would look down Market Street, past the Ferry Building and across the continent, and wonder why BSA national headquarters wasn't seeing the same thing.[2]

RESISTANCE

What Scouters on both coasts—and everywhere in-between—understood was that the Boy Scouts of America wasn't the same organization in 1925 as it had been in 1913. And it wasn't just the growth of the membership rolls, or the final rationalization of ranks and requirements, or the geographic expansion of troops, or even the ongoing experimentation with a new "Cub" program for younger boys.

No, Scouting had changed because the world had changed. The movement had been born in the Progressive Era, that tenuous marriage between scientific empiricism and romantic environmentalism, buoyed by the belief that the world had entered into a more enlightened age of continuous progress. Boy Scouting had been devised in part in the belief that even boyhood was a problem that could be solved.

But that confidence had died in the flooded trenches of Passchendaele on the Western Front and in the Hall of Mirrors with the signing of the Treaty of Versailles. What was left now was either disillusionment (as exemplified by the Lost Generation wandering about Europe) or a new, less-idealistic pragmatism.

Scouting, by its very nature, was destined to choose the latter. The days of ad hoc groups meeting in barns and playing Indians or Frontiersman were gone. Scouting was now a giant organization, as big as any domestic corporation, and one of the largest institutions in American life. Thanks to the efforts of James West, whose 30 years as chief Scout executive would provide the stability and continuity the organization needed, Scouting had been organized, systematized, and recognized.

The requirements for each of the ranks had now been set and made universal across the program. The number of merit badges had continuously increased in both number (by 1930 there would be 92) and scope (new badges included Zoology, Weather, Salesmanship, and Railroading).[3] And the "patrol method" from which Baden-Powell had first built Scouting had now evolved into a sophisticated and multi-tiered management structure for troops that included patrol leaders, senior patrol leaders, instructors, and even librarians and chaplains. The adult volunteer/professional apparatus of districts and councils, Scoutmasters, committees and commissioners was now largely complete as well.

Purists, not least Ernest Thompson Seton, complained that Scouting had lost something important—the innocence and freedom of childhood that had characterized the movement at its conception—in its transformation to respectability. But West's answer was a simple one: under his leadership Scouting had both survived and thrived . . . and would soon be delivering its experience to 1 million American boys. None of that would have been possible with the 1910 version of Scouting. Scouting's extraordinary success was the prima facie counterargument to any of its critics.

But, West could also point out, much of Seton's original vision of Scouting had, in fact remained. It had merely been packaged into, or channeled through, the more formal organization. Thus, Seton's vision of younger Scouts was emerging as Cub Scouting, his worship of Native American culture had been the foundation of Scouting's camping fraternity—the Order of the Arrow (created in 1915)—and when it came to his belief that boys should spend time in the outdoors, how could he argue with hundreds of thousands of American boys now out camping and learning woodcraft skills at least one weekend per month?

Scouting may have lost some of its innocence (though not in the public's imagination) but it had also gained something far more important than good bookkeeping: a new purpose.

The transformative event had been the First World War. Here again, the conflicting visions of the BSA founders had unwittingly forced the best possible compromise. It was a middle ground between Seton's pacifism and Beard's jingoism—a position that could best be described as staunchly patriotic *nonmilitarism.*

What this meant in practice was that the BSA was deeply committed to the war effort as a U.S. organization and went to enormous lengths to instill the values of duty and love of country into its young members. It was also dedicated to teaching its young charges the kind of skills—bravery, resourcefulness, first aid, camping and hiking, and survival—that would make them *become* superior soldiers. But Scouting itself refused to take the next step of teaching American boys to *be* good soldiers. Scouts wore uniforms, but they weren't military uniforms. They marched, but never with weapons. They played war-like games, but never held war games.

This was, at least initially, a difficult position to maintain. As the fighting intensified in Europe, and as older brothers—and eventually older Scouts themselves—began to volunteer or be drafted, considerable pressure from the highest levels was placed on the BSA to become a kind of Junior ROTC and assume some of the duties of military basic training.

Scouting resisted—and that, other than the actual founding of Scouting in America—may have been the single most important decision the BSA ever made.

By not following the path that led to being merely an extension of the armed forces, BSA made itself much less vulnerable to the cultural swings between promilitary and antimilitary eras that characterized American life during the rest of the twentieth century. Radicals of different decades still accused BSA of being a paramilitary organization—an argument that would have had a lot more teeth had the BSA chosen the other path—but those claims found little support.

By taking the position it did, the BSA never faced the danger of being hijacked by political interests pursuing a sinister objective. There were no *Hitler-Jugend* or Soviet Young Pioneers in the future of American Scouting—in the end those who tried, like the German-American Bund with its *Jugendshaft,* were obviously transgressive imitations.

BSA's choice to resist was so important because it also forever changed the *orientation* of Scouting. Until the outbreak of the First World War, Scouting had remained a comparatively introverted organization, focused mainly on camping, woodcraft, and advancement. What encounters these early Scouts had with their communities was mostly restricted to those daily "good turns"—hence the eternal association of Boy Scouts, especially younger ones, with walking little old ladies across the street—and merit badge instruction.

SAVE A SOLDIER

And so it might have remained had war not erupted. Now the Boy Scouts of America faced an existential challenge: how could it, as a patriotic organization, help the nation in its war efforts while still remaining true to its nonmilitaristic charter?

One last time, the parent Scouting organization in the UK provided a model solution. From the beginning, Baden-Powell's program had been accused of being too militaristic. He was, in fact, still on active duty in 1907. Ultimately, several competing organizations formed in reaction to this perception—the Order of World Scouts, which still exists today in 14 countries, and the British Boy Scouts (BBS), which at one point represented one-third of Scouts in the UK. There were even British Peace Scouts. The success and growing internationalism of these organizations—indeed, the BBS appears to have only failed because of financial mismanagement—had forced Baden-Powell to move Scouting away from a strong military connection, a stance he was in no position to abandon in 1914. Instead, he directed Scouting to immerse itself in service on the home front.

Baden-Powell's definition of home "service" was a pretty fluid one—perhaps not surprising given either his background or the fact that Britain was under direct attack. British Scouts not only joined agricultural work and other activities, but also served as military messengers and coastal guards. One Scout, 15-year-old George Taylor, was killed during the siege of Scarborough—and was buried with full military honors at a service filled with his fellow Scouts. Taylor was the only active Scout known to have been killed during the war.

As for Baden-Powell himself, he placed himself before the War Office in search of a command. But Lord Kitchener refused to give him one, saying he "could lay his hand on several competent divisional generals but could find no one who could carry on the invaluable work of the Boy Scouts."[4] Whether or not that was the real reason, it was a wonderful publicity message, and it underscored the importance of British Scouting to the war effort. During the war, it was regularly rumored that Baden-Powell was engaged in espionage activities—an activity never proven, but also shrewdly never denied by intelligence officers.

Three years later the Boy Scouts of America, facing the same challenge, chose the same solution—and with a vengeance. Scouting had already begun to find its public footing with Scouts (many of them Eagles) who had served on the honor guard and support staffs at the Star-Spangled Banner Centennial ceremonies in 1914 and at various sixtieth anniversary reunions of Civil War Veterans beginning in 1913. It had also found considerable success with its National Good Turn, begun in 1912 with a "Sane and Safe Fourth of July" initiative.

On June 15, 1916, the BSA finally reached its goal of a congressional charter. From now on, it would be the sole Scouting organization of the United States. Henceforth, it would be an official American institution.

Now, with America entering the war—and with their big brothers, including former Scouts and Eagles like Arthur Eldred, heading off to France—Scouts were anxious to do their part. The BSA, filled with its own patriotism and recognizing a unique opportunity, quickly created programs to help the boys do so.

First was the Veteran Scout program begun in 1917 to help retiring Scouts, wherever they were, maintain contact with Scouting. Then, when the United States declared war at last, Scouting was ready with a "Help Win the War" campaign. This campaign, which was built on the BSA's ready-made motto—"Be Prepared," incorporated a wide range of programs designed to empower even the youngest Scouts to be part of the war effort. For example, the "Every Scout to Feed a Soldier" initiative instructed Scouts to plant their own victory ("war") gardens—a total of 12,000 were created. In another program destined to become a trivia question, Scouts collected 100 railroad cars' worth of nut hulls and peach pits to be used to make charcoal for gas masks. They also identified and charted the location of 21 million board feet of black walnut trees for use in gunstocks and airplane propellers and distributed 30 million pieces of government literature to the citizenry.[5]

These achievements were impressive enough and did much to capture the public imagination, but they paled in comparison to the showpiece initiative for Scouting during those years—war bonds.

It began with the huge government-sponsored "Wake Up, America!" rally held in New York City on April 17, 1917. Ostensibly held to commemorate the 1775 Battle of Lexington, the rally was in fact a military recruiting event. In an enthralling photograph from that day published in the *National Geographic* (and used nine decades later by the U.S. Post Office to promote a stamp series about the decade), scores of Scouts in full uniform and carrying tall staffs bearing American flags can be seen running down Fifth Avenue as if leading the charge of the 60,000 parade participants into battle.

War bonds—officially "Liberty" Bonds—were an array of government script ranging in valuation from $50 or more for the official money-like bonds, down to just 25¢ for War Saving Stamps. Strictly speaking, these bonds were IOUs covering the principle and interest for the loan made to the government by citizens with their purchase.

War bonds quickly became synonymous with "doing something for our boys 'over there,'" and Liberty Bond rallies often drew thousands—especially when the entertainment featured the likes of Charlie Chaplin, Mary Pickford, or the Ziegfield girls. Boy Scouts across America were enlisted into the program as foot soldiers for the bond drives: handing out promotional flyers, going door to door to either sell bonds or seek out rally attendees, serving as ushers, and perhaps most of all, acting as the very embodiment of "what we're fighting for."

This last was most brilliantly visualized in one of the most celebrated (and collected) posters of the era (called "Weapons for Liberty"). It was created by J. C. Leyendecker for the third Liberty Bond drive in 1918, and as was often the case, began its life as a March 1918 *Saturday Evening Post* cover. It is still a knockout: Lady Liberty atop her plinth has come to life and is now draped in an American flag and carrying a golden shield bearing the Great Seal of the United States (which looks like a giant military officer's dress uniform button). Girded for war, Liberty gazes out into the distance, apparently at an emerging threat and, without looking, is reaching down for her giant broadsword. That sword has been etched with the words "Be Prepared," and it is being lifted to Liberty by a kneeling young Boy Scout wearing a campaign hat, neckerchief, and khaki shorts. On the plinth has been carved: "Weapons for Liberty."

As a piece of propaganda, the poster for the third Liberty Bond drive is a masterpiece. As a bit of over-the-top patriotic theater in poster form (perhaps driven by Leyendecker's self-consciousness about his German birth), it is one of the best ever done by an American illustrator. It is so influential in the Scouting story because of a critical aesthetic decision made by the artist.

Leyendecker was and is justly famous for his images of impossibly handsome men (he did invent the iconic Arrow Collar Man, after all). But with the Scout set beneath the battle-tested, androgynous Lady Liberty, Leyendecker makes a very different choice: he portrays a *real* boy: skinny, a bit gawky, and a bit overwhelmed by the situation in which he finds himself. To understand why this is important, you need only imagine the Scout replaced by a classic Leyendecker square-jawed young man out of an Interwoven Sock or Pierce-Arrow ad: what would be gained in artistic coherence would be more than lost by distancing the viewer. The genius of Leyendecker in putting the real-life boy in the poster is that, for adults, it placed Boy Scouts at the heart of American life during wartime; and for boys, it enabled them to see *themselves* in the poster.[6]

A third impact of this famous poster wouldn't be seen for almost two more decades—in Leyendecker's most faithful follower, Norman Rockwell, who was already painting covers for *Boys' Life*. Rockwell, who would one day be a pallbearer at his mentor's funeral, learned much from this poster . . . not least that no matter how mythical the subject, the Boy Scout in the image had to look like the kid next door.

In the first Liberty Bond drive, held in April 1917, the Boy Scouts under the slogan "Every Scout to Save a Soldier" (the Girl Scouts ran an identical campaign) stunned everyone by raising $23 *million*. They topped that in October, in the second campaign, by raising $102 million.[7] By now, Scouting was becoming as synonymous with Liberty Bonds as Douglas Fairbanks and Al Jolson—not a bad place to be in 1917—and the best was yet to come.

For the third campaign, to be held in April 1918, Scouting went all out. Secretary of the Treasury William Gibbs McAdoo made a special appeal to James West that Boy Scouting shift from the high-profile/high-ticket fundraisers and focus instead on a house-to-house appeal. President Wilson himself asked that Scouting be the "gleaners and reapers" of the Liberty Bond drive, focusing on private citizens and small organizations that the national campaign might not reach—and then to sell the lower-cost instruments like the War Savings Stamps.

The third campaign kicked off with a major rally for Scouts at Liberty Loan Park in New York at Madison Avenue and Thirty-Eighth Street. Afterward, Scouts, armed with their new Government Printing Office pamphlets instructing them on successful salesmanship using the points of the Scout Law, and under the banner of the Leyendecker poster, fanned out across America to do their patriotic duty.

What happened next cemented Scouting forever into American life. A few weeks later, when the numbers were tabulated, it was found that the Boy Scouts of America had sold a seemingly superhuman $205 million *more* bonds—nearly all in the smallest denominations available.[8]

By war's end, over the course of five Liberty Bond drives, America's Boy Scouts sold 2,328,308 bond subscriptions for a total of $354,859,262. They also sold more than 2 million War Saving Stamps worth $43,043,698.[9]

In just 20 months, the BSA had mobilized its 400,000 members, reoriented its energies towards the community and supporting the war effort and, in the process, had raised almost $400 million—more than $5 *billion* in 2010 dollars—toward that effort.[10] The organization then made a quick turn and provided nationwide first-aid service during the 1918 Spanish influenza epidemic.[11]

Together, this was the largest youth service initiative in American history to date. It is little wonder, as the decade ended, that the Boy Scouts were almost heroes as celebrated as the nation's returning doughboys.

PROTAGONIST

Where were Eagles during this great transformation in Boy Scouting? As always, they were in front, leading. But, at this point in the Scouting story, only other Scouts and their leaders noticed.

After just a decade, Boy Scouting was one of the most celebrated new cultural institutions in the land; and the boys who wore its uniform were instantly recognizable almost anywhere. This new celebrity was driven home in 1923 when, joined by Jackie Coogan, the most famous child star of the age, Scouting took part in the national Milk Campaign that made the humble carton of milk a standard feature of school cafeterias for generations to come.

But beyond that, to the general public the Scouts themselves were essentially indistinguishable. They were young and a little older, short and tall, and they all wore khaki uniforms, neckerchiefs, campaign hats, and a variety of patches and pins of obscure meaning.

It would be several decades more before the badges and ranks—especially Eagle—of Scouting would be distinguishable to most Americans. And that process would begin in the 1920s in the world of entertainment and the media.

Scouts emerged from the war years as both amusing and heroic figures— amusing because they were so young and ardent, heroic because of their extraordinary service to the country—and the stories created about Scouting for a hungry audience in the 1920s reflected that schizoid perception.

Beginning with silent films, first in the UK (*Scouts to the Rescue*, 1908) and then in the United States (*Universal Boy Joins the Boy Scouts*, 1914), Scouting was basically a new leitmotif on which to play out traditional adventure stories. Early fiction on Scouting was much the same, notably the Boy Scout series of books begun by author Herbert Carter in 1913 (e.g., *The Boy Scouts through the Big Timber, The Boy Scouts in the Maine Woods, The Boy Scouts' First Camp Fire*). In these productions, the Scouts are young and competent, but usually played to comic effect. This narrative thread has continued right up to the present, constantly adding new layers—postmodernism, cynicism, social conflict, optimism, technology—to essentially the same tale of do-good Scouts made to look foolish out of a combination of too much sincerity and naivety, but ultimately succeeding through their unique skills and determination.

The "good deed daily" Scout stereotype found in the earliest movies, books, and cartoons about Scouting, survives to this day—often slightly disguised to circumvent Scouting's copyright demands—in everything from TV episodes of *The Simpsons* and *South Park,* to comic strips featuring "Calvin and Hobbes" and the "The Berenstain Bears" series of children's books. A more nuanced version of this Scout can also be found in productions such as the classic film *Mr. Smith Goes to Washington*, and even in the guise of a drag queen in the musical *Rent.*

But there is a second, more complicated narrative thread about Scouting that began to emerge during the First World War, exploded in the 1920s, and has made subtle and often unexpected appearances ever since. In these books, movies, and television shows, the Scout is older, more accomplished and almost never a fool—on the contrary, he is often the hero and protagonist of the story. And though it is rarely said—at least not until the last 30 years when the title finally distinguished itself in the public mind—the Scouts are most certainly Eagles. And when their title is stated—as with the Will Smith character in *Men in Black*, or Captain Jonathon Archer in *Star Trek: Enterprise,* or even the Professor on *Gilligan's Island*—"Eagle Scout" is almost always code for clever, brave, and resourceful.

This fictional Eagle first appears in a spate of very popular books published through the 1920s with titles like *Boy Scouts on Motorcycles*, *Boy Scouts in the Northwest Fighting Forest Fires*, and *Boy Scouts of the Air on Lost Island*—potboilers all. But also classic ripping yarns, in which older Scouts behave like proto-action figures (soon-to-be-invented Eagle Scout Indiana Jones comes as no surprise to anyone who has read these books) taking on adult responsibilities, acting bravely, and using their unique Scouting skills to best their evil opponents.

These stories introduced an older, more responsible, and more adventurous image of Scouting not just to the American public, but also to Scouts themselves. And they wanted to be those heroic characters. The 1920s saw the birth of the first glimmerings of Scouting's future high adventure program, as these same older Scouts began testing themselves with 50-mile hikes, wilderness survival camps, and other feats.

One positive result of the influenza epidemic for Scouting had been that the BSA had taken a hard look at its emerging collection of summer camps (military camps had been the breeding ground of the epidemic), concluded that too many were unacceptable, and established a set of standards for these sites—which in turn laid the groundwork for a growing number of special outdoor programs (climbing, rappelling, and so on) at these camps. Needless to say, Eagles soon found their place serving on camp staffs and running these programs.

Other older Scouts migrated to specialty versions of Scouting, notably the Sea Scouts, where they could be with their chronological peers and take part in activities that were riskier, more demanding, and more rugged than most of what traditional Boy Scouting could offer. Besides the Sea Scouts, a number of other specialty Scouting programs emerged over the next 20 years. In a brochure for "Senior Scouts" published by the BSA in 1938, Chief Scout Executive West noted "the surprising fact" that more than 200,000 registered Scouts were more than 15 years old:

> There has never been any upper age limit to Scouting. Hundreds of thousands of young men have carried on as Junior Assistant Scoutmaster, or Assistant Scoutmasters, upon reaching the age of sixteen or eighteen respectively and then have become Scoutmasters. Many others have preserved their membership with their Troop even while away at college as associate Scouts.

During the years, Sea Scouting as a program for older Scouts, has steadily grown in its appeal until today there are 29,500 young men and leaders registered in this branch of the Movement. The experiences gained in our contact with these young men, has been invaluable.

In recent years there have been experiments with Rovering throughout the country. On the college campus, the Alpha Phi Omega, an honorary society for Scouts who are in institutions of higher learning, has come into being. In addition, certain Local Council organizations for older Scouts have come into existence. In the far West, much success was attained in the experiment with an Explorer Program for older Scouts.[12]

The passive language ("have come into being") betrays an organization faced with a fundamental paradox—one that still bedevils Scouting. As its name suggests, Boy Scouting is about *boys*, essentially between the ages of 10 and 14—that is, roughly between fifth and eighth grades, or in Scouting terms, the final "Webelos" year of Cub Scouting and, in Boy Scouting, the achievement of First Class and the leadership position of Patrol Leader. Everything before is basically an after-school program for children; everything after is an adventure/senior management/career training program for young adults.

This isn't to say that the activities on either ends of this spectrum are superfluous to Scouting. On the contrary, the Pinewood Derby for Cub Scouts is as iconic to American life as anything in Scouting. And much of the glory of Boy Scouting lies in its high adventure camps (such as Philmont) and, as we shall see, in its Eagle service projects. But the mass of Scouting will always lie within those four years, with its focus on the patrol, the troop, weekend campouts, and outdoor skills. *That* can never be compromised.

And there is the problem. The better Scouting does its job, the more Scouts who will want to stick with the program after they turn 14, when troop meetings and fourth time around at some of the same campsites is no longer enough. Demography plays a part as well: one reason Scouting (and the rest of America) found itself in a crisis in the late 1960s was because the mass of baby boomers had rolled through and were now in their late teens.

Not wanting to lose this vast source of intellectual capital today, and adult leadership tomorrow, institutions inevitably responded by creating specialty programs for its veteran members that walked a fine line between allowing them a certain amount of independence while still keeping them tightly bound to the organization.

And that is exactly what Scouting did, with those various Senior Scout programs—some of which, such as Sea Scouting and Exploring still survive today.

But these separate programs inevitably bring with them a whole new set of problems. For one thing, they draw away talent and resources from the main organization—a major problem for Scouting in the 1920s when it was short on leaders, and in the 1930s when it was short on money. Another problem is that, if successful, these operations tend to exacerbate the very difficulty they were created to solve: that is, if all of the older Scouts run off to join Rovering (a high adventure camping program) or Sea Scouts, who is left to lead the troops?

Finally, there is the problem of expectations: young men joined senior Scout organizations to live out the dreams of adventure they read about and watched in movies—could Scouting provide that? Did it want to? At the same time, almost by definition, these senior Scouts were the members most committed to advancement—did Scouting want to allow them to continue their march through the ranks even if, strictly speaking, they weren't involved in Boy Scouts anymore? Or did each of these groups need its own advancement program?

Scouting's answer to the first—high adventure—proved to be brilliant. The Senior Scout organizations came and went according to the interests of that age cohort and were free to develop their programs in any way, as long they didn't violate Scouting rules. As for the second, advancement, Scouting mostly failed. Each program did develop its own ranks and supreme award, many of them more difficult than Scouting's own, but the Sea Scouting Quartermaster Award, and the Exploring/Venturing Silver Medal (to name the most popular) never achieved anything like the public acclaim afforded to the Eagle medal—a fact that no doubt led the majority of Scouts to stick with their Boy Scout troops, even as they became increasingly irrelevant to their teenaged lives.

It is hard not to conclude that this was exactly the way the Boy Scouts of America wanted it. It understood the desire of these older boys to continue their Scouting experience (or join and catch up on what they missed), and was happy to allow these institutional "safety valves" to pop up on the fringes of the program. But each year, a half-million excited new 11-year-olds were showing up at troop meetings around the country—and the BSA's first duty was to engage those boys, give them an experience they'd remember the rest of their lives, and help them reach the summit of basic Scouting—the First Class rank.

But there was one other group of older Scouts who shared the same desire to stay engaged with Scouting, combined with a desire to create their own special program, that was so central to Scouting that the BSA could neither ignore nor marginalize it: Eagle Scouts. As the finest flowering of the Scouting philosophy and the ne plus ultra of the movement, Eagle Scouts were too important for Scouting to lose—and yet, by the mid-1920s, several thousand were aging out every year.

The BSA had rested its hopes on the belief that, being among the most committed of Scouts, Eagles would want to stay associated with the program straight through into adulthood—hence West's almost wistful comment about older Scouts becoming Junior Assistant Scoutmasters, Assistant Scoutmasters, and then Scoutmasters in the years to come. Certainly that would prove true for many Eagle Scouts—but often after an interregnum of decades. The flaw in Scouting's logic—once again it had been surprised by its Eagles—was that it had failed to understand that overachievers rarely stick around to admire their handiwork; instead, they race off for the next mountain to climb.

Still, if Scout headquarters did not yet understand the problem, a continent away there was one Scouting professional who did: a born entrepreneur who would have felt right at home in the world of high-tech start-up companies that would define his community a half-century hence. And he would build the most mythic (literally and figuratively), among the most influential, and the least celebrated, organization in Scouting history.

A RETINUE OF KNIGHTS

Raymond O. Hanson was the right man for the challenge. A slight man with horn-rimmed glasses who most resembled a college professor, Hanson was in fact—in the great Northern California tradition—one of the great mavericks of American Boy Scouting. And as he pondered the conundrum of the Lost Eagles, it slowly dawned on him that the solution might not be to reform Scouting, but to lead a friendly revolt against it.

In early 1925, the BSA was not only experiencing spectacular growth, but was also looking forward to even more as a baby boomlet created by the war was about enter its teenage years. This expansion in both membership and units combined with the chronic shortage of leaders was putting considerable stress on the organization—and the last thing it had time to worry about was either the retention of older Scouts or the care and cultivation of Eagles. Meanwhile, most of the senior Scouting programs described in the 1938 brochure were either just being born or as yet unimagined.

As Hanson studied the situation, he realized that the wealth and youthful excitement of the Roaring Twenties was sparking the creation of a number of new organizations for young people, and many—his attention was particularly drawn to the phenomenally successful Masonic youth society DeMolay, founded in 1919—seemed to be doing a much better job at attracting and keeping older teens than Scouting.

Investigating these competing organizations, Hanson discovered several common themes: exclusivity, a commitment to service, "adult" activities such as dress balls and dinners, rituals and ranks of distinction, membership that continued to age 21 and beyond, and a small amount of mystery.

On April 19, 1925, Hanson invited 10 local Eagle Scouts (Jack McDonald, Lou Mulloy, Clement Schnabel, Scott McDonald, Raymond Moyle, Ralph Gilley, Stewart Ebner, Prescott Blatterman Jr., Joseph Roger, and Ted Blockley) to his Market Street office and presented his thoughts to them. He was shrewd enough to leave just enough of its elucidation to the boys to give them ownership of the idea, while still keeping the plan within the boundaries of his own thinking, notably in terms of an overarching mystical theme. With Indians, pioneers, explorers, pilots, and sailors already taken, Hanson took a cue from DeMolay and chose knighthood—an inspired choice given the implicit chivalry of the Eagle Scout image.

This wasn't the first such meeting Hanson had attempted. Nine years later, the organization's newsletter would recall that "several other meetings previous to this one were held at which ways and means were discussed to bring about a permanent organization. Several attempts failed. Something was lacking . . ."13

Reading between the lines, it seems pretty obvious that rather than tripping over the idea for this new organization through trial and error, Hanson was in fact slowly moving the boys toward a consensus . . . and on that Sunday night (the day is important to show that, from the beginning, this was a nonofficial group) he got it.

The program was to be called the Knights of Dunamis—the final term derived from the Greek word for "power" or "spirit."

The Knights of Dunamis, Hanson suggested and the boys agreed, would follow the theme of the Knights of the Round Table with swords, capes, and even on occasion, helmets. New members were to be called Squires, and established members were designated Knights (and addressed as "Sir Knight") or Knight Commanders (chapter presidents), and there would be a series of requirements, initiations, and award ceremonies for each position. Eventually the Knights of Dunamis (KD) would create its own ultimate rank, Knight-Eagle, which would unofficially become the highest honor for a boy in Scouting.

It was also agreed by the little group that:

1. The Knights of Dunamis would be an honor society dedicated exclusively to service to both Scouting and the community.
2. Membership would only be open to Eagle Scouts.

These two little spur-of-the-moment decisions would prove to be momentous in the story of the Boy Scouts of America. The first would turn Scouting, for the first time, permanently away from its hermetic world of camping and woodcraft and dedicate it to full-time public service . . . a move that would eventually lead to the Eagle service project and a permanent transformation of the face of America. The second would, also for the first time, make Eagle Scouting a distinct entity, part of Scouting yet apart from it, and a lifelong brotherhood. "Once an Eagle, always an Eagle" began that day in Raymond Hanson's office.

Having completed their vote, the 10 Eagles were then presented by Hanson with a preliminary program for new member initiation and other rituals, as well as for new ranks and their requirements. Scribed in the KD newsletter in 1934, "The plans were enthusiastically received and it was voted to organize a chapter immediately and to adopt a Constitution and by-laws."[14] The 10 Eagles then selected the officers for Chapter Number 1 of the Knights of Dunamis and named Hanson Patron General in perpetuity. After this, Hanson led the newly elected Commander Jack McDonald into another room and read him the ritual and administered the oath of office. He followed that with similar ceremonies for each of the Chapter's new officers. The secret side of KD, a source of consternation in years to come, had begun.

The 10 new Sir Knights ended the meeting by performing the newly written closing ceremonies for the first time and then made their way home in the darkness. The Knights of Dunamis had been formally founded.

In the months ahead, the details of the society's rituals and regalia were elaborated. It was classic secret society mumbo jumbo; here's a scene from an induction ceremony that sounds to modern ears like something out of Dungeons & Dragons:

Senior Councilor: Has he satisfied you that he is qualified to do this?

Third Guard: He has proven himself worthy of our confidence.

Senior Councilor: Very well. We will escort him further—(to Candidate) but I warn you, my friend, that you have not yet reached the goal of your ambition, and that beyond this door, Seven Knights who are seated at the Round Table will demand further proof that you are a true Eagle Scout and that you are continuing to practice daily the Scout Oath and Law.

The Senior Councilor knocks five times and the same is answered in like fashion by the First Sir Knight of the Castle, after which the door is opened with sound effects.[15]

One of the founding Sir Knights, Clem Schnabel, designed the emblem of the Order: an Eagle, taken from the BSA medal, clenching a broadsword ("the sword of Galahad") in its talons, atop a triangular shield bearing "KD" in blue letters. According to the Order's history, the Eagle symbolized service, the sword symbolized leadership gained in that service, and the three sides of the triangular shield stood for the three parts of the Scout Oath.

This emblem, as a lapel pin, jacket patch, neckerchief and slide, and even on the end of a blue-and-white uniform pocket "dangle" (similar to that presented by the Order of the Arrow), would come to distinguish the Knights of Dunamis from the rest of Scouting and extend the image of the Eagle further in public life. Eighty years later, they would also become among the most prized and valuable Scouting collectibles.

(The Knights of Dunamis wasn't the only Eagle organization to emerge during this period—only the most successful. A number of adult Eagle groups popped up in the mid-West to offer their help to local councils. Across the Bay from the KD in Oakland, the "Ohitekah Tribe" had a brief existence. And most interestingly, the Diocesan Troop, created by the Roman Catholic archdiocese of Chicago, was created to serve as honor guards at priest ordinations and to provide future candidates for the priesthood.)[16]

That October 27th, chosen because it was the birthday of early Scout supporter Theodore Roosevelt, the KD held its first public installation. It took place at the Golden Gate Commandery (Knights Templar Hall) in San Francisco and featured public speeches, a music concert, and a new Eagle Scout Court of Honor—very different from traditional Scouting events and a first glimpse of the new organization's new trajectory. So too were the semiannual past-commander's banquets, first held in January 1926, and the annual semiformal balls, both dress-up affairs in which a Scout uniform was a rare sight.

By December 1929, when the Bay Area chapters met to create a Grand (Headquarters) Chapter, the Knights of Dunamis had 13 chapters, including Chapter 3 in Atlantic City, New Jersey. By 1933, the KD had 27 chapters across the United States, mostly around major cities, 750 members and 130 adult associates, and a new slogan: "Power and Service."[17]

By "power," KD was playing off the meaning of the "Dunamis," but the underlying message was clear: the Eagles who now comprised the Knighthood were the zenith, the princes, of Scouting—and as such, they wielded considerable power inside Scouting as leaders and role models and outside Scouting as its shining emissaries.

As for "service," this was an evolving notion for the Knights. During its first decade, this meant service to Scouting. The Order regularly published for its members long lists of ways in which they could help Scouting, from hosting Courts of Honor to serving as merit badge counselors, and from working as summer camp staff to even serving as temporary Scoutmasters for orphaned troops. Said a 1936 flyer:

> No one can deny the lack of adult leadership at the present time. This is due not so much to [a] lack of volunteers but rather to their lack of experience . . . The Knights of Dunamis can aid Scouting in great measure by serving as leaders, instructors, and examiners in Troops where the Scoutmaster is handicapped by his own inexperience, and by a lack of efficient junior leaders.[18]

This contribution by the Knights of Dunamis to Scouting in the BSA's difficult middle years during the Depression and the war has largely gone unrecognized. But that certainly wasn't the case at the time with its recipients. In the late 1930s, when Hanson decided to audit the impact of the KD and requested comments from executives of councils where the Knights had a chapter, he was inundated with letters lauding the KD for its contribution. Sir Knights filled the staffs of summer camps, merit badge midways, Scout circuses (a popular advancement gathering of the era), and camporees. They also served as Assistant Scoutmasters to new troops and staged nearly all of the Eagle Courts of Honor.

QUEST

The Knights of Dunamis now seemed perfectly positioned to move ahead of the other pretenders and claim ownership of the now-empty 18- to 21-year-old wing of Boy Scouting. Raymond Hanson could look on with satisfaction that his little brainstorm had grown in just a dozen years into the most visible, and in many ways the most influential, new movement in Scouting. The organization was still Western-heavy, but new chapters that were popping up in Washington, DC; Boston; and Kansas City were beginning to change that as well.

The future of the Knights of Dunamis looked very bright indeed.

What Hanson didn't realize was, almost from day one, he had made a strategic blunder that would one day prove fatal to the KD. In fact, in many ways he was already at the climax of the KD story . . . because he was about to crash into two roadblocks unique to his Eagles, which no one had foreseen.

Hanson's strategic mistake dated all of the way back to that first meeting in his office. He had imagined an independent organization, part of the BSA but still detached from it in terms of ranks, rituals, and membership requirements. In this way, Hanson believed, the Knights of Dunamis could be a tremendous asset to Scouting, bringing its unequalled intellectual capital to bear wherever the BSA's operations were weak.

And, as the letters to Hanson showed, the KD was just that. However, James West and the staff at BSA's National Headquarters in New York City saw a lot more. Beyond the standard East Coast skepticism that anything new and of value could come from the West Coast, the BSA also saw other problems: an exclusive club inside an organization that stressed its lack of exclusivity; a group that often behaved as adults with dates, dances, cars, and parties when Scouting was designed to be a final respite from the complexities of adulthood; a new locus of power—a praetorian guard with unmatched credentials—that could eventually challenge Scouting's leadership; and perhaps most important of all, an organization of the elite of Scouting that was so appealing that it was actually drawing young leadership talent *away* from troops.

Secret societies for good (Elks, Shriners, Rotary, and Lions) and evil (the KKK, European fascists) were all the rage in the 1920s and 1930s, but Scouting, probably rightly, feared them. And if the Knights of Dunamis was obviously benign, there was no guarantee it would stay so, or that this valuable asset wouldn't one day prove a parasite on the organization.

Had he been as calculating as he was clever, Ray Hanson would have traveled to New York at the very beginning of the KD, built support, and lobbied to have the Knights fully recognized as part of Scouting. Instead, by the time he requested that certification it was already too late. To read the minutes of the annual KD conferences of the 1930s shows, in the midst of all of the good news, a persistent effort by the Knights toward recognition by the BSA turning into a forlorn hope. It's not that the KD didn't try: Chief Scout Executive West was invited, and attended, the KD national convention one year in San Francisco. Other senior Scout executives were invited to join the KD national council. And even the Chief Scout of the World, Lord Baden-Powell was invited, and accepted, an honorary membership, while stopping in San Francisco in 1935 on his last world tour.

The aging founder responded to the honor with a message that was, in part, a warning:

> *I have been watching with interest the growth of the Knights of Dunamis among Eagle Scouts, and am especially gratified to see its members have realized the truism that it is one thing to be in a state of mind for doing things but that it is quite another to do them.*
>
> *The Knights of Dunamis have a hunch that it is a good thing to render service, in some form to Scoutcraft . . . This is of great potential value to the Scout movement; it not only prevents the Knights of Dunamis from becoming a class of superior beings distinct from their younger brothers, but also it is a big help to our organization as a whole in keeping the older boys still under the influence of Scouting.*[19]

In other words, *Don't get above yourselves.* Dedicate yourselves to Scouting, and Scouting will find a place for you.

But that place was still up in the air. For all of KD's efforts, the BSA continued to keep the Order at arm's length—even as it began to embrace other peripheral organizations. In 1938, in what was perceived as a breakthrough, Boy Scouts finally recognized the Knights of Dunamis . . . but nothing more. The KD was now officially a member of the Boy Scout family—but with limited support and almost no recognition.

Still, it was assumed that full recognition was just a matter of time. In fact, it would be more than 30 years before Scouting fully embraced the Knights of Dunamis—and that was only as a prelude to killing it.

If Hanson had pressed for full recognition early, the history of the Knights of Dunamis may have been very different. As it was, the organization ended the 1930s watching helplessly as it was eclipsed by Exploring—open to all older Scouts, even accepting new Scouts—as the BSA's new favorite organization.[20]

It didn't help that its own success was making it increasingly difficult for the Order even to fulfill Baden-Powell's admonition and stick to service to Scouting. Thanks to the KD, the general public was beginning to discover this singular breed of super-Scout . . . and even as the Order's members were busy with their service commitments to Scouting, individual chapters increasingly found themselves asked (often by local Scout councils) to serve as honor guards at parades, speeches, conventions, and conferences. KD members themselves also increasingly treated the Knighthood as an extension not just of Scouting, but also of their high school service clubs—and began volunteering at hospitals, soup kitchens, and during disasters. In time, the KD armband would become as well known as the neckerchief or pocket dangle.

These community service activities provided immediate and immeasurable goodwill for the Boy Scouts of America. In the long term, they did even more: they set the stage for the Eagle Scout service project. Indeed, with the perspective of 75 years, it can be said that the modern Eagle Scout award most resembles in its requirements and difficulty, the Sir Knight title (requiring as it did both the traditional Eagle plus extensive service). And if there is a historic precedent for the Adams Award for best Eagle service projects in the nation, it is probably the Knight Eagle award.

But in the short term, these activities drew the KD away from its Scouting activities—making it less vital by the year to the BSA, and opening the door even further to the Order of the Arrow; Exploring; and other more ecumenical, Scoutcraft-oriented groups.

Still, the Knights of Dunamis, given its rapid growth—it peaked at 110 chapters—and immense contribution to Scouting, might still have eventually forced itself on Scouting by its sheer size and importance. However, that is when the two roadblocks appeared that couldn't have been bigger obstacles.

The first was the Great Depression. Even at its zenith, the KD found itself begging its chapters to pay their dues—not a major problem for the Chapter 1 kids going to Berkeley or Stanford, but a real burden on other chapters from Northern California and elsewhere. Making the situation worse was the unexpected reality that while parents might scrape together enough money for their 11-year-old's Scout uniform; their 20-year-old Eagle son was on his own. And, because the BSA didn't even allow the Knights to run a capital campaign until 1939, the KD was almost always nearly broke and unable to finance a national recruitment campaign.

In the end, even the Great Depression didn't prove to be the biggest threat to the survival of the Knights of Dunamis. Rather, it was World War II. The KD hit a challenge that traditional Scouting had never faced: its members were all of military age. And, being Eagles—indeed, *beyond* Eagles: Knight Eagles had to earn 36 merit badges, restore a Scout troop, and perform prodigies of leadership and service—they were the perfect candidates for military officer training.

By mid-1942, the ranks of the Order had been decimated by the draft and enlistment. The KD had performed one last great service to the country. In the hours after Pearl Harbor, members of the Honolulu chapter of the KD rushed to the scene of the attack and volunteered their help. It was a fitting end to the first era of the Knights of Dunamis.

COMING HOME

When the KD was reborn after World War II, it was a radically different organization. Not only had the first generation of Knights disappeared with the war, but so had the founder himself. Ray Hanson retired from Scouting for health reasons in 1942. He died two years later, at age 54.

Almost nothing survived of the old order but its symbols and rituals— and the latter were increasingly honored in the breach. Arthurian sagas and secret societies no longer had as much attraction in the Atomic Age.

The newly emerging chapters—and those that survived, including Chapter 1—increasingly dispensed with the robes and the rococo titles. The ceremonial sword was now rarely hauled out, and only for investitures and

Eagle Courts of Honor. The new Knights of Dunamis now looked less like DeMolay and more like a college service fraternity.

That was no coincidence: if the KD was never lucky with Scouting, it was certainly blessed with leaders. Hanson's eventual replacement, who would serve the Order for the rest of its history was Dr. Lester R. Steig, a San Francisco school administrator who, tellingly, had been a major figure in the story of Alpha Phi Omega, the national college service fraternity based on Scouting's principles and officially recognized by the BSA in 1931.

Steig would go on to become one of the most honored figures in Scouting history—serving as national president of Alpha Phi Omega and earning its National Distinguished Service Key. In Scouting, he would not only become the national president of the Knights of Dunamis, but also earn Scouting's two highest awards for adults: the Silver Buffalo and the Distinguished Eagle Scout Award.

KD II, as it might be called, was almost exclusively a service organization, now dedicated as much to being the face of local Scouting to the community as to Scouting itself, where the task had now largely been assumed by the others. And though it never grew again to more than a few thousand members, its impact was far out of proportion to its size. In the Golden Age of Boy Scouting, the Knights of Dunamis was the BSA's most famous (if uncredited) public face.

For example, a typical year for the reborn Knights of Dunamis Chapter 33 in San Jose, California, in the early 1970s included serving as master of ceremonies for more than 30 Eagle Courts of Honor; honor guard duties at Christmas, Veterans Day, and Cinco de Mayo parades; flag honor guard at several county supervisor meetings, State of the City, and other events; holding a Christmas party for children at a local hospital; packing emergency supplies; *and* cooking and manning a wedding reception for a local Scout executive (the fees donated to charity).

Once again, in such a list, one can see the template for the Eagle service projects to come.

But, for all of its achievements—and its tenacious endurance—the Order was still viewed with suspicion by a BSA that still believed the KD to be too independent, too exclusive, and too much of an attraction drawing

Eagles away from troops. In other words, the Knights were trapped: whether succeeding or failing, the BSA deemed them a failure and withheld its support.

Well, not always. In 1956, the BSA National Executive Board at last—after 30 years—gave its blessing to the KD. Two years later, shifting its support to the new national rollout of Exploring, it rescinded that certification. And the dreams of two generations of Sir Knights were dashed again.

It is a measure of both the organizational strength and the internal morale of the Knights of Dunamis that, despite this devastating turn, it not only endured, but also continued to grow in both size and influence. Boy Scouting may not have believed in the KD, but Eagle Scouts still believed in the Knights of Dunamis.

Remarkably enough, thanks to an interesting confluence of events, the KD was given one last chance at legitimacy. Les Steig was a mild-mannered, courtly man, but he had a will of iron, and he surrounded himself with a young national chapter leadership filled with future college presidents and corporate executives. Steig began by completely restructuring the KD, stripping out the last remnants of the 1920s secret society and making it into an association. Then, in the late 1960s this leadership group, leveraging Steig's own reputation at BSA National Headquarters, made one last attempt at acceptance. Amazingly, they got a welcome reception.

The explanation was pure serendipity. In 1967, Alden G. Barber was appointed the fifth chief Scout executive. He is remembered today for having led Scouting not only at its peak in membership, but also through one of the most culturally challenging periods in its history. That Barber was a maverick and risk taker was not surprising given that he had learned adult Scouting from a similar character: Ray Hanson. Alden G. Barber had been in fact, a KD chapter commander in Chico, California, in the mid-1930s, and in time, national commander of the Knights of Dunamis.

Barber was not only the ultimate advertisement for the value of the Order; he also understood it better than anyone. And now, at last, he gave the Knights of Dunamis its break. Suddenly, Scouting was talking about the KD, its surviving chapters were given national support, and there was even a page in the Scout Uniform catalog dedicated KD gear. In November

1967, the BSA Executive Board passed a resolution stating, "the Boy Scouts of America recognize the Knights of Dunamis and cooperate with them in achieving their objectives." The KD had waited 52 years for those 18 words.

To the surviving Knights—and especially chapter alumni—this sudden realization of a half-century-old dream was staggering. Perhaps now the Knights of Dunamis would take its rightful place in the Scouting family. Chief Scout Executive Barber even came and spoke at the Order's 1968 convention—another first.

THE LAST BATTLE

But it was too late. By now, the KD had shrunk to just 44 chapters (many of them inactive) in 22 states. Meanwhile, Scouting itself was beset with its own problems: a toxic combination of trying to be too relevant and urban, combined with changing rank requirements, and the departure of the baby boomers from teenagehood, had devastated Scouting's membership rolls. It had little time or patience to wait for the KD to come around. In giving its support to the Order at last, it was also giving it one last chance.

And so, in 1971, even as the KD was holding meetings and conferences to come up with a strategy to regain its storied past, the BSA was already working on its own study about what to do with its Eagle Scouts. Leading the charge were two members of the BSA National Council, Donald H. Flanders and J. Kimball Whitney. The concept they developed, the National Eagle Scout Association, would abandon almost all that had made the Knights such a singular program—guaranteeing it would never again steal away young Eagles from their troops—in exchange for full BSA support and (because all Eagles of any age were welcomed) a massive increase in membership.

The bomb was dropped on the KD at its conference in Asilomar, California, in 1973. Steig, accepting the inevitable, agreed to join the NESA transition team and use his influence to convince the Knights to accept the change. Flanders would later say of Steig, "He was a big help to me in trying to fold the Knights of Dunamis into NESA." NESA's new *Eagletter* would go so far as to say, "Les Steig, probably more than any other single individual, provided the impetus for the birth of the National Eagle Scout Association."[21]

Though he would live until 1995, dying at the age of 91, there is no record of Dr. Steig's opinion of that appraisal. He had saved the Order at the cost of its identity. Brokenhearted Knights joined the staff of the two national jamborees in 1973 and put on happy faces as they announced to giant crowds of Eagles the creation of the new NESA. Most wore their KD neckerchiefs and armbands as they did so.

A few KD chapters, notably the one in Long Beach, held out for a few more years. But by the late 1970s, the Knights of Dunamis was gone. Even the board members who joined NESA had moved on.

Today, except among collectors who prize the rare surviving items from the organization and among a few gray-haired men who still pointedly wear fraying dangles on their uniform shirts or KD pins on their suit jacket lapels, the Knights of Dunamis is long forgotten.

A KNIGHT'S FAREWELL

Nine decades after Raymond O. Hanson called that meeting in his San Francisco office, there is one surviving memorial to his creation. It stands 80 miles north of that office in the "Knights of Dunamis Grove" at the San Francisco Council's Camp Royaneh.[22]

Hanson built Camp Royaneh during his tenure as council executive, and each summer from the mid-1920s to the late 1950s, the members of KD Chapter 1 would travel up to the camp and hold a big Saturday night ceremony in front of the other campers. In that ceremony, as many as 50 Eagles would march singing down the hill from their encampment in the grove with their banners and white neckerchiefs, with the robed chapter commander in the lead, and sit at special tables in the mess hall with their Chief Knight Ray Hanson. Later that evening, the KD would put on a campfire program for the younger Scouts, often featuring chapter alumni who had gone on to careers in the arts.

The Grove was dedicated in 1942, two years before Hanson's death.[23] Many years later, a black marble headstone was placed there. It still stands and reads:

In Memory of
RAYMOND O. HANSON
1890-1944
FOUNDER
KNIGHTS OF DUNAMIS
Eagle Scout Service Society

Above those words is carved the last surviving public image of the Knights of Dunamis logo.

Raymond Hanson didn't invent the Eagle rank. But more than anyone, he invented modern Eagle Scouting. And even though his name and the Order he created may be now long forgotten, his legacy is stronger than ever.

CHAPTER FOUR

FIRE AND ICE

ON AUGUST 13, 1928, THE *NEW YORK TIMES*, THE
NATION'S MOST INFLUENTIAL NEWSPAPER, CARRIED
THE HEADLINE "SCOUTS IN RACE FOR
HONOR OF JOINING BYRD'S EXPEDITION."

Scouting's most famous adventure had begun. The story picked up by numerous other newspapers electrified Boy Scouts across the country. Soon, thousands of applications flooded the New York offices of Commander Richard E. Byrd. And what had begun as something of a publicity stunt quickly became a national obsession.[1]

It was the era of polar exploration—and Byrd was one of the most celebrated of its adventurer-explorers. He had come a bit late to the game. As early as 1908 American Frederick Cook claimed to be the first to reach the North Pole, but his claim was generally disputed, and today the credit is usually given to the team led by American Robert Peary and that included Matthew Henson and four Inuit men. They reached the North Pole on April 6, 1909.

The South Pole, by comparison, was first reached by Norwegian Roald Amundsen on December 14, 1911, just 34 days before the doomed second expedition of the British Robert Falcon Scott.

Each of these heroic—and harrowing—journeys made the history books and fired the world's imagination. All of these men were prodigies of human endurance. In terms of impact on mankind's future, Byrd's expeditions to the South Pole—which began 15 years later—were far more influential.

Seen from today's perspective, Byrd's polar assaults seem auguries of the future, in which cutting-edge technology and careful project management (at the time credited to "Byrd's Luck") enabled the Commander and his crew to not only embark on high profile expeditions, but also to conduct scientific research along the way . . . and return alive. From the elaborate staging, to the regular radio communications, to the triumphant returns, the Byrd expeditions seem like primitive rehearsals for the Apollo missions.

In the first of these adventures, on May 9, 1926, Byrd and his co-pilot Floyd Bennett, flew a Fokker Tri-motor over the North Pole—just three days before Amundsen and his American sponsor Lincoln Ellsworth did the same thing in the airship *Norge*. For this feat, Byrd and Bennett were awarded the Congressional Medal of Honor.[2]

It is a measure of the inherent danger in this kind of adventuring that a year later co-pilot Bennett, in a practice run with Byrd and a third pilot in their pursuit of the Orteig Prize for flying across the Atlantic (won by Lindbergh a few weeks later), was seriously injured a crash. The resulting injury would lead to pneumonia that would kill Bennett a year later during an equally daring flight to northern Canada to save the downed crew of the airship *Bremen*. Byrd was heartbroken by the loss. His co-pilot on Bennett's final flight, Bernt Balchen, would be the chief pilot of Byrd's aerial assault on the South Pole—and the plane they flew would be named the *Floyd Bennett.*

Most of these details are long forgotten in twenty-first century memories; but they were in the forefront of every boy's dreams in the mid-1920s (as late as the early 1930s, Amelia Earhart would hire Balchen to fly her Lockheed Vega—using his fame to distract the world from her own secret planning for an Atlantic crossing.) Once Byrd had conquered the North Pole, it seemed inevitable he would take on Antarctica and the South Pole. But when, in announcing the adventure, he added that he would be taking along an American boy—a Boy Scout—the result was frenzy.

From among the thousands of applications, the Boy Scouts of America winnowed out all Scouts who had not met the basic requirements for the honor: the applicant had to be between 17 and 20 years old; he had to have been a member in good standing for two years in the BSA; and he had to have earned either the First Class or Able Sea Scout rank. The applicant also was required to have completed a 500- to 1,000-word essay stating his reasons for wanting to be part of the exhibition and his explanation of why he was uniquely suited for the honor.

To these requirements, the BSA added that preference would be given to Scouts with merit badges whose skills would directly support the expedition, including astronomy, carpentry, hiking, photography, signaling, surveying, and taxidermy. Boating and winter camping experience were also expected.

Given all of these stipulations, the local councils were able to quickly narrow the applicant pool down to just 88 boys. Then, in turn, the national office—making heavy use of the applicants' essays—cut the list to just six boys representing the absolute best of Scouting— Donald H. Cooper, Sumner D. Davis, Jack Hirschmann, Paul Siple, Alden Snell, and Clark Spurlock.[3] All the finalists were Eagle Scouts, *and* all were veteran winter campers and had earned at least 31 merit badges. One had earned the Honor Medal for saving a life, another had summited Mount Rainier, and a third had paddled a canoe 180 miles. They also came from hometowns as different as Birmingham, Alabama, and Tacoma, Washington. Arguably, there were no better candidates for this expedition under the age of 21 in the United States.

In August 1928, the six were invited to New York City for the final stage of the competition. There, they spent 10 miserable days undergoing a battery of tests in complex skills, the Army IQ test, physical examinations, and personal interviews. Then, with the media in tow (one reporter, Russell Owen of the *New York Times*, would even join the expedition to cover the story), the candidates were rushed around the city for a week to be part of various media events—including a trip to Byrd's flagship, *The City of New York*, to meet its captain.

The culminating event was a luncheon hosted by Commander Byrd himself. Like any great leader, Byrd had an ulterior motive for the gathering:

it enabled him to watch the six candidates alone and together, and in interaction with perceived subordinates, peers, and superiors. During the course of the luncheon, Byrd made a point to go up to each boy, introduce himself, shake the boy's hand, and look him in the eye. Just from that brief moment, Byrd largely made his choice. It was finalized when he compared his own judgment with that of a quick poll taken of the finalists—asking which two other finalists each would pick to go with them on the expedition—and found that the results were unanimous. Every Scout had named one boy as his first choice: Paul Siple. Byrd had his Eagle.

SCOUTING'S BEAU IDEAL

If Paul Siple hadn't existed, Scouting would have invented him—and, in a way, it already had. The 19-year-old whose image appeared under the headline, "Erie Scout with Byrd" on the front of the *Erie Dispatch-Herald,* could have stepped out of one of those potboiler Scouting novels of the era as the resourceful and fearless hero. And he would prove to be more than that.

Born in Montpelier, Ohio, in 1908, Paul's family moved to Erie, Pennsylvania, when he was nine. Three years later, in 1920, he joined Boy Scout Troop 24. With impressive speed—no doubt in part because he was skillful at the one merit badge subject that ruined the dreams of three generations of early Scouts: Bird Study—Siple earned his Eagle medal when he was just 15.

As if his Eagle was merely a prelude rather than a culmination, Siple then turned around and joined the Sea Scouts, becoming an Able Sea Scout. Because Sea Scouting allowed him to advance as a Scout, Siple continued to earn merit badges, until by his 18th birthday, he had earned 59 merit badges—nearly all that were available, making him one of the highest-achieving Scouts in the country. (Because Scouting retirement rules were different then, Siple would go on to earn a total of 61 merit badges.)

In June 1926, Paul Siple graduated from Erie's Central High School and went to work as an assistant draftsman at the Pennsylvania State Highway

Department. That job helped him pay for tuition at Allegany College in nearby Meadville, where he enrolled that fall.

And there Paul Siple might have remained, ultimately becoming a laboratory scientist at some local company, had that article not appeared in the *Times*. As with many young men his age, Commander Byrd had been a hero of Siple's. He had followed the great man's exploits through his high school years and had dreamed of being along with him on a polar expedition. And now, the opportunity was there before him.

There was every reason for Siple *not* to apply. He was, strictly speaking, out of Scouting now, in college and with a job. But he also knew, as did his family and the people who supported him in this quest, that he was not an ordinary Scout. The early Eagle and the three score merit badges proved that—as did Paul's skills in cold weather camping, taxidermy, and sailing. Looking at the requirements for the honor, Siple figured he had as good a chance as any Scout in the country.

But there was more than that; and this was the distinction that made Byrd take notice at that luncheon: Paul Siple was huge. Six feet tall and 180 pounds in an era when the average adult man was six inches shorter and 20 pounds lighter, photos show him as a Boy Scout sitting on a bench towering over the Scouts around him. He also had the overdrawn features of a hero: a large and long face with hawk-like features, a wide mouth with almost comically large teeth, and huge hands that suggested immense reservoirs of hidden strength. If you were to imagine an Eagle Scout joining a company of tough veterans on a polar exploration mission, he would probably look a lot like Paul Siple.

What the photographs don't capture is what Byrd saw in Siple's eyes. Where many of the other candidates were visibly nervous meeting their hero for the first time, Siple, no doubt at least as frightened, swallowed his fear and stepped forward, looked the legend in the eye, and firmly shook the Commander's hand. At that moment, Byrd knew that Paul Siple was a hero, awaiting his call. And Siple would show his bravery and cool judgment under the most stressful conditions imaginable in the months—and decades—to come.

After a few brief days in Erie, where friends, neighbors, and civic leaders feted their now-famous native son, Paul Siple headed back to New York City. On August 25, the first of Byrd's four-ship flotilla, the wooden square-rigged *City of New York*, carrying 200 tons of cargo (everything from thumbtacks to airplanes) as well human passengers—scientists, engineers, expedition veterans, and one Boy Scout—weighed anchor and started down the Hudson River.

Hundreds of people lined the dock waving farewell, including two of the major underwriters of the $500,000 expedition ($25 million in 2010 dollars), John D. Rockefeller and Edsel Ford; representatives of the other sponsors, including Maxwell House coffee and Beechnut chewing gum; Paul Siple's parents and older sister, and, much noted by the media and on-lookers, a contingent of Scouts from Troop 24, Erie, Pennsylvania.

For the next two years—he would return in June 1930 to a very different America—Paul Siple would not only participate in, but would play a major role in one of the epic adventures of the twentieth century. He would be tested every step of the way—and on more than one occasion would use his Scouting skills to save his own, or another person's life. And the callow youth would return as a veteran explorer and researcher, ready to embark on a career that would make him the most famous of all polar scientists.

ON DECK

With his legendary organizational skills, Commander Byrd had planned for each of his four ships to arrive in New Zealand at the same time. That meant a staggered start, with the old *City of New York* given a head start, followed six weeks later by the steel-hulled *Eleanor Bolling* (named after Byrd's mother) carrying 300 tons of supplies, sailing out of Norfolk, Virginia. Following it, but catching up quickly, would be two smaller whaling boats filled with men and dogs, steaming out of Southern California.

Over the two months of the cruise, Paul Siple endured the usual indignities of a long voyage in an old boat—seasickness, tight quarters, a bunk too small for his huge frame, cabin bullies, vermin, hazing, and practical jokes. He was also initially assigned duty as a messmate in the ship's galley, which meant long days in a cabin without a porthole, breathing greasy smoke and sundry smells, and peeling thousands of potatoes. But he was tough and single-minded, and he learned to endure the misery.

Then, in a bit of good luck, a stowaway was discovered on board. By tradition, the stowaway had to earn his stay on the ship until he could be dropped off at the nearest port—in this case, Panama. When he was made a messmate, Siple was promoted to the duty of port watch. He had at last made it to the open air—though in a job that provided little sleep.

It only got more challenging from there. Just a few weeks into the voyage, the old hull sprung a leak that flooded the engine room—the salt water damaging the boiler, fouling much of the stored fresh water. Siple and others fought to plug the leak—and then spent days pumping out the water and working, via added shifts, to repair the engine. Meanwhile, the remaining water was reserved for drinking, so the crew soon grew filthy, wearing salt-encrusted clothes. It was not a promising beginning.

Then Byrd's Luck returned; although, it didn't begin very well. A fire broke out in the radio battery storage room that threatened to engulf the entire wooden ship in an inferno. The crew worked for hours putting out the fire—and then collapsed in exhaustion. It was a windless night with a glassy sea, and with no one noticing, a current took the ship nearly 80 miles off course. They awoke to a strangely calm sky . . . and then learned on the radio that a savage hurricane had passed just behind them, hitting Puerto Rico and Florida with tornados in its train. Had the *City of New York* not drifted off course, it would have been trapped—and likely destroyed—by the storm.

After a stop in the Panama Canal, where Siple was met and escorted about by the local International Scouting Commissioner—and where he learned to put limes and lemons in the ship's drinking water to improve its antibacterial acidity and to fight scurvy (a useful bit of knowledge for the years ahead)—the crew sailed on into the Pacific.

After the tumult of the Atlantic and Caribbean, the immense Pacific was a relatively easy passage. On crossing the equator, Siple tried to escape the Davy Jones ceremony by hiding in a ventilator pipe, but was caught and with the others, sentenced to have his head shaved and to be thrown into a tank of water.

When he wasn't on shift, Siple used his time wisely. The expedition had brought with it a library of 3,000 books, including encyclopedias and technical manuals. And during the long, equatorial passage, Siple studied the books to learn more about astronomy, navigation, bird study, and zoology.

He had also come to appreciate more than ever the value of his Scouting skills, especially knots, rope splicing, and compass work—knowledge that many of the younger expedition members didn't have. Siple would later write that these skills proved to be the difference between being "a humble servant and being recognized as a leader."[4]

The *Eleanor Bolling* caught the slow-moving *City of New York* in Tahiti, and the two ships sailed on into rough weather toward New Zealand.

At one point in this passage, Paul Siple was nearly killed. Caught in high seas in the "Roaring Forties"—strong westerly winds in the Southern Hemisphere—he rushed to answer an "all hands on deck" call. However, the moment he climbed up from the gangway, he was hit in the head by an unstowed wooden crate sliding across the deck. He revived just in time for a huge wave to crash over him, which sent him sliding along the deck towards the scuppers. Still dazed, he managed at the last second to grab the rail before being washed overboard.

He was still clinging to the rail when he heard the chief officer shouting, "Make the upper topsail fast!" Without thinking, Siple made his way to the shrouds and started to climb. At the top of the mast, more than 100 feet above the rolling deck, he joined other crewmen in tying down the flapping sail.

Just as they did, the great ship, hit by a giant wave, heeled over so far that the mainsail, far below Siple, dipped into the ocean—threatening to snap the mast with the men on it. Everyone on deck stared in horror . . . then, just as suddenly, the ship righted itself, and the mast rose to vertical again. An exhausted and thankful Paul Siple made his way back down the shrouds—and, as he later wrote, was never so happy to be standing on a solid, if pitching, deck.

In late November 1928, the *City of New York* was the last of the flotilla to arrive in New Zealand. On the first day of December, the repaired and restocked ships set sail for Antarctica. On Christmas Day, they reached the great Ross Ice Shelf. They had arrived—now the real adventure would begin.

COURAGE ON ICE

The expedition eventually dropped anchor at the Bay of Whales. Byrd judged this the best place from which to take off on his polar flight. And, not far from Amundsen's old camp, he set the crew to building what would become famous as "Little America."

The location, like everywhere else in Antarctica, was far from safe and secure. Soon after arriving, Siple—who had just been named assistant to the scientific staff—joined Commander Byrd and several others in a lifeboat investigating black specks in the water just beyond the edge of the ice shelf. As they were searching, a lookout atop the edge of the ice began shouting, "Killer whales!"

The men started paddling back to the ice wall—slowly, so as not to arouse the attention of the pod of three orcas. But the orcas saw the lifeboat and began to swim toward it. The men quickly changed direction and headed for the shore . . . ominously, the orcas turned and followed.

Now it was a race. As Siple and two other men rowed frantically, Byrd drew his pistol and prepared to fight.

The boat reached the shore first—and the men scrambled out onto the low ice. Siple was last out, and as he dove onto the ice, the lead orca lunged, just missing him with its huge teeth. Falling backwards from the attack, Siple nearly lost his balance on the ice and slid back into the water. The other men, sprawled on the ice beyond, looked back just in time to see the orca disappear back into the depths.

The ice too was an ever-present threat. The two big ships had anchored up against a low section of the ice shelf and had begun unloading the next morning, stacking the items from the hold atop the ice "dock." Then, in the middle of this rushed work, the ice shelf suddenly began to crack under the weight and calve off a section of ice bearing much of the supplies. Within seconds, the entire expedition was at risk.

The men on shore raced to the edge of the shelf and then scrambled down toward the water, the most intrepid jumping onto the nearest large piece of ice and then leaping from floe to floe toward the cargo. They managed to get there in time and haul the goods back aboard the ships.

After that near-disaster, Byrd decided that the low shelf was just too fragile to handle the stress of serving as a dock—and ordered the ships moved to a new location against the full-height ice wall. Unloading there would be a lot more difficult—indeed, at their new anchorage, the top of the ice shelf towered high over the decks of the two ships, which were lashed side-by-side against the ice. This was deemed to be safer; but in fact, the expedition had merely replaced one threat with another.

Realization of this fact took only another 36 hours. The men were again busily unloading from the decks of the ships to the ice above . . . when there was a tremendous groan of ice, and a rumbling in the ice wall that knocked the men above off their feet. Below, the men of the *Eleanor Bolling* looked up helplessly to see a giant sliver of ice break loose and come hurtling down to crash on their ship's deck. The concussion and the sheer weight of the ice rocked the ship so far that only the lines to the *City of New York* kept the ship from capsizing.

But no one felt the crash more than the two men actually standing on the section of ice when it broke loose. One of them, seaman Benny Roth was literally catapulted over the *Eleanor Bolling*—a distance of well over 100 feet—and into the freezing water. Miraculously, Roth surfaced still alive—but not knowing how to swim, could only cling desperately to a small ice floe that kept slipping out of his grip. Commander Byrd and several other crewmen heroically leaped into the frigid water to save Roth, but they quickly had to retreat before they too drowned.

The second man, meteorologist Henry Harrison, who had been standing just inland from Roth, felt the ice disappear beneath his feet . . . and suddenly found himself sliding down a sheer ice face to the water. With amazing presence in such a shocking situation, Harrison as he slid spotted the *Eleanor Bolling*'s anchor chain—it had been attached to the top of the ice shelf—beneath him. He managed to grab it as he passed and clung for dear life—only to have the chain pull taut as the shipped rolled and drifted out, leaving Harrison dangling 50 feet in the air above the icy water.

As Byrd and the men on the ships scrambled to help Roth, whose location was lost in the sun's glare off the water, Paul Siple and the expedition's physician Dr. Francis Coman ran to save Harrison. In the single most important application in his life of his Scouting skills, Siple grabbed a length of rope and tied a loop in it using that bane of Second Class Scouts everywhere, the bowline. Shouting for Harrison to slip the loop under his arms—the meteorologist, hanging with frozen hands from the chain, was getting the benefit of the many pull-up competitions during the voyage—Siple flung the rope.

Harrison somehow managed to catch the rope and loop it under his arms. Next came the dangerous part. Unsticking his bleeding hands, Harrison let go . . . swinging down and slamming into the face of the ice wall. Siple and Coman then pulled with all of their might, dragging Harrison up the jagged wall face and up onto the top.

Within minutes, Roth too was located and dragged from the water by men in the *City of New York*'s lifeboat. Both rescues had taken less than 20 minutes. Harrison and Roth were in bad shape—the former with much of the skin ripped from his hands, the latter with severe frostbite—but they had survived and would soon be back at work.

As for Paul Siple, the Eagle Scout had used his skills to save a man's life—and once again had proven his value to the expedition.

COLD COMFORT

Having (barely) survived the disembarkation, the expedition now set about constructing its home for the next year.

The original plan for Little America had been comparatively elaborate—certainly by Antarctic standards—with a half-dozen separate buildings that included sleeping quarters, mess hall, library and scientific areas, and a gym. Half of those buildings, all of the food, and most of the supplies had arrived with the expedition; and now, unloaded on the ice, it all had to be transported the eight miles to the Little America site.

Byrd divided the team into three groups: one to manage and unpack the supplies, a second to transport the items inland via dog teams, and a third to do the on-site construction at Little America. When one of the sled drivers was hurt, Paul Siple was assigned his sled. It was yet one more promotion for the young man, but a mixed one, as he found himself with a team of dogs—troublesome huskies and mongrels that no one else wanted.

However, Siple had always been a natural with dogs, in part because of his almost superhuman patience, and he quickly formed his motley pack into an enthusiastic team. Sometimes too enthusiastic: on one occasion, caught in a whiteout in which earth and sky, and near and far, were all but indistinguishable, Paul turned his team the wrong way and headed down a slope toward the ice shelf cliff. The dogs, refusing to stop, only ran faster toward oblivion. It took the quick-witted intervention of Dr. Coman—who used his own sled team to cut off the runaway group, and then dove out and grabbed Siple's gang line to the dogs—to avert disaster.

No doubt in part because of his increasing importance to the expedition, when the time came for Byrd to select the 42 men to winter over at Little America, Siple was among of those chosen. And, because he had made himself so popular with the crew with his cheerfulness, competence, and bravery, there was little rumbling about the "kid" getting special treatment by those who had to leave. Indeed, as at the New York luncheon, there seems to have been a general consensus that Siple had earned the right to stay.

With the weather starting to turn, Byrd ordered the *Eleanor Bolling* to be quickly manned—there wasn't even time to get the last three buildings out of its hold—and made ready for a quick dash to New Zealand. The hope was that if it could get away fast enough it might be able to return with supplies in time before the sea ice locked up.

But it wasn't to be. As the men who remained at Little America learned—listening to the radio signals picked up by the three tall masts they had just installed—the *Eleanor Bolling* endured a hair-raising voyage of storms and high seas and barely limped intact into Wellington Harbour. Meanwhile, at the Bay of Whales, the sea quickly froze with thick ice. The *Eleanor Bolling* had gotten out just in time. It would not be able to return now until spring.

The immediate impact of this change of plans was that the original six structures of Little America had now been reduced to three. That meant a long winter of crowded quarters (exacerbated by the fact that the reindeer skin clothes shed and quickly covered everything in fine hairs), greater human friction, and reduced shelter from the elements. It also created a pressing need to get the last remaining supply items inland from the ice shelf, especially as the items had already disappeared beneath the increasingly deep snow.

And so, as soon as there was a break in the weather—that is, when the howling wind had reduced to less than 60 miles per hour—three teams of dogs, sleds, and drivers raced for the coast. The three drivers of one team, Paul Siple and his two new friends, Quin Blackburn and surveyor Mike Thorne, agreed to stay within visual contact for safety.

But within minutes, the snow flurries grew so blinding that the three lost sight of each other. A few minutes more and they were lost in a whiteout. Siple was on the brink of turning back when he spotted one of the markers—an orange flag atop a long bamboo pole—he had emplaced days before to mark the route. He pressed on, knowing he was just a few hundred yards from the supply cache.

When the three sled teams reached the cache, they found the members of the two teams that had preceded them huddled together against the storm. Siple, Blackburn, and Thorne did the same. Linking arms and hunching down against the wind, they searched about until they found the buried 50-pound barrels of fuel. Though the blizzard was worsening by the minute, the three young men didn't stop until they had loaded the barrels on their sleds.

Now they had to get back, and the trail was beginning to disappear under the piling snowdrifts. Once again shouting to each other to stay together, the three sleds took off, Thorne in the lead, Blackburn in the middle, and Siple taking up the rear. But this time, the wind was quartering into their faces, and whatever cohesion they had disappeared within seconds.

Now alone, Paul Siple did his best to navigate by the orange markers, driving from one to the next, 100 yards away, by trying to keep the team moving in a straight line. Within minutes, his eyes were nearly frozen shut from squinting—so he closed his eyes and tried to navigate with his feet by feeling for the more compressed snow of the path.

But it was a doomed strategy. Soon, Siple found himself nearly blind in a perfect whiteout, his visibility down to a few inches, lost in loose snow with no idea how to get back to the trail. There was no other sled, no orange marker—no feature of any kind—in sight. It was more than 40 degrees below zero—but Paul Siple began to sweat with fear. In Antarctica, this was how men died.

He remembered his Scouting training: when lost, the first step was to stop, stay calm, and evaluate your situation. Holding back his rising panic, Siple did just that. What vital bit of information was he missing?

Then it hit him. His dogs, given the chance, would always turn downwind to keep from having to drive into the teeth of the storm. And they had begun to do just that. So, fighting his own impulse to bend away, he turned his dogs and sled back until the wind was pounding against them. Within minutes he had found the trail and the marker.

But was he going the right direction? If he and the dogs were mistakenly headed again for the ice shelf, they would never have the strength to get back. Siple stopped again. Scouting had taught him to be observant. He remembered: the wind always struck the left side of his face when driving toward the camp. It was doing that now: he was still headed in the right direction. Within minutes, to his relief, he had caught the other two sleds. Once again, the now-terrified young men agreed to stick closely together.

But it wasn't to be. A half-mile from Little America, just as the trail turned directly into the storm, Blackburn's dogs, believing they were almost home took off from the trail in a straight line for the buildings. Blackburn couldn't hold them back, and he disappeared into the storm.

Siple and Thorne reached Little America at last. Siple, his eyes still nearly frozen shut, and with a ring of blisters around his wrists from snow getting under his gloves, was rushed to Dr. Coman. It was only then that he, assuming that Blackburn had already arrived, discovered that his friend was still lost in the storm.

They rushed to Byrd to mount a rescue—but the commander, worried he might lose more personnel, refuse to let anyone leave the buildings until the storm abated. The men waited, praying that the winds would slow before darkness fell.

The storm broke at last, with only a couple hours of light to spare, Thorne and Byrd himself went out in search. Siple begged to go along, but Byrd refused, telling him to recover from his hyperthermia instead.

Byrd and Thorne eventually returned: no sign of Quin Blackburn. Now there was only an hour of light left. There was one last chance: now Byrd sent out four teams, each in a different direction. This time Siple was allowed to go.

In the end, it was Thorne's team that found Blackburn. Overwhelmed by the storm, he had buried himself and his dogs in a hole in the snow, using the sled as a windbreak. He was carried back to Little America, where he joined Paul Siple—who had been ordered back into the dispensary—under the care of Dr. Coman. In the next few days, sharing their stories, the two young men became fast friends.

THE ENDLESS NIGHT

After these near-fatal experiences, the bigger adventure—wintering over in Antarctica—was something of an anticlimax.

Outside, in the perpetual darkness, the temperature fell below −40F and stayed there—bottoming on July 28, 1929, at −72F. Inside, in buildings almost completely buried in snow, life slid into a daily routine of meals, workouts, lectures, and reading time in the library, work shifts, and evening poker. As could be expected in such tight quarters, the occasional fight broke out to relieve the tension, and the men soon came to live for their Sunday night movie and the radio broadcasts from the USA carrying messages from wives and families. When the claustrophobia grew too great, the men would step outside, accepting the bitter cold in exchange for a few minutes of privacy.

Through all of the long weeks, Paul Siple's reputation grew among both the men and the leaders of the expedition. He had begun this journey as a little more than a publicity exercise, a novelty. But he had proven himself over and over as a man on whom others could depend. He was also a model of uprightness and perpetual cheerfulness. He helped break up fights, never started them. He spent long hours in the library improving his skills, or watching the expedition's tailor and sail maker, Martin Ronne, creating custom clothes out of leather and reindeer skins. And, because he didn't smoke and ate his chocolate ration the moment he received it, Siple had nothing to bet in the endless poker games—so he never joined in, sparing himself the biggest source of team tension.

Commander Byrd, as always, was watching. He saw the endless care with which Siple had dug out a tunnel for the dogs, how tenderly he cared for them, and how patiently he trained them. In reward, he gave the young man a second job of using his Scouting merit badge skills to perform the taxidermy of seals and other specimens promised for delivery to the American Museum of Natural History. Siple took to the work with his usual enthusiasm.

Finally, the sun reappeared on the horizon and the weather began to improve. In surviving the winter, Byrd and his crew had made history—though they were now too occupied to give it much thought. Siple was as busy as anyone in the crew. Byrd had given the 20-year-old another promotion—this time to scientific researcher for the expedition. Now, often teaming up with Quin Blackburn, who had been named surveyor, the pair traveled to the unexplored regions of the Ross Ice Shelf. Blackburn mapped the area and Siple surveyed the birthrate of baby seals and their growth and behavior—a process that often led to unfriendly encounters with mother seals.

OVER THE POLE

At noon on November 28, 1930, the Ford TriMotor *Floyd Bennett* rose from the runway at Little America into a clear sky and headed toward the South Pole. In the camp's radio room, the rest of the expedition crew, minus the five men on the plane, gathered around the speaker to follow the flight.

At the last moment, Byrd had ordered an extra 100 gallons loaded onto the plane—a decision that proved to be another case of Byrd's Luck.

The best known of these 1930s Eagles was **Milt Caniff**, the celebrated cartoonist. He earned his Eagle in 1923 at age 16 in Hillsboro, Ohio. By age 23, he had landed a job as an illustrator for the *Columbus Dispatch*. But when the Depression arrived and he was laid off from the paper, he briefly considered an acting career—until an older cartoonist, Billy Ireland, told him, "Stick to your inkpots, kid, actors don't eat regularly."[5]

He did stick with cartooning—and by 1934 he had found a job with the *New York Daily News*. There, he created one of the iconic comic strips of the twentieth century, *Terry and the Pirates*—its powerful images, strong plots, noir shading, and exotic locales inspiring generations of cartoonists that followed. At the beginning of World War II, Caniff created a hugely popular armed forces-only version of *Terry* called *Male Call* that is still noted for its realistic depiction of military life.

After the war, chafing at his lack of ownership of his own creation, Caniff killed off *Terry* and replaced it with the Air Force-oriented *Steve Canyon*, which proved almost as popular as its predecessor. It only ended with Caniff's own death in 1988. At that time, the National Cartoonists Society named its lifetime achievement medal after him, and he was also inducted into the Comic Book Hall of Fame.

The only known Eagle Scout to be nominated for sainthood was **Francis J. Parater**, who had earned his Eagle in 1913 from a Virginia troop. Just a decade later, as a young seminarian, he was sent to study in Rome, where he contracted rheumatic fever and died at only 23. He was nominated for canonization in 2001.

The third celebrated young Eagle of the pre-war years—he earned the rank at age 13 in a troop from Ridgefield, New Jersey—was a musician whose first big hit, "And Then Some," hit number one on the pop charts in 1935. Later that year he married his duet partner, Harriet Hilliard, with whom he had two sons. When his music career began to fade, **Ozzie Nelson** tried films—and then, anxious to spend more time with his family—created a radio show-turned-television program that employed all of them. *The Adventures of Ozzie and Harriet*, which ran on radio and TV from 1944 to 1973 was one of the most enduring comedy shows in television history.

The most famous Eagle Scout of the era was a fictional character, the product of Broadway and Hollywood. Henry Aldrich was the most minor, but also most interesting, character in the 1938 comedy *What a Life*, written by Clifford Goldsmith and produced and directed by the legendary George Abbot. Audiences loved Henry (played by Ezra Stone), a cheerful, energetic, and consistently misdirected teenager who seemed to embody the whole "bobby soxer" ethos.

The next year, an Aldrich family radio show, again starring Stone, and with its iconic opening of Mrs. Aldrich calling her son's name—and Henry shouting back "*Com*-ing Mother!"—was an instant hit, joining Bob Hope and Jack Benny at the top of the radio ratings.

Not surprisingly, the radio show in turn spawned a series of mid-budget films from Paramount revolving around the adventures of the increasingly more responsible and mature Henry. The first two Henry Aldrich films featured major child star Jackie Cooper, as Henry. For the rest of the nine films of the series, the role was assumed by Jimmy Lydon, who quickly became synonymous with the character.

Audiences had always known that Henry was a Boy Scout. But with the ninth film of the series, *Henry Aldrich, Boy Scout* (1944), this participation moved to the forefront. More than that, in a shorthand for Henry's growing maturity during wartime, the one-time troublemaker became an Eagle Scout and patrol leader, shouldering the responsibility for a troublesome Scout who resembled his younger self.

Meanwhile, Jackie Cooper, having established the series, moved on to his own Scouting-related production, the hugely popular 12-part serial *Scouts to the Rescue* (1939). In it, Cooper played Eagle Scout Bruce Scott who, after his Scoutmaster has to leave a camping trip because of a family emergency, leads his troop into a series of wild adventures involving a ghost town, counterfeiters, and even a lost Inca tribe. Not only is this serial an interesting precursor to *Indiana Jones and the Last Crusade* a half-century later, but it even takes place the same year.

Henry Aldrich and Bruce Scott, in their theatrical way, represent a last glimpse of the first era of Scouting. By the time these films appeared, the world had already changed, the young men who had filled theaters to watch them were gone—and like everything else in America, Scouting was being transformed into a very different organization.

EAGLES OF WAR

Pearl Harbor was attacked at the very moment the first generation of America's Eagle Scouts reached middle age and the second generation became old enough to fight. And because, among its other attributes, war elevates both heroes and natural leaders to prominence, it is not surprising that America's Eagles assumed high profile roles in the war and were recognized for some its most famous acts of heroism.

Among the thousands of highly decorated Eagle Scouts who fought in the Second World War, eight stand apart because their extraordinary heroism— some at the cost of their own lives—earned them America's highest military award, the Congressional Medal of Honor.

Lt. Colonel Aquilla J. "Jimmy" Dyess earned his Eagle in 1925 with a troop in Andersonville, Georgia. In 1928, already showing his courage, Dyess was awarded the Carnegie Medal for saving the lives of two swimmers off the coast of Charleston, South California—he remains the only American to receive the nation's highest civilian and military awards for heroism. Joining the marines in 1936, Dyess, a crack shot, quickly became a member of the Marine Corps Rifle Team.

In February 1944, during the brutal battle for Kwajalein Atoll in the Marshall Islands, Lt. Col. Dyess led a company of Marines in a flanking attack on the last Japanese position on Namur Island. As always he led from the front, driving his troops forward against withering enemy fire. As he stood atop the parapet of an antitank trench waving his men forward, he was cut down by a machine gun burst.

Today, the Georgia-Carolina Council of the BSA holds an annual Jimmy Dyess Day at Fort Gordon—and the four-line highway the Scouts take from Augusta to the Fort is named after Dyess as well.

2nd Lt. Robert Edward Femoyer had only been in the European theater six weeks when he found himself, as the navigator of a crippled B-17 Flying Fortress in a raid over Merseburg, Germany, wounded and bleeding, with the pilot and co-pilot dead. Struggling to remain conscious in the face of massive blood loss, the West Virginian Eagle refused the morphine offered by crewmates—despite agonizing pain described as "almost beyond the realm of human endurance"—to keep his head clear enough to pilot the plane.

For the next two-and-a-half hours, Femoyer piloted the damaged plane through six course corrections around antiaircraft flack. It was only after the plane reached the English Channel that Femoyer finally accepted a shot of morphine. He successfully landed the plane . . . and died of his wounds just 30 minutes later. He was 23 years old.

Rear Admiral Eugene Fluckey earned his Eagle Scout in Washington, DC, but left for the Naval Academy before it could be awarded. After commissioning, he served on a battleship and a destroyer before finding his permanent home in the U.S. Navy submarine fleet. He assumed command of the USS *Barb* in April 1944 and embarked on what is often considered the greatest career of any submariner.

The USS *Barb*, under "Lucky" Fluckey, sank more tonnage than any other submarine in the war—including a carrier, a cruiser, a frigate, and 14 other ships and Fluckey is also credited with the only military landing on the home Japanese islands in WWII: when a Barb landing party blew up a 16-car train passing along the coast. For the raiding party, Fluckey specifically asked for former Boy Scouts because of their resourcefulness.

Fluckey had already earned the Navy Cross four times when he and the Barb crew embarked on their 11th—and most celebrated—mission. During this raid, Fluckey invented a new way to attack night convoys by sneaking into the line of escort ships. The *Barb* attacked two convoys of Japanese ships and then, while escaping and under attack, set a then world speed record for submarines.

In later years, Fluckey was commander of the United States Pacific Fleet's submarine force and Director of Naval Intelligence. He was finally awarded his Eagle in 1948.

Charles P. Murray, a 1st Lieutenant leading a patrol near the medieval town of Kayserburg on the border of France and Germany on December 16, 1994, came upon a 200-man German unit shelling a nearby American force.

Moving forward alone to get a better view, Murray called in artillery—but when its aim was off and he tried to call in corrections, Murray found his radio was dead. The German force was too large attack directly, so Murray decided instead to pin it down until he could get support.

Returning to his patrol, he gathered up automatic weapons and grenade launchers and went back alone to his outpost. There, despite drawing extensive fire, Murray attacked the Germans, killing ten, scattering the rest, and even destroying a truck loaded with three mortars. He then led his patrol forward, capturing its bridge objective and capturing ten more of the enemy. At that point, another German soldier, who was pretending to surrender, threw a grenade that seriously injured Murray who refused aid until he had properly positioned his unit.

Murray would stay in the U.S. Army through the Vietnam War era, ultimately, as a Colonel, commanding the Old Guard, which guards the Tomb of the Unknown Soldier. When it was learned in 1971 that Murray had never officially completed the paperwork for his Eagle, the BSA awarded him an honorary Distinguished Eagle Scout Award, one of the first ever given.

On October 13, 1943, **Captain Arlo L. Olson** performed feats of bravery that would seem unbelievable had they not been witnessed. Having led his company 30 miles into enemy territory in Northern Italy, Olson waded chest deep across the Volturno River under nearly point-black machine gun fire, climbed the opposite bank and threw two hand grenades into the enemy gun position and killed its crew.

Soon after, a second enemy machine gun opened up 150 yards away. Olson, according to his Medal of Honor citation, "advanced upon the position in a slow, deliberate walk. Although 5 German soldiers threw handgrenades at him from a range of 5 yards, Capt. Olson dispatched them all, picked up a machine pistol and continued toward the enemy. Advancing to within 15 yards of the position he shot it out with the foe, killing 9 and seizing the post."

For the next 13 days, Olson continued these superhuman feats, often leading attacks directly into machine gun fire, despite the fact that the enemy gunners were specifically targeting him. Finally, his luck ran out during an assault on Monte San Nicola. Greviously wounded, Captain Olson still finished his reconnaissance, put his men in position and ordered that his wounded fellow soldiers be tended to first. He died of his wounds while being stretchered down the mountain.

In October 1942, **Colonel Mitchell Paige** was a 22-year-old platoon sergeant in the Battle of Guadalcanal when his unit came under heavy fire. Paige commanded the counterattack. Then, when all of the other Marines in his unit had been killed, Paige continued the fight himself—running from one machine gun to another to return fire. When reinforcements arrived, Paige organized them into a line and led a bayonet counterattack, driving the attackers back and punching a hole in the enemy's line.

Paige, the son of Croatian immigrants had earned his Eagle in 1936 from a troop in Charleroi, Pennsylvania, but graduated high school and immediately joined the marines. He finally received his Eagle medal just before his death in 2003. Paige also lived long enough to see a GI Joe modeled after his younger self.

Lt. Colonel Jay Zeamer, Jr. earned his Eagle at age 13 with a troop in Orange, New Jersey. A year later, he left for military school and then went on to the Massachusetts Institute of Technology. In 1941, even before the war began, he earned his pilot's wings and officer's commission in the U.S. Army Air Corps. In April 1943, now a captain and a veteran of 46 missions, Zeamer volunteered to pilot an unescorted B-17 on a reconnaisance mission of an island near Bougainville. The Japanese had assembled a force of an estimated 400 fighters in the region—and Zeamer's assignment was to discover where they were.

Zeamer and his crew made the 600-mile flight to their target, took the photographs . . . and were quickly set on by an estimated 20 fighters, five of which made a devastating first attack that severely damaged the bomber. The severely wounded bombardier, who would also win the Medal of Honor, managed to shoot down two of the fighters before bleeding to death while still manning his guns. Zeamer, covered with shrapnel wounds and with a broken leg, managed to shoot down another fighter even as he evaded the attackers.

For the next 45 minutes, Zeamer flew evasive maneuvers as his crew fought off 17 more fighters. Bleeding heavily and drifting into unconsciousness,

Zeamer refused treatment until the bomber escaped the attacked. Then, realizing the plane wouldn't clear a mountain pass in its path, his last order was to crash land the plane on a nearby runway.

When the rescue crew reached the crashed bomber, Zeamer had lost so much blood that he was at first believed dead. But he survived and lived a long life. When he died in 2007 at age 88, he was the last surviving Army Air Corps Medal of Honor recipient.

Captain Benjamin Salomon never expected to see combat. He was a dentist, assigned to frontline surgeon duty during the battle of Saipan in July 1944. An Eagle from Milwaukee, Wisconsin, he had graduated from the University of Southern California dental school in 1937 and opened a practice.

Drafted in 1940 as a private, he was eventually commissioned as an officer in 1942. Dr. Salomon saw his first combat two years later when he went ashore on Saipan with the 105th Infantry. With little need for his dental services, Salomon volunteered to replace the battalion's wounded doctor. His surgical station was just 50 yards behind the front foxhole line—and when that line was overrun, Salomon found his surgical tent filling with Japanese soldiers who had run in through the tent fly and crawled under the sides. Salomon fought them off—kicking the knife out of one's hand, shooting another, bayoneting a third, and rifle butting at fourth—even as he ordered his staff to evacuate the wounded. Without a second thought, Dr. Salomon stayed behind to provide cover.

When Salomon's body was found the next day, it was slumped over a machine gun, with *98* dead enemy soldiers lying in front of him. Salomon's body had 76 bullets, and multiple bayonet, wounds—as many as two dozen of them received while Dr. Salomon was still alive.

Sadly, after this mind-boggling act of heroism, the War Department resisted awarding the Medal of Honor to Salomon. One reason was doubt about his eligibility as an official noncombatant. But just as important was institutional anti-Semitism: at this point in the war, only two other Jews had received the Medal of Honor (one of them the uncle of musician Lenny Kravitz), and none would again for the rest of WWII and Korea. Where Scouting hadn't hesitated to give Ben Salomon its highest award, the U.S. Army had failed in its duty.

In 1951 a nomination for the award was made, but turned down. In 1969, the surgeon general of the U.S. Army made the nomination . . . and was turned down without explanation. The next year the secretary of the army made the same nomination—again without luck.

In 2002, 58 years after the death of Captain Ben Salomon DDS—thanks to a nomination by the USC Dental School, supported by a local Congressman—the nomination was finally accepted and the award signed by President George W. Bush. The Eagle Scout had earned his true honor at last.

COLOR BLINDNESS

Benjamin Salomon's story is a reminder of the prejudices that still divided America at the beginning of the Second World War—and that would begin to crack at its end.

Though the Boy Scouts of America didn't entirely escape the racism and biases of early twentieth century America, to its eternal credit, it set at the very core of its philosophy that *every* Scout of sufficient character, discipline, and ambition—no matter their race, intelligence, or physical ability—could earn the rank of Eagle. That meant the Eagle rank was, in the end, not just a measure of skill or competence or ability, but most of all, of *character.* And character had no prejudice.

Thus, from the very beginning, even when communities still demanded that Scout troops be segregated, young men of otherwise marginalized racial, religious, and ethnic groups could still make the run for Eagle. And they did just that.

THE AFRICAN AMERICAN EAGLE

There was one group of American Scouts whose entry into the ranks of Eagles was long overdue: African Americans. It took 16 years, but in mid-1926, in the face of enduring Jim Crow and the second rise of the Ku Klux Klan, a small group of black Scouts scattered around the country earned the rank at last.

Records have long been murky, but it is believed that the first African American Eagle Scout was **Edgar Cunningham, Sr.** He earned his Eagle on June 8, 1926, as a member of Troop 12 Waterloo, Iowa, of the Wapsipinicon Area Council. As great as his achievement was, it was certainly equaled by his Scoutmaster, **James Lincoln Page**, a World War I veteran who had organized the first all-black Boy Scout troops (Troops 9 and 12) in February, 1925. For his work, Page received a presidential citation from President Calvin Coolidge, while Cunningham also received a handwritten letter from the president.

Scoutmaster Page spent the rest of his life in Scouting, mentoring numerous other Eagles. When asked by younger Scouts about his early Scouting experiences, Page replied, in words that can serve as his epitaph: "We were tough, we didn't give up."[6]

Francis "Tick" Coleman was the third African American Eagle Scout, earning the award in October, 1926. He joined Troop 181 at his local Episcopal Church in Philadelphia mainly because his mother insisted he do something to fill his afternoons after school. But Tick took to Scouting, just as he did the YMCA—the only other local organization that looked past his race—and, in thanks, he would stay loyal to both organizations for the next 80 years.

In the course of his long life (1911–2008), Coleman, even as he worked as an educator and school counselor, set a standard for community service that few have ever matched by working in the Boy Scouts, Peace Corps, YMCA, Boys Club, Salvation Army, the local Hebrew Center, and many others—all to help the disadvantage youth of his city.

At his death, at age 97, Coleman was believed to be the oldest African American Eagle Scout. To honor his service, the BSA created the Coleman Service Award to honor Scouting paraprofessionals.

But, like Paul Siple, Tick Coleman was a singular case: a man before (and indeed, after) his time. It would take World War II, and a social revolution, before America's black Eagles would begin to make their mark.

TUSKEGEE AIRMEN EAGLES

And that mark would first be made by the Tuskegee Airmen of the 332nd Fighter Group. The Airmen, with their historic fight against military prejudice, and sterling record in their red-tailed P-51s in the skies over Germany, remain one of the most compelling stories of the war. What was rarely noticed—at least not until recent years—was the presence of at least three Eagle Scouts in their ranks.

Lt. Colonel Eugene C. Cheatham Jr. was born in Georgia, but at a young age joined his Episcopal missionary father and family on trips to Africa and Europe. Eventually, the family settled in New York City, where Cheatham joined a troop and completed his Eagle requirements by age 15.

But his family was too poor to ever buy him an official Scout uniform. And so, when the time came for young Eugene to appear before an Eagle board of review, he was too embarrassed to go.

After flying with the Tuskegee Airmen in the Second World War, Cheatham went on to fly 150 more missions in the Korean War. The Air Force had been good to Cheatham—and he returned the favor, remaining in the service and retiring as a Lieutenant Colonel in 1977.

In 2001, at a Veterans Day event where he was a guest of honor, Cheatham watched the Boy Scout honor guard and casually remarked that he regretted never having finished his Eagle. One of his companions, an organizer of the event who happened to be an Eagle, decided to rectify the situation. When a search found that Cheatham's Scouting records were long gone, the BSA decided to allow the 80-year-old to participate in an Eagle board of review that met the tough 1930 standards.

On September 18, 2004, just seven months before his death, Eugene Cheatham was awarded his Eagle medal at a Court of Honor held at the San Diego Air & Space Museum.

Colonel Charles E. McGee, who earned his Eagle in 1940, had a military career that extended almost three decades beyond the Tuskegee Airmen. A career officer in the USAF, he holds an Air Force record of 409 combat missions in three wars (WWII, Korea, and Vietnam)—136 of them with the Airmen. At the time this is being written, he remains deeply committed to the Air Force, even flying to Iraq at age 86 to meet with and inspire the current generation of fighter pilots.

One distinction that separates McGee from his peers is that not only was he a Boy Scout—in a troop in Cleveland, Ohio—but he has also continued his affiliation with Scouting throughout his adult life, holding both district and regional positions with the BSA.

Like the other Tuskegee Eagles, McGee has been awarded the Distinguished Eagle Scout Award—in his case, appropriately enough, at the 2010 Centennial Boy Scouts of America Jamboree.

Percy Sutton may have had the most remarkable and varied life of the three Tuskegee Eagles.

Born in San Antonio, Texas, the last of 15 children, Sutton's father had been born a slave and had become a farmer, entrepreneur, high school principal, and early civil rights activist.

Percy joined Scouting in San Antonio—and at age 16, achieved the rank of Eagle. He would later say that Scouting played a key role in shaping his life.

All of the Sutton children, including Percy who was the youngest and apparently the wildest, attended college. Once out in the world, Sutton took up stunt flying and barnstorming, but quit after a friend crashed. The outbreak of war found him at the Tuskegee Institute, and it was a natural next step for him to join the Airmen. He earned battle stars in both the Italian and Mediterranean theaters as the squadron's intelligence officer.

But for a many like Percy Sutton, a place in the Tuskegee Airmen was just a prelude to adult life for an ambitious 25-year-old.

With the war's end, Sutton set out to become a lawyer and attended both Columbia and Brooklyn Law Schools. Brilliant, black and fearless, he was soon one the best-known civil rights lawyers in the country. His most famous client was Malcolm X, whose widow he supported after that leader's assassination. He was also jailed for his vigorous defense of black radical Stokely Carmichael.

Sutton used the credibility this work had gained for him in the African American community to enter politics. He co-founded the "Harlem Clubhouse," a Democrat power center that still dominates Harlem politics—and has produced over the years such important African American politicians as New York Mayor David Dinkins, U.S. Congressman Charles Rangel, New York Secretary of State Basil Paterson and son New York Governor David Paterson.

In time, Sutton entered politics himself—and served in the New York assembly and as Manhattan borough president. In 1977, he ran for mayor of New York, but lost to Ed Koch. But that didn't stop the irrepressible Percy Sutton. He had already co-founded the Inner City Broadcasting Corporation and purchased New York's first African American radio station, WLIB. Now he expanded his media empire: after helping drive the restoration of Harlem's famed Apollo Theater, Sutton produced a popular syndicated television series, *Live at the Apollo,* originating from there.

Percy Sutton was a legendary figure in New York—especially in Harlem—when he died at 89 in 2007, leaving Leatrice, his wife of 66 years. But if New York City had been his stage, in the end the old Tuskegee Eagle went home to San Antonio. There he is buried, not far from where he had once camped as a Scout.

HOME FRONT

Scouting during the Great Depression and World War II was a very different organization from that of the preceding boom years.

Massive unemployment and widespread poverty placed heavy pressure on families in the 1930s. The more elaborate troop activities and summer camping trips of the 1920s were now often replaced by weekend campouts nearby using improvised tents and bedding. As with Eugene Cheatham, many Scouts couldn't afford uniforms, much less the traditional accoutrements— knife, compass, and hatchet—of Scouting.

Moreover, many families were on the move, searching for work, which bedeviled unit cohesion. Many older Scouts, recognizing the economic burden they placed on their families, dropped out of school and hit the rails or roads searching for work. Others joined the Civilian Conservation Corps (CCC) or other government programs. Not surprisingly, the annual number of new Eagles, which had more than doubled from 4,500 in 1927 to 9,200 in 1932, slumped the next year to 7,000—and stayed there until the end of the decade.[7]

In 1934, President Roosevelt, recognizing in Scouting an established mechanism to organize young people to both get them off the streets and help contribute to the nation's rebuilding, publicly called on Scouting to help the distressed and needy. The result was a National Good Turn that ultimately netted 1.8 million items of clothing, food, household furnishings, and supplies.[8]

And if the number of new Eagles fell—underscoring the impact of the Depression on older teenaged boys—Scouting itself continued to grow, passing 1 million members in 1935, the BSA's silver jubilee year.[9] Even the two-year postponement—because of an infantile paralysis (polio) epidemic—of the first national jamboree in 1935 failed to slow Scouting's growth.

The New Deal once again transformed the image of Scouting. Ever since the bond drives of WWI, Scouting had largely returned to its camping roots. But now it was back in the community—collecting clothes, visiting the needy, serving as a kind of de facto Youth Auxiliary of the national recovery effort. The BSA had long since become an institution identified with American life—but now that image was sealed forever . . . and immortalized in Frank Capra's *Mr. Smith Goes to Washington* (1939).

Tellingly, the Boy "Rangers" in that movie, organizing in support of a bill to create a national boy's camp—proposed by their old leader, now a U.S. senator—is largely led by older boys, the movie's surrogate Eagles. To a Depression audience, this scenario, with a troop led by older Scouts while the grown-ups are off trying to save the country, would have seen far less unlikely than it does today.

As for the national boy's camp, that idea too was one of the moment: even as the movie was opening, oil baron Waite Phillips was in the process of donating 128,000 acres in New Mexico's Sangre de Christo mountains to create Philturn (later Philmont) Scout Ranch, still Scouting's premiere summer camp—and a source of employment for generations of young Eagles.

By the time Philmont opened, the Eagles were there to fill its many counselor and ranger positions. With the economy improving, more older boys were able to stay home—and, inevitably, the number of new Eagles again rose, to 10,000 in 1939.[10]

Needless to say, when war came two years later, Scouting was again challenged . . . and again found a vital role. Once again, President Roosevelt called on Boy Scouts to serve as a homefront auxiliary.

By war's end, the federal government had made 69 specific requests for assistance from the BSA for the war effort. They included the collection of rubber in the form of spare tires and other consumer products—in a two-week drive Scouts collected 30 million pounds; Victory gardens—20,000 Scouts earned the General Douglas MacArthur Victory Garden medal; the distribution of pledge cards for war bonds and saving stamps; the distribution of stamp and Victory posters; the collection of aluminum, waste paper, and salvage; the management of defense housing surveys; and the distribution of air raid posters. Scouts also served as firewatchers, emergency medical personnel, and messengers and dispatch bearers.[11]

If mainstream Scouting became a kind of pre-boot camp for future soldiers in WWII America; the process of becoming an Eagle Scout served as a prep for Officer Candidate School. Uncelebrated, because largely unnoticed, the great Scouting service initiatives of the early 1940s were largely managed by Eagles and other Scouts in senior leadership roles, because most of the fathers who would have normally led Scout troops had gone off to war. This presented a tremendous challenge, as even the Eagles typically had only a year or two to lead the younger Scouts before they too went off to war.

Even the BSA itself was suffering a shortage of senior leadership. An aging James West, the only chief Scout executive that Scouting had ever known, retired in 1942. Chief Scout Dan Beard died at age 90 in 1941. Ernest Seton would die in 1946. And, most traumatic of all, Lord Baden-Powell, Scouting's founder, died in Kenya at age 83 in 1941. The men who had built Scouting and led it for three decades were suddenly gone from the scene.

It was inevitable now that dramatic changes were in store for Scouting—and its Eagles—in the postwar world. There would be new leaders, new priorities, and most of all, a gigantic new wave of postwar baby boomer boys heading in Scouting's direction. Scouting would soon have to reinvent itself several times to keep up with this new, and rapidly changing, America.

THE ARCTIC EAGLE

And what of Paul Siple, the "Eagle on Ice" as his biographers would call him?

Home from the Byrd Expedition in June 1930, he was feted in both New York and at home in Erie, Pennsylvania. Within three months, he returned to the life he had once led as if nothing had happened. In September, he went back to Alleghany College to complete his degree.

But everything *had* changed. Siple had left an America kicking up its heels at the height of the Roaring Twenties—and had returned to a stunned nation sinking ever deeper into the Great Depression. America, especially young people facing an uncertain future, needed heroes. And Paul Siple, having been part of one of the great adventures of the century while still a teenager, fit the bill. Soon, he found himself giving speeches—three years' worth—to Scouting organizations and other groups throughout the Northeast, often sharing the stage with (now Rear-Admiral) Byrd himself.

And, despite appearances, Paul Siple had been changed by his experiences. He now seemed a young man in a hurry. Even as he was touring and giving speeches, he raced through the remaining three years of his bachelor of science degree in biology, with a minor in geology. At the same time, he *also* managed to author two best-selling books on his experiences. Then, soon after graduation, Siple took off on a two-year backpacking tour of the world, traveling to England, Western Europe, Russia, the Middle East, and North Africa. Erie, Pennsylvania, had grown too small to keep him.

He returned from his travels to an invitation by Byrd to join a second Antarctic expedition. Byrd, who in the years to come would show that he had boundless trust and faith in the young man, asked Siple to join him on his personal staff and help him plan the voyage—then, once it was underway, made him the expedition's chief biologist. During this expedition's two years in Antarctica (1933–1935), Siple led the Marie Byrd Land Sledging Party, which identified and catalogued 90 new species of moss and lichen.

Siple returned to the States to two more years of lectures; hundreds of them now, around the country. He also found time to write his third book. In 1936, he enrolled in graduate school at Clark University in Worcester, Massachusetts. He had found his life's work now: the adaptation of human beings to their physical environment—and would earn a PhD in geography and climatology three years later. Also in 1936, he married Ruth

Ida Johannesmeyer—and between 1940 and 1946 they would have three daughters.

It's amazing they had the time. Between 1939 and 1941, now-Admiral Byrd was named head of the U.S. Antarctic Service and embarked on yet another expedition. He asked Paul Siple to be his assistant. Ultimately, Siple became supervisor of all Antarctic expedition logistics and supply, senior geographer of the Service, leader of the west base of Little America III and—again putting his Scouting training to good use—official navigator on all Antarctic exploratory flights.

With the outbreak of war, Siple was hired by the U.S. Army to help design cold weather clothing and gear, as well as develop maps. Within a year, he was commissioned as a captain in the U.S. Army Quartermaster Corps, where he directed research on clothing and environmental protection for troops in all climates. He had come a long way from those days in Little America I watching Martin Ronne sew reindeer skins.

Ultimately, Siple founded the U.S. Quartermaster Corps' Climate Research Laboratory. The revolutionary clothing the Laboratory invented—notably the cold weather parka and the thermal barrier boot—saved thousands of lives and earned Siple both the Legion of Merit medal and an honorary knighthood (MBE) from the King of England. Those designs still define outdoor clothing to this day.

With the war's end, Siple did field research in the Arctic and Greenland and then traveled to Little America IV as the scientific advisor to the War Department. In 1946, he left the army as a Lt. Colonel—and immediately rejoined the army's general staff as a civilian expert in science and geography, and the acknowledged world's expert on human adaptation to all of the Earth's diverse climates.

One of the most celebrated feats of U.S. military leadership is General Matthew Ridgeway's command of the NATO and UN forces during the Korean War. Ridgeway arrived to find his troops demoralized, in retreat, and literally freezing to death. One of his first command decisions—one which both saved lives and restored morale—was to order new winter clothing for the troops . . . Siple and his design would travel twice to Korea during those years, traveling into combat zones to test and perfect the technology. There, he would also put to use a scientific discovery he had made with a colleague in 1946: "wind chill," a term now used casually by the general public.

In 1953, now generally recognized as the greatest of all polar scientists, Siple was named director of scientific projects and environmental living for the task force preparing for Operation Deep Freeze I, which would begin the construction of research facilities across the Antarctic. This initiative was in turn the kickoff for 1958's Deep Freeze II, the first great international (67 nations at 40 stations) exploration of the Antarctic and South Pole. Soon, he was named deputy to the rapidly fading Admiral Byrd—after 30 years, this would be their final partnership.

On December 31, 1956, Eagle Scout Paul Siple appeared on the cover of *Time* magazine as part of a larger story about Deep Freeze II, the first-ever attempt to winter-over at the South Pole. Siple had been named scientific leader of the 18-man expedition, which would spend six months at Amundsen-Scott South Pole Station.

They emerged in late September 1956 to acclaim as great as the first Scott expedition. In the months that followed, Siple would receive five honorary doctorates, medals from the U.S. Army and Defense Department—and most prized of all because he now joined the ranks of the most famous Polar explorers—the *National Geographic* Hubbard Medal.

In making the award, Chief Justice Earl Warren, after listing such names as Peary, Amundsen, Scott, and Byrd, said, "Our Hubbard medalist today is of the same stature as the great explorers I have just mentioned. Six times he has journeyed to the forbidding continent of Antarctica, the first time with Admiral Byrd as a young Eagle Scout."

Now, Justice Warren continued, Paul Siple had led the team that survived "the longest, darkest and coldest winter yet endured by man."[12]

Paul Siple accepted the medal with typical humility, "on behalf of all those who have taken part in the exploration and uncovering of a continent."[13]

In his final years, Siple continued to work with little thought to retirement. Like his beloved sled dogs, he remained in harness to the very end. In 1966, while serving as the first scientific attaché to the U.S. embassies in New

Zealand and Australia, he suffered a stroke. He was only 58, but after the physical stresses of living in the most inhospitable places on the planet, Paul Siple's body had begun to wear out.

He returned to Washington as special scientific advisor to the army's research & development office. And there on November 25, 1958, he died, at his desk, hard at work on his next adventure. In his memory, the U.S. Army created the Paul A. Siple Award, a silver medallion awarded biannually to an Army scientist or scientific team for excellence in scientific research.

But Paul Siple's greatest legacy is Antarctica. Today, travelers to that frozen continent can visit Mount Siple, Siple Island, Siple Ridge, and Siple Station—and even the Siple Coast of New Zealand—all honoring a great explorer, a great scientist, and the most famous young Eagle of Scouting's first century.

================ CHAPTER FIVE ================

SHOOTING THE MOON

THEY WOULD ONLY GET ONE CHANCE.

The targeted landing area was on the southwest edge of the Sea of Tranquility. The two men, after saying goodbye to Michael Collins in the command module, had climbed through the tight passage into the lunar excursion module (LEM), sealed the hatches, and readied the LEM for separation.

That was almost an hour ago now. Collins was now 70 miles above them, listening intently to the radio, and hundreds of NASA employees were monitoring their progress back on Earth from the Houston control room. And—almost impossible as it was to imagine—all over the surface of that little blue marble hovering above them, a billion or more people were listening as well in living rooms and auditoriums and public marketplaces.[1]

None of that mattered now. All that counted was a successful touch down.

At 6,000 feet, a yellow caution light flared on the console. Neil Armstrong and Ed "Buzz" Aldrin glanced at each other. "Program alarm," said Armstrong brusquely, "It's a 1202." Twenty miles above, Collins dove for his checklist and began thumbing through its pages. But before he could find the designation, he heard a voice from Houston—it was fellow astronaut and designated capsule communicator Charlie Duke—saying, "Roger, we're GO on the alarm."

Collins found the listing: "1202: Executive overflow." It meant that the onboard computer, little more powerful than an electric adding machine, was now being overwhelmed with so much input from so many sources that it was postponing some of the calculations for later.

What calculations? When? Was the computer now putting off calculating a critical piece of information?

At 3,000 feet above the surface, another yellow caution light appeared. The computer now read "1201," yet another kind of program overflow alarm.

Recalled Aldrin later: "Back in Houston, not to mention on board the Eagle, hearts shot up into throats while we waited to learn what would happen. We had received two of the caution lights when Steve Bales, the flight controller responsible for LM [lunar module] computer activity, told us to proceed, through Charlie . . . We received three or four more warnings but kept on going."

The Apollo 11 lunar module was now fully committed to a landing—and with little extra fuel on the descent engine, Armstrong knew he had to pick the final landing site quickly and commit to it. There would be no time to change his mind.

Hands on the controls and looking out the LEM's window, Armstrong began bringing the LEM down, adjusting the descent rate to make minute course corrections. He checked the landscape off to his starboard—good, they are on track.

Armstrong looked out ahead. To his horror, he saw "an NFL stadium-sized crater, with a large number of big boulders and rocks for about one- or two-crater diameters around it." That is exactly where they *didn't* want to land. And the LEM's autotargeting landing system was taking them right for it. The LEM risked landing at an angle on the crater's wall and perhaps tipping. Worse, on the rippled surface at the edge of the crater, Armstrong risked the worst nightmare of all: *stubbing a toe*, as he called it—catching one of the legs of the LEM on the ground or on one of the many boulders that strewed the area while the lander was still moving sideways . . . a potentially fatal mistake.

Without a second thought, Armstrong switched off the autotargeting system and grabbed the controls. He'd have to land the craft manually. But at only a couple hundred feet up now, there seemed to be no safe place to go. He scanned the horizon for a better landing spot that he could reach with the 60 seconds of fuel that still remained, working the rockets to slowly bring the craft closer to the lunar surface. To use a modern analogy, it was like a computer game playing four different variables at once—only this time the cost of failure was everything:

540 feet, down at 30 [feet per second] . . . down at 15 . . . 400 feet down at 9 . . . forward . . . 350 feet, down at 4 . . . 300 feet, down 3½ . . . 47 forward . . . 1½ down . . . 13 forward . . . 11 forward? coming down nicely . . . 200 feet, 4½ down . . . 5½ down . . . 5 percent . . . 75 feet . . . 6 forward . . . lights on . . . down 2½ . . . 40 feet? down 2½, kicking up some dust . . . 30 feet, 2½ down . . . faint shadow . . . 4 forward . . . 4 forward . . . drifting to right a little . . .[2]

LIFTOFF

At that moment—July 20, 1969, at the controls, hovering a dozen feet off the surface of the moon in the lunar excursion module with just seconds of fuel left—no human being was better suited for the task at hand than 39-year-old Neil A. Armstrong, a former test pilot and aerospace engineer from Wapakoneta, Ohio.

Armstrong was born on August 5, 1930, just five weeks after Paul Siple's return from the Antarctic. He was the oldest of three children born to Stephen Koenig Armstrong and Viola Louise Engel. Because his father worked for the state of Ohio, and was regularly transferred to a new town, the Armstrongs lived an itinerant existence for most of Neil's childhood—living in 20 different places in his first 15 years.

Such a childhood teaches a young man to adapt quickly to new surroundings, immerse himself immediately into daily life, and to be prepared to move on with little advance notice. And so, somewhere in the middle of those moves, Neil Armstrong at age 13 joined a newly-formed Boy Scout troop in his town. And, because his father made his last forced move—to Wapakoneta—when Neil was 14, the young man finally got the stability he needed to stay with a troop and complete his Eagle at age 17.

Neil left for college at Purdue that August. He had also been accepted at MIT, but chose to stay in the Midwest. He proved to be a merely average student those first two years, no doubt in part because he fully enjoyed campus life—including being a member of the Marching and Concert Bands—and perhaps because he also knew that a job was already waiting for him: he'd gone to Purdue on the Holloway Plan, which meant he was now also an apprentice seaman and owed the U.S. Navy three years on active duty and two more, during his final years in college, in the Naval Air Reserve. It was an interesting career choice because Armstrong had a history of motion sickness.

Fulfilling that commitment, Neil Armstrong joined the navy in 1947 as a midshipman. Eighteen months later, a week after his 20th birthday—after he had made six carrier landings in a propeller trainer and six more landings in a propeller fighter aircraft—he received his wings. Six months after that, in June 1951, now an Ensign, he made his first carrier landing in a jet. And three months after that, just weeks after his 21st birthday, Ensign Neil Armstrong saw his first action over Korea as an escort on a reconnaissance mission.

Five days later, on a low-altitude bombing attack in a valley, Armstrong's F9F Panther was hit by anti-aircraft fire. The damaged plane, flying at 350 mph, headed directly toward a cable the North Koreans had strung between the walls of the valley 500 feet above the floor. As Armstrong struggled to regain control of the plane, it clipped the cable, slicing off six feet of one wing.

The young pilot somehow still managed to regain control of the plane before it crashed, and then to fly out of the valley for home. But now he realized that, because the wing's aileron was gone, it would be impossible to land. And so, after Armstrong limped his plane to the nearest friendly airfield—he flew directly over it, aimed the plane for the nearby ocean, and hit the ejection seat.

Neil's plan was to parachute into the water and wait to get picked up by rescue helicopters. Instead, as he ejected, Armstrong ran into an onshore wind and his parachute was blown back over land. Amusingly, he found himself picked up by a Marine officer, sent out in a jeep to find the parachuting pilot . . . and who just happened to be his old flight school roommate.

Ensign Neil Armstrong left the navy in August 1952, having flown 78 combat missions, which earned him an Air Medal with two gold stars. He went home to finish his degree at Purdue. Like Paul Siple before him, Armstrong was a changed man. This time he hit the books, becoming an honors student . . . yet still found time to join a fraternity.

He finished his aeronautical engineering degree in 1955. Two years later, he was a married man with the first of three children on the way. He was working for NACA (soon to be NASA) at Edwards Air Force Base in the Southern California desert. Edwards, of course, was the home of the nation's best test pilots including Chuck Yeager, the first man to break the sound barrier.

Armstrong flew on his very first day at Edwards and was soon piloting chase planes and co-piloting the B-29 Superfortress assigned to perform high-altitude drops of the new jet-powered experimental planes. He quickly learned the dangers of his new profession. During one of his first flights, one of the B-29's engine propellers went out of control and cut through both the engine nacelles and the fuselage—and severing the pilot's control cables. Armstrong was co-pilot on this flight, his job to fly the airplane while the pilot supervised the drop sequence activities. Armstrong flew as pilot and sometimes co-pilot on more than 100 of these launch flights.

Nosing the plane down to pick up speed, Armstrong managed to launch the test plane attached to the B-29's belly. Then, cutting one more engine to keep the plane flyable, Armstrong, with only his controls intact, brought the big bomber down from 30,000 feet in a series of slow circles and landed it safely—despite having lost three engines and landing on the sole remaining, outer left hand engine.

Less than 18 months later, Neil Armstrong had joined the elite of test pilots flying the rocket-powered planes. In August 1957, manning the controls of a Bell X-1B—the successor to Yeager's record-breaking plane—Neil dropped from the belly of the bomber and climbed to an altitude of more than 11 miles. Completing the flight, he had a momentary thrill when the plane's nose gear broke on landing.

Within a few years, Armstrong was flying the premiere experimental plane of the pre-space age: the X-15. In April, 1962, in a famous flight, he pushed the X-15 to 207,000 feet—the brink of space, and the highest Armstrong would fly until he joined the Gemini program. But on the descent, he left the nose of the craft high for too long—and suffered the singular experience of literally bouncing off the outer edge of the lower, thicker atmosphere. The X-15 was reportedly flung back up to 140,000 feet (though Armstrong isn't sure it reached quite that height), where he had to attempt a second re-entry.

By now, Armstrong was already over Edwards Air Base, rocketing along at 2,000 mph. Legend has it he was all the way to the Rose Bowl in Pasadena (a bit of an exaggeration, according to Armstrong) when he finally banked the X-15 back around to land at Edwards.

Neil Armstrong's career reached a turning point in 1962. After seven flights in the X-15—and ultimately having tested more than 50 different aircraft, Neil's career as an experimental test pilot was nearing its end. He had been named one of the six engineer-pilots chosen to fly a proposed new space plane.

His life was also marked by tragedy. In late January that year, his only daughter, Karen, died from complications from brain cancer. That may have been why, when NASA announced that it would recruit a second group of astronauts (after the Mercury group) for the planned Apollo missions to the moon, Armstrong's letter of application arrived a week after the June 1, 1962, deadline. Luckily, Dick Day, who had worked with Neil at Edwards before joining NASA, spotted Armstrong's letter and slipped it into the applicant pile.

In March 1966, Neil Armstrong was the commander of Gemini VIII. It was to be a flight of firsts—not least that Armstrong himself was the first American civilian in orbit. Gemini VIII would also be the first spacecraft to ever dock with another—in this case, an unmanned Agena target vehicle— and the third to feature a spacewalk.

However, it wasn't a flight without controversy. Soon after the successful docking—and out of contact with ground stations—the joined pair of spacecraft began to roll. Armstrong decided the only solution was to undock and try to get the capsule under control. But it only got worse . . . until the capsule was rolling once per *second*.

In the end, because the craft was out of radio/telemetry contact with Houston, Mission Control was unable to assist the crew in diagnosing the system failure. So, left to his own devices, Armstrong executed an emergency maneuver that stopped the rolling—but that also required the mission to end before his co-pilot, David Scott, could take his spacewalk.

Afterwards, Armstrong was depressed because the spacecraft failure had prevented the crew from doing all of the things it had planned. Still, he consoled himself with the knowledge that had he not taken the decisive action he did, none of them might have survived. NASA ultimately concluded that the error had been its own and that Armstrong had made the right decision.

And so, at age 36, Neil Armstrong found himself assigned to the Apollo program. On December 23, 1968, even as Apollo 8 (for which he had been backup commander) was circling the moon, Armstrong was offered command of Apollo 11.

The entire world watched as Apollo 11, atop a gigantic Saturn V rocket, lifted off from Cape Kennedy on the morning of July 16, 1969. Millions had watched the three astronauts, looking cool and confident, walk from the control center to the special vehicle that would carry them to the launch pad. Millions of viewers also knew that the previous May, in a test run of the LEM landing process, Armstrong had ejected from a failing system just 100 feet from the ground—and scientists had determined that if he'd ejected *one-half second* later, he would have been killed. It was just one more close call in a career filled with near-death experiences.

The Saturn V, bearing its tiny capsule, roared into the sky. In the next few days, the world would learn more about the three men in that capsule, especially the command pilot, Neil Armstrong. It would also learn the name of the lunar excursion module—the "Eagle"—a name chosen for the symbol of the United States of America. But for millions of Americans who knew Armstrong's Scouting history, the LEM's name took on a second meaning.

Now, at 20:17 UDT, Neil Armstrong, manually directing the controls of the LEM as it hovered over the surface of the moon, needed every one of the skills he had learned in his remarkable career—Boy Scouts, fighter pilot, test pilot, and astronaut—to touch down safely. With the fuel indicator saying the tanks were nearly empty, Armstrong knew he had just seconds left.

At last, Neil found his spot and cut the engines. Would, as some feared, the moon dust prove so fine and deep that the spacecraft would just sink beneath the surface? The two astronauts held their breaths.

A sensor on one of the lunar module's legs registered contact with the lunar surface. In turn, a panel light on the control panel lit up.

"Contact light," said an excited Aldrin, "OK, engine stop . . . descent engine command override off . . ."

"Houston," said Neil Armstrong, "Tranquility Base here. The Eagle has landed."

MAKING UP FOR LOST TIME

In 1946, America's dads—current and near-future—came home from the war. Armed with their GI Bills, and exhibiting unusual maturity and worldliness for men of their age, several million American men hit the States running and ready to make up for lost time. They wanted college degrees, a career, marriage, and a house full of kids—and they wanted them in a hurry.

And even more than most American institutions, the Boy Scouts of America was anxious for their return. For a quarter century, Scouting had been suffering a shortage of adult leadership. From 1911 to 1929, the BSA's explosive growth had outstripped the number of available volunteers—which is why many troops, like Arthur Eldred's, had been largely created and run by boys. In the 1930s and during the Depression, as fathers searched for work, they had little free time to contribute. And in the 1940s, almost every able-bodied adult male was either off at war or working extra shifts in war-related industries—leaving Scouts to be led by old men and young Eagles who would soon themselves head off to boot camp.

But now America was suddenly awash in men aged 20 to 50—and, even as these members of the Greatest Generation raced to turn themselves into organization men, they also were committed (to an unprecedented degree) to making sure their children wouldn't suffer the same deprivations and abandonment they had. And if they couldn't be on hand to do so, they would hire surrogates to take their place. It didn't take a prophet to recognize that Scouting (and every other youth organization in America from the Little League to Campfire Girls) was about to be overrun with a vast demographic wave of new young members—the baby boomers—led by an army of anxious and engaged parents.

To its great credit, and perhaps better than at any other time in its history, the BSA exhibited considerable prescience as it prepared for the postwar world. With its new generation of leaders, the organization seemed to intuitively recognize that not only would the new world be very different from what came before—the Atomic Age, the Information Age, the Space Age, and an economy increasingly defined by a giant demographic bulge of children—but that for Scouting to maintain its presence at the heart of boyhood, it too must radically transform itself. Scouting, for the first time, also had the funds to implement these changes, in part because of Irving Berlin's stipulation in 1940 that the royalties from "God Bless America" be divided between the Girl and Boy Scouts.[3]

That transformation had already begun during World War II. The 1943 *Handbook* saw a burst in the number of merit badges, as Scouting recognized that the Trail to Eagle now needed much more than just perfecting outdoor skills (though they were still there in the "required" merit badges); it needed adult and professional skill development.

The result was an explosion in the number of merit badges: 100 by 1948, including 23 related to agriculture (a vital skill during this era of national rationing and home gardens) and four dealing with aviation, the most exciting new technology of the war.[4]

Then, as if in recognition that the future now truly belonged to the young, the BSA also made plans to remove adults from the rank process—a new rule it officially announced in 1952. No longer would an adult Scouter be able to continue to work toward the Eagle rank; from now on the cutoff would be the Scout's 18th birthday (resulting in generations of scrambling 17½-year-old Life Scouts). However, in a later codicil to that new rule, Scouting made one of the most enlightened— and ultimately, as we will see, the most moving—decisions in its history: it waived the 18-year-old retirement rule for mentally, and otherwise permanently, disabled Scouts.

Americans were also beginning their great migration to the suburbs. And Scouting followed, moving its New York City headquarters to New Brunswick, New Jersey, in 1954.

Finally, in 1948 Scouting made what one of its historians called "a seemingly innocuous change . . . that foreshadowed the next major step in the Eagle Scout award's evolution."[5] It was simply an elaboration of the longstanding requirement for Eagle that the Life Scout perform six months of "satisfactory service."

The new rule stipulated that the Life Scout spend those six months actively working:

> *As a leader in his troop's meetings, outdoor activities, and projects;*
> *his best to help in his home, school, places of worship, and community;*
> *and take care of things that belonged to him and respect the property of others.*[6]

Practically speaking, for a Life Scout in an active Boy Scout troop working on various merit badges such as Citizenship, the precise words of this requirement were all-but superfluous as the boy was likely performing this sort of work already. But philosophically, it was a major step: for the first time, the BSA was unequivocally stating that its vision of what constituted a true Eagle Scout now included a deep engagement with his community—family, school, church, and neighborhood. It established a position from which Scouting has not deviated for more than 70 years.

Less than two decades later, Scouting would refine that requirement one more time . . . and in doing so, give itself a brand new purpose.

SECOND LIFE

Appropriately enough, Scouting launched its second era in 1950, at the midpoint of the century and Scouting's 40th anniversary. The kickoff was a second national jamboree, held at Valley Forge, Pennsylvania, in mid-June. The site selection was brilliant: Scouting underscored its status as an iconic American institution by placing itself at one of the most inspiring of American locations—one with particular resonance for millions of new American veterans.

This second jamboree drew an astounding 47,000 Scouts, nearly twice that of its 1937 D.C. predecessor—and in the process attracted considerable national attention.[7] Its official theme (casting back to the famous Leyendecker poster) was "Strengthening the Arm of Liberty," which the BSA promoted by donating 200 eight-foot copies of Lady Liberty to organizations around the country. But the implicit message of the event was: *Scouting is back, and it is bigger and more important than ever.*

But what kind of Scouting? Young Scouting. The Knights of Dunamis, Exploring, Air Cadets and all of the other older Scouting programs were busy reconstituting themselves and enjoying impressive growth. But really the attention—as with every other part of American society—was focused on the boomers . . . and the first of that cohort was just now entering elementary school.

Not surprisingly then, Cub Scouting got most of the attention from both the BSA and the general public. In fact, seeing what was coming, Scouting had spent much of the 1940s restructuring Cubbing, most notably added the Webelos rank—that critical, hybrid transition rank for 11- (later, 10-) year-olds between Cub Scouts and Boy Scouts. The Webelos "Arrow of Light" bridging ceremony smoothly transferred boys between the two programs, minimizing dropouts. At the same time, Den mothers, who had been allowed as optional leaders beginning in 1936, were allowed to be officially registered after 1949.

But in terms of capturing the imagination of both boys and their dads, Cub Scouting's greatest recruitment tool would be invented in 1953: the Pinewood Derby. This annual race of small wooden cars, constructed by the boys themselves, was the brainstorm of Cubmaster Don Murphy of Pack 280 in Manhattan Beach, California. Quickly adopted nationally, it would go on to become one of the most famous annual events of American boyhood.

Cub Scouting enjoyed explosive growth throughout the 1950s—and, inevitably, the image of the Cub Scout in his blue uniform, yellow neckerchief, and baseball cap, became ubiquitous in the culture. As for Boy Scouts, their profile was much lower . . . except during the jamborees. The third such jamboree, held in 1953 in Irvine Ranch, California, managed to draw more than 45,000 Scouts despite being held on the West Coast—underscoring that Scouting, if anyone still wondered, was now a continental phenomenon. In 1957, it was back at Valley Forge—and this time drew nearly 53,000 Scouts.[8]

Where were the Eagles? Anyone who was looking saw more of them than ever. Throughout the mid-1950s, more than 14,000 Scouts each year earned their Eagle awards—double that of both the 1930s and the war years. And they were busy: providing leadership for inexperienced new troops, and swollen older ones, through the Knights of Dunamis, helping build new campgrounds with the Order of the Arrow, spending a season in the Antarctic with the National Science Foundation (and sometimes meeting Paul Siple), presenting the annual Scouting report to the president of the United States, and working on the staff of Philmont Ranch. Others were helping to build the new Explorer program for older Scouts, which earned official backing from the BSA in 1959 as the official senior Scouting organization. Exploring also offered (until 1972) a back door to Scouts to continue to pursue their Eagle until age 21. That was one reason why the Exploring's membership more than tripled from 1949 to 1958 to 220,000.[9]

It could be said that any great adventure or initiative—mountain climbing, hiking in the wilderness, helping with disaster relief—by a team of Americans in this era, if it included teenage boys, inevitably featured an Eagle Scout.

THE NEW ARISTOCRACY

Meanwhile, adult Eagle Scouts continued their march through American life. With the war over, it was time for other older Eagles in the civilian world to make their way into the limelight.

Barber Conable, an Eagle Scout from Warsaw, New York, and a veteran of Iwo Jima, embarked on a political career that would make him an 11-term Republican congressman. A close friend of Richard Nixon, he broke from that president because of Watergate—in the process adding the indelible phrase "smoking gun" to the political lexicon. In 1984, President Reagan named him president of the World Bank.

John Creighton not only served as CEO of Weyerhauser and United Airlines, but also as the national president of the Boy Scouts of America. Commenting on the last, Creighton said: "Scouting has always reflected the expectations of the American family. That so many American parents have chosen to involve their children in Scouting is a powerful testament to Scouting's effectiveness in building character in American youth."[10]

James Daughdrill resigned as president of a successful carpet and textile company to study to become a Presbyterian minister. He ended up as Secretary of Stewardship for the Presbyterian Church, USA. Then he successfully took on the challenge of saving struggling Rhodes College in Memphis, raising the endowment from $6 million to more than $200 million during his quarter-century tenure there.

Tom C. Clark, who earned his Eagle at the dawn of the BSA (1914), was named U.S. Attorney General in 1945 by President Harry Truman. Four years later, Truman nominated him again to the United States Supreme Court, where he served—voting on such landmark cases as *Brown v. Board of Education*—until 1967, when he resigned because the nomination of his son, Ramsey, as U.S. Attorney General posed a potential conflict of interest.

Ross Perot was one of those extraordinary young men who earned his Eagle medal at age 12. After attending Annapolis and serving his time in the U.S. Navy, Perot went to work at IBM, becoming a top salesman. Leaving Big Blue in 1962, Perot founded Electronic Data Systems (EDS). The company initially only survived because of Perot's sheer tenacity—he finally landed the company's first contract after 77 turndowns. By 1984, when General Motors bought EDS, Ross Perot was a billionaire. By then Perot was already becoming famous for his swashbuckling patriotism—including organizing a raid into Iran to free two imprisoned EDS employees. By then, he was deeply involved in politics—culminating in his 1992 and 1996 runs for president of the United States. The former was the most successful third-party presidential run (He garnered 18.9 percent of the popular vote.) in 70 years.

Michael Dukakis, an Eagle from Brookline, Massachusetts, served twice as governor of Massachusetts, as a U.S. Congressman, and most famously, was the Democratic candidate for the U.S. presidency in 1988. His running mate was another Eagle, **Lloyd Bentsen**, four-term U.S. senator from Texas and later secretary of the treasury. **Murphy Foster** was governor of Louisiana; **Lamar Alexander** was governor of Tennessee and secretary of education; **Richard Lugar** was elected senator from Indiana; **Jack Murtha** was a 27-year congressman from Pennsylvania; **Sam Nunn** served four terms as senator from Georgia; **Samuel Pierce** was Reagan's secretary of housing and urban Development. **Warren Rudman** was a two-term senator for New Hampshire. And **Donald Rumsfeld** was a two-time secretary of defense. **Terry Sanford** was governor of South Carolina, senator from that state, and president of Duke University.

William S. Sessions, who earned his Eagle in Arkansas in 1947, went on to become director of the FBI (1987–1993). His son **Pete Sessions**, a Texas congressman, also became an Eagle, as did Bill Sessions' grandsons. Bill Session's father was the author of the *God and Country* religious medal handbook for the BSA.

John Caldwell became chancellor of North Carolina State; financier **John Anderson** funded the UCLA School of Management that bears his name; **Norman R. Augustine** was CEO of Martin Marietta; **Stephen Bechtel** became chairman of his family's giant corporation, as was **J.W. Marriott**; **Daniel Evans** was governor of Washington and U.S. senator; Washington Congressman **Tom Foley** became Speaker of the House and U.S. ambassador to Japan; **Howard Hunter** and John **Groberg** were leaders of the Mormon Church; attorney **William Gates Sr.** became CEO of the giant Foundation created by his son, Bill, and daughter-in-law Melinda; **General Robert Herres** was chairman of USAA and first commander of the United States Space Command.

Dudley Herschbach, who earned his Eagle in Campbell, California, in 1946, became a noted science professor at Harvard—and in 1986, won the Nobel Prize in Chemistry for his experiments with crossed molecular beams. **Frederick Reines**, the son of Russian Jewish immigrants, earned his Eagle at age 16—and the Nobel Prize in Physics six decades later for his co-discovery of the neutrino. **Robert Richardson** wrote about his Scouting experiences in the biography he submitted to the Nobel Committee after receiving the 1996 Nobel Prize in Physics for his discoveries in the behavior of Helium-3 at supercold temperatures.

Ewing Kauffman founded Marion Laboratories and owned the Kansas City Royals. The wonderfully named General **Charles H. Bonesteel III** commanded the U.S. Army in South Korea in the late 1960s. Oklahoman **Glen McLaughlin** became a noted Silicon Valley venture capitalist and head of the 1,000-year-old Catholic Order of Knights of St. John. **Major Gen. Charles Metcalfe**, who earned his Eagle in 1949, became director of the National Air Force Museum, while also serving as vice president of the BSA central region. **Jim Mora** became a much-traveled NFL head coach and

The First Eagle Scout in This Country.

ABOVE LEFT: The nation's first Eagle Scout Arthur Eldred in 1912. (courtesy of Dr. Terry Grove) ABOVE RIGHT: Famed child actor Jackie Coogan receives the key to the city of Detroit from an Eagle Scout in the 1920s. Coogan, who began a notable career in silent films, co-starred with comic genius Charlie Chaplin in 1921 in the movie *The Kid*. Coogan later portrayed "Uncle Fester" in *The Addams Family* television show in the 1960s.

Evangeline Lindbergh, the mother of famed aviator Charles A. Lindbergh, receives a bouquet of roses from Lt. Hegenberger (second from the left, and an Eagle Scout himself) and two Eagle Scouts at Boston's Hotel Statler in March 1928.

ABOVE LEFT: Nicknamed "Eagle Scout #1" in the 1930s, Paul Allman Siple earned the Eagle medal in 1923 along with 59 total merit badges. He was the first BSA youth member to travel to the South Pole in 1928 with Admiral Richard E. Byrd. ABOVE RIGHT: Siple (left), with Admiral Byrd (right), at the South Pole's Little America base. BELOW: In 1956, 18-year-old Eagle Scout Richard Lee Chappell (left) of Eggertsville, New York was chosen to accompany Dr. Siple to the Antarctic.

ABOVE: A rare image of Astronaut Neil Armstrong (left) as an Eagle Scout on a souvenir stamp with BSA's former honorary president Dwight D. Eisenhower (right) that celebrated the 13th World Jamboree in Japan. BELOW: Armstrong, the world's first Moonwalker and 1973 Distinguished Eagle Scout, makes a statement to the press at the 13th World Jamboree held in Japan in August 1971.

ABOVE: Astronaut and former Boy Scout from Mitchell, Indiana, Virgil I. "Gus" Grissom, shows two Explorer Eagle Scouts around the Kennedy Space Center in the mid-1960s. RIGHT: Actor Jimmy Lydon portrays all-American youth Henry Aldrich in the 1940s *Aldrich Family* film series. *Henry Aldrich-Boy Scout* reveals Henry to be an Eagle Scout with 36 merit badges. In this movie, actress Mary Malone plays his sister, Mary Aldrich. FAR RIGHT: Explorer Eagle Scout Paul Rettberg holds aloft the torch for the 1959 Pan American Games held in Chicago. Designed as a cross-continental relay utilizing Boy Scout runners, it was not without incident. Lit on a mountaintop outside Mexico City, Mexican Scouts got it to the U.S. border at Laredo, Texas without issue. However, when it reached McAlister, Oklahoma, it was stolen from the Scout honor guard outside city hall but was recovered two hours later. And in Alton, Illinois, the torch's wooden base was lost when the car carrying it rolled into the Mississippi River while unattended.

TOP LEFT: Bill Bradley, a U.S. Senator from New Jersey, a 1964 Olympic gold medalist, and NBA Hall of Fame member, received his Eagle Scout rank in 1957 and the Distinguished Eagle Scout Award in 1982. TOP MIDDLE: William Hanna, half of the cartoon animation team of Hanna-Barbera, received his Eagle medal in 1924 and was presented with the Distinguished Eagle Scout Award in 1980. His creations included *The Jetsons*, *The Flintstones*, *Scooby-Doo*, and *Tom and Jerry*. TOP RIGHT: In 1913, American biologist and scientific researcher Alfred Kinsey earned the rank of Eagle Scout as a 19-year-old (since there was no age limit to prevent him from doing so). ABOVE: Legendary American bandleader and television dad, Ozzie Nelson (bottom middle) of *The Adventures of Ozzie and Harriet*, earned the Eagle medal in 1920 at the age of 14. He received the Distinguished Eagle Scout Award in 1973. His clean-living lifestyle, strong moral code, and natural charm led the Nelsons to the top of the charts as the nation's #1 TV family in the 1950s and 1960s.

ABOVE: Surrounded by four Eagle Scouts, Congressional Medal of Honor recipient Gen. Douglas MacArthur receives BSA's Silver Buffalo medal in New York in May 1963.
BOTTOM LEFT: Graduating the U.S. Naval Academy in 1954, Robert T. "Bob" Herres went on to earn the rank of full general in the U.S. Air Force in 1984 and serve as the nation's first Vice Chairman of the Joint Chiefs of Staff in 1987. General Herres earned his Eagle Scout rank in 1946 and received the Distinguished Eagle Scout Award in 1990.
BOTTOM RIGHT: Texas billionaire H. Ross Perot founded his financial empire with a $1,000 loan made to him by his bride, Margot, which initially funded Electronic Data Systems in 1962. The 1943 Eagle Scout and 1970 Distinguished Eagle Scout transformed it into a multi-billion dollar company that he sold to General Motors in 1984.

ABOVE: President Franklin D. Roosevelt was one of the nation's strongest supporters of Scouting throughout his tenure as BSA's honorary president in the 1930s and 1940s. This landmark image of the President examining the Eagle medal of one of his Scout escorts was taken during the welcoming parade for BSA's 1937 National Jamboree in Washington, DC. Seated with the President are Chief Scout Executive James E. West (middle) and National Scout Commissioner Daniel Carter Beard (right). LEFT: Our future President Gerald R. Ford (right) earned his Eagle rank in November 1927 as a member of Troop 15 in Grand Rapids, Michigan. As the only U.S. President ever to have done so, he remains the icon of integrity that escorted the country through the immediate aftermath of the turbulent Watergate years.

sportscaster. **Walter Wriston** became chairman of Citicorp and an influential business writer.

Not all Eagle Scouts of that (or this) era lived out the stereotype of the upright and culturally mainstream Scout. As with any group of superachievers, Eagle Scouting also produced its own share of mavericks and revolutionaries. **Clive Cussler**, who grew up in Alhambra, California, and earned his Eagle in 1946 at just 14, went on to become a best-selling adventure novelist and marine archaeologist. **James "Red" Duke** became a successful surgeon and founder of Houston's Life Flight helicopter emergency medical service program. **Lawrence Ferlinghetti** became a noted poet of the Beat era and was co-owner of that most famous of Beat publishers and gathering places, City Lights Bookstore. **"Big Daddy" Don Garlitz** earned his Eagle in 1946. He invented the rear-engined, top fuel eliminator dragster on his way to becoming the "Father of Drag Racing." Saturday morning television featured **Dick "The Destroyer" Beyer**, a masked wrestler and Eagle Scout, class of 1946. **Admiral Elmo Zumwalt** commanded Swift boats in the Vietnam War, then became chief of naval operations in 1970 and embarked on a series of radical changes—including improved racial relations—that were loved by enlisted men, but often drew criticism from his fellow officers.

William Hanna, who earned his Eagle in 1924, teamed with Joseph Barbera to found one of the most successful of all animation companies. Hanna-Barbera earned seven Oscars and eight Emmies in the course of creating *Tom and Jerry, The Flintstones, The Jetsons, Scooby-Doo, Yogi Bear,* and the *Smurfs.* Through all of this, he also managed to serve as a Scoutmaster to a local Culver City troop. Another animator, who earned his Eagle the same year, was **Alfred Harvey**, founder of Harvey Comics.

Philo Farnsworth, born in a log cabin in Utah, earned his Eagle medal in 1932. By then he had already scratched on a piece of notebook paper the design for one of the most influential inventions in human history: the television. In the course of earning more than 300 patents, Farnsworth also made seminal contributions to the electron microscope, the telescope, gastroscope, baby incubators, and nuclear fusion.

L. Ron Hubbard earned his Eagle in 1924 with a Puget Sound troop. He would not be remembered solely for his work as a pioneering science fiction writer because he also founded a controversial new religion, Scientology, with its self-help system, Dianetics. Scientology claims to have several million adherents around the world.

Along with Hubbard, probably the most controversial Eagle Scout to enter the public eye in the 1950s was **Dr. Alfred Kinsey**, the pioneering researcher into human sexuality. The child of devout parents and a fan of the outdoors, Kinsey was active as a boy in the YMCA until a Scout troop was founded in his community. Supported by his parents, and despite a weak heart, Kinsey earned his Eagle in 1913—making him one of the very first Eagle Scouts—and continued to be an active hiker for the rest of his life. Scouting was even the source of Kinsey's college senior undergraduate thesis, which was on the group dynamics of boys. Surprisingly, given his later notoriety, Kinsey first gained fame for his research into gall wasps, and as the author of a hugely popular high school biology textbook and (again based on his Scouting experiences) a classic on edible plants. **Wallace Stegner**, the "Dean of Western Writers" earned his Eagle about 1925 as a Presbyterian boy who joined a Mormon troop in Utah. His great love of the outdoors, begun with Scouting, filled both his writing—he won the Pulitzer Prize for Fiction in 1972 for *Angle of Repose* and the National Book Award in 1977 for *The Spectator Bird*—and his environmental work. Stegner also founded and ran for many years the influential creative writing program at Stanford University.

E.O. Wilson, a 1944 Eagle from Alabama not only became one of the premiere biologists of his generation with his research into the social behavior of ants—but the often-controversial Harvard professor then went on to become one of the great writers about natural science, earning two Pulitzer Prizes for nonfiction.

Sam Walton, who earned his Eagle with a troop in Kingfisher, Oklahoma, in 1934—the youngest in the state's history—was one of the greatest entrepreneurs of the twentieth century. Walton worked through much of his childhood to help his family make ends meet; then went on and worked his way through the University of Missouri. After leaving the military in 1945, Walton took $5,000 of his military pay, combined with a $20,000 loan from his father-in-law, and bought a small variety store in Arkansas. There he experimented with many of the innovations that would make him a retailing legend. By 1962, having turned this store into a chain, Walton opened the first true Wal-Mart. By the time of his death in 1992, Wal-Mart had 2,000 stores—and was on its way to becoming the largest retailer in the world.[11]

There were also Eagles who achieved national fame while still young. Perhaps the most notable example in the 1950s was **Ernest Green**. He earned his Eagle from a troop in Little Rock, Arkansas, in 1956. A year later, at age 17, he received national attention as a member of the "Little Rock Nine": African-American students who tried to attend the segregated Little Rock Central High School. When the Nine attempted to integrate the high school, they were attacked by students and their way was blocked by the Arkansas National Guard. In the end, President Eisenhower called in the Army's 101st Airborne division to escort Green and the others. Ernest Green, who received a Congressional Gold Medal, went on to be the first black graduate of Little Rock Central. Martin Luther King Jr. attended his graduation. He was later assistant secretary of housing and urban affairs in the Carter administration.

AMERICA'S ARTIST

As impressive as these real-life figures were, none better personified the Eagle Scout more in the public eye than those anonymous Eagle Scouts who appeared in the works of the most famous illustrator—and most popular American painter—of the century.

Norman Rockwell was 18 years old when he walked into the offices of *Boys' Life* magazine, in his native New York City, looking for work. Having left public high school to bounce around the city's art schools—Chase Art School at age 14, then the National Academy of Design, and finally the Art Students League (the last, ironically, given Rockwell's intense realism, would become the heart of American abstract expressionism)—young Rockwell had proven himself to be something of a prodigy at illustration.

Boys' Life itself was just a couple years old, and had only been purchased (for $6,000—or $1 per subscriber) the year before by the Boy Scouts of America.[12] The magazine was still edited by boys . . . so it was not surprising that Rockwell, with his portfolio of sketches, was not only hired, but named art director—a position he held for three years. It was the beginning of his relationship with the magazine and with Scouting, which would last six decades.

During his time on the *Boys' Life* staff, Rockwell painted several covers for the magazine. The first, a grisaille (black & white) image for the September 1913 issue, showed a Scout in captain's hat standing at the large wheel of a ship. Interestingly, unlike Leyendecker's Scouting images of the same era— which Rockwell admired and often emulated—this Scout is much older, almost an adult. And though, as with many Rockwell images of Scouts over the next 60 years, the boy's rank badge is hidden, given his age and position of authority—perhaps not coincidentally, there is a photograph of Paul Siple in the same pose taken 15 years later—this painting might be seen as the first public image of an Eagle Scout.

Anxious for action, turned down when he first tried to enlist in World War I, the underweight Rockwell gorged himself on food until he was accepted . . . and still ended up spending the war stateside as a military illustrator. He used the time to perfect his craft—which now had begun to reflect the patriotic values that would characterize his art—move with his family to New Rochelle, New York, and get married two years later. Rockwell was given an early discharge in exchange for painting a portrait of his commanding officer.

It was during this period, thanks to an introduction by his studio mate, that Rockwell began to work for the *Saturday Evening Post*. Between the *Post* and *Boys' Life*, Rockwell would ultimately publish more than 400 covers—as well as, through the latter, produce 50 years of hugely popular Scouting calendars. And it was with this pair of magazines (and later *Life* magazine) that Norman Rockwell would cement his reputation as the most beloved illustrator of American life.

Part of the appeal of Rockwell's paintings—and what distinguishes them from more mawkish imitators—is that their sentimentality is usually checked by superb technique and absolute precision in the details. Vladimir Nabokov famously complained that Rockwell wasted his great technique on "banal" subjects, but he didn't appreciate the artist's extraordinary understanding of the world he painted. His Scouts always *look* like real Boy Scouts: their uniforms always have the correct color and badges, they wrinkle like real cotton twill, and they hang just right on skinny young frames. The same is true for the tents, backpacks, and cooking gear. In the late (1969), famous self-portrait of Rockwell standing before an easel in the field being watched by older Scouts, the boys themselves stand like real teenagers: slumped, hands in pockets, with neckerchiefs slightly askew.

This same discernment enabled Rockwell to see Scouts essentially as they saw themselves. Looking across his scores of images of Scouts over the six decades, it is apparent that Rockwell divided Scouts into three general categories. The first are the little ones: the young Tenderfeet, distinguishable from Rockwell's Cub Scouts mostly by their oversized khaki uniforms. In these images (the most famous being "Can't Wait"—the little boy trying on his older brother's Scout uniform and saluting into a mirror), the theme is inevitably excitement, bewilderment, and earnest effort.

Next are the "middle-aged" boys. These are the First Class and Star Scouts who do the day-to-day heavy lifting in Rockwell's paintings, just as they do in Scouting. In Scouting, they lead the patrols, manage the meetings, and teach the basic Scout skills to the little ones. In Rockwell's paintings they demonstrate how to tie knots; put bandages on injured children and pets; manifest the 12 tenets of the Scout Law, Oath, Motto, and Slogan; and promote the next big Scouting event or initiative. Most of these images, being instructional, are usually also far less memorable—and in this area, Rockwell's early images are usually better than the later. The painter himself used to complain, "The Boy Scouts are simply going to have to devise some new deeds or Brown & Bigelow [the calendar printer] will be in a stew."

Finally, there are the Eagles. Often they aren't identified as such—Rockwell liked to position his subjects to hide the rank patch on their breast pockets—but it's usually quite evident who they are. The messages in these paintings are almost always inspirational: the older Scout is presented as noble, heroic, and confident. Most of the time—and unlike the other two types of Scouts—these older Scouts are looking off into the distance, typically upward, as if being called to glory.

The most iconic image in this last group is "We, too, have a job to do" in which a stern-faced older Scout in a campaign hat, stands before an American flag and salutes directly toward the viewer. This image, painted for a WWII campaign poster, has regularly reappeared in Scouting, most recently on the patch for U.S. Scouts attending the 2008 World Jamboree in Chelmsford, England. But there are many other memorable images, some nearly as famous: the older Scout striding across the cover of the 1960 *Scout Handbook*; the young Eagle receiving his medal from his mother, father, and Scoutmaster in 1965's "A Great Moment"; the older Scout being pointed in the right direction by George Washington in "A Scout is Loyal" (1962); and in 1929's "Spirit of America" of an older Scout in profile in campaign hat and red neckerchief standing with half-toned images of Washington, Lincoln, Teddy Roosevelt, and other heroes.

In the words of the Rockwell Museum, Norman Rockwell became the "visual spokesperson for Scouting." But that only captures part of his appeal. Boy Scouting is an organization built on ideals—none more than its idealized image of itself. Norman Rockwell began his career by painting this idea of Scouting. But as the years passed and his understanding of Scouting grew, Rockwell came to realize that there was another, equally real, ideal of Scouting: the one of young men struggling—often humorously, sometimes foolishly, and always movingly—to make themselves into something better. At his best, Rockwell caught these moments with breathtaking technique . . . and gave Scouting a mirror from which to view itself.

But when it came to Scouting's elite, its Eagles, Rockwell's early perspective never really changed. Here, the old ideal was very much real—and the artist seems to imply that to pursue the Eagle was to choose the same path taken by the greatest of American heroes. In his Eagle paintings, Rockwell offers not a mirror to Scouting, but a telescope to see the loftiest vistas. If Norman Rockwell's Scouting paintings amuse and entertain both Scouts and the general public, his Eagle paintings quietly haunt them. *This is what it is possible to become*, they whisper.

In the early 1950s, Rockwell was treated by the legendary German psychologist Erik Erikson, the man who first defined "identity crisis." Erikson reportedly told Rockwell that he painted his happiness, but did not live it. It is not difficult to conclude that, in painting his Eagles so nobly, Norman Rockwell secretly dreamed of being among their ranks.

FATED TO SUCCEED

Demography is destiny—especially if you are an institution with strictly defined age limits.

It was easy to predict that the explosion of Cub Scouts in the 1950s would lead to a massive expansion in the rolls of Boy Scouting in the Sixties as the great baby boom bulge passed through American life. What wasn't so apparent was that that the sheer size of this generational cohort would not only begin by giving American Scouting its Golden Age, but end by so transforming American culture that Scouting would find itself alienated from—even an enemy to—large segments of the population.

Scouting hit the 1960s running. By 1954, Scouting had already passed 20 million total members in its history, 4 million current members, 1 million volunteers, and 100,000 units. *Boys Life's* subscription level crossed 1 million that year.[13]

Three years later, the fourth national jamboree—again at Valley Forge—drew more than 50,000 Scouts and leaders. By then, 15 million copies of the *Handbook* were in print.[14]

And so, as the 1950s ended, the BSA—rich, swollen with members, increasingly synonymous with American youth—was ready to break out. The election of John F. Kennedy, the first Scout ever to be president of the United States, seemed prophetic: this was going to be Scouting's decade.

Norman Rockwell, as usual, led the way. His cover for the new *Handbook* was a tall, waving—implicitly Eagle—Scout striding into the future. His more melodramatic than usual February 1960 cover for *Boys' Life* showed a Scout in a 1910 BSA uniform handing an open scroll bearing the words of the Scout Oath to a modern Scout—this time the Eagle medal is explicit—who has his other hand on the shoulder of a Cub Scout, who in turn is looking down at a globe.

That year, American Scouting's Jubilee, the BSA also began the process of formally looking back, and archiving and preserving its past, by opening the Johnston Historical Museum at its headquarters in New Brunswick, New Jersey. In time, earning pride of place, would be Arthur Eldred's battered Eagle medal. The fifth national jamboree ("For God and Country"), held in Colorado Springs, would—despite its less accessible location—draw more Scouts and Scouters than ever: 53,400.[15] It would never be so large again . . . nor again mention the Almighty.

This was Scouting at its most triumphant: an American institution thriving in the heart of the American Century. And it could only get better, at every level. Cub Scouting was still growing; and Exploring, now capturing the vanguard of the boomers, was seeing record growth. And, most important for the future of Scouting—because from its ranks would come many of the adults who would lead the BSA into the new century—the number of new Eagle Scouts continued to climb. By 1963, 27,000 Eagle medals were being awarded each year; reaching 30,000 by decade's end.[16]

But 1965—coincidentally the year when the 40 millionth Scout would join the BSA[17]—was the year that would prove to be the most important of the decade for Scouting. And the BSA would make the one decision, seemingly minor at the time, that would prove among the most important in its history . . . and may well have saved the organization.

Confident organizations make confident moves—and that is what the BSA did at its zenith: it rewrote the requirements of its ranks.

The first print runs of the new 1965 *Handbook* contained two sets of requirements for Scouting advancement; one set that had been in effect with few changes since just after the war; the other that made changes to almost every rank, but most of all to the top ranks of Star, Life, and Eagle. Scouts who were completing a rank were allowed to finish it according to the old rules, but then had to switch to the new requirements for all future ranks.

For Tenderfoot, Second Class, and First Class, this was an almost invisible transition. The most notable change dealt with a requirement at each rank for a "Scoutmaster Conference": a final meeting with the leader of the troop to make sure the Scout had truly met the requirements, and learned the skills, of that rank. This gave Scouting a "product" quality control that it had never had before—yet still did so within the troop itself, where it belonged. Over the next three decades, though occasionally abused by overzealous Scoutmasters, the conference would profoundly improve the overall quality and consistency of Scouting across its thousands of troops.

The second change, also at all ranks, dealt with participation—and essentially formalized what was already a de facto characteristic of most Scout troops: all Scouts, Second Class and above, were required to hold a "warrant" position—that is, a role of responsibility in the troop (patrol leader, senior patrol leader, instructor, and so on). If the Scoutmaster Conference was designed to codify and improve the quality of the skills and ranks, the goal of the participation requirement was to underscore that leadership and management skill training were an inextricable part of the Scouting experience.

This second requirement also had the planned secondary effect of forcing high school-aged Life Scouts to stay engaged with their troops — even though they were already distracted by the larger world, not to mention the demands of working on their Eagle. The result was that, after a decade of having adults running the show, many troops again enjoyed the salutary improvement of a cadre of senior Scouts in charge.

The third change dealt with merit badges. In the 1948 *Handbook,* the BSA took the hundred merit badges available at the time and grouped them into 15 subject areas: animal husbandry, aquatics, arts, building, campcraft, citizenship, communication, conservation, crafts and collections, nature, outdoor sports, personal development, plant cultivation, public service, and transportation.[18]

These categories may seem a bit arbitrary and overlapping; but they served a larger purpose. Eagle candidates still had to earn the traditional core of 10 required merit badges—Camping, Swimming, Nature, Public Health, Firemanship, Cooking, Lifesaving, Personal Fitness, Safety, and First Aid— that had been in place for decades (and would be for decades more); but they also had to earn one badge from conservation, three from citizenship, one from outdoor sports, and one from animal husbandry, plant cultivation, communication, transportation, or building categories . . . as well as five more merit badges of their choice to reach the traditional total of 21.

One half-million Scouts had earned their Eagle medal along this path (the 500,000th Eagle medal was awarded in 1965).[19] But, to the innocent eye, it was the obvious product of a half-century of modifications, edits, and bolted-on ideas. Shockingly, but shrewdly, the BSA swept it all away. Henceforth, there would be no more merit badge categories: just 11 required badges (Firemanship disappeared, Citizenship became four badges for Home, Community, Nation, and World) and 10 that each Life Scout chose. With over 110 merit badges then available, it was rightly felt that the 10 optional badges would be sufficient to give any Eagle a broad range of life skills and career experiences.

But if that change simplified the path to Eagle, the addition of one new requirement made that path much, much more difficult—and changed Scouting forever. This fourth change added a service component to all of the ranks. At the lower ranks, this requirement was just for a few hours of contribution to the community. For Star and Life, this requirement had two components: a conservation project and a community service project. Both remained comparatively general in subject and brief in duration.

But the Eagle service project was a whole different matter. It returned to a single requirement—and it was unlike anything Scouting (or any other American youth group) had ever seen before.

In the words of the 1965 *Handbook*, the Life Scout had to:

> ...plan, develop, and carry out a service project helpful to [his] church or synagogue, school or community approved in advance by [his] Scoutmaster.

The Eagle Scout service project had begun.

Over the next few decades, as the details of its scope, duration, magnitude, and approval were teased out through the iterative process of hundreds of thousands of examples, the "Eagle project" came to stand as not just the last requirement, but the culminating achievement of a Scout's career. In time, it even began to stand outside of the rest of Scouting as the great transitional experience from youth to adulthood. And if earning the Eagle Scout rank was indeed "the PhD of boyhood," then the service project was now its dissertation.

Over time, the Eagle project would transform Scouting. But, literally in a million small ways, it would also change the face of America.

Still, in 1965, as they read this new requirement and scratched their heads over its implications, only America's Life Scouts had even a glimmering of what was to come.

EAGLE AT THE TOP

Of all of the Eagle Scouts who rose to prominence in the postwar world, probably none cherished his Eagle rank more than the boy born in Michigan in April 1913, named Leslie Lynch King Jr.

Leslie Jr.'s early childhood was, by any measure, a nightmare. His paternal grandfather was a significant individual in early 1900's America: Charles Henry King was an Omaha banker and entrepreneur who had founded several cities in Nebraska and Wyoming in the course of making money off the railroads. He was a very rich man for the era and lived in a famous Omaha mansion. King's wealth at its peak was estimated at nearly a quarter-billion in today's dollars.[20]

One of the businesses King created was a wool brokerage, and he brought his son Leslie (Sr.) into the business with him, probably to launch him on a career. This might seem like your typical tycoon setting up his ne'er do well son; but Leslie King Sr. was much more than that . . . he was a monster.

In 1912, Leslie Sr. married Dorothy Gardner, the daughter of a small town mayor. He had been visiting his sister at college—and Dorothy, the girl's roommate, found the young man smooth and charming.

However, the marriage went bad almost from the first day. On their honeymoon, Leslie reportedly thought he saw his new wife smiling at another man—and promptly beat her. Upon returning to their new home in Omaha, Dorothy quickly realized that her new husband was also an alcoholic and inveterate liar. Unfortunately, by then she was already pregnant. Little Leslie Jr. arrived eight months after their wedding day. And the beatings returned immediately thereafter. Leslie Sr. even threatened his new bride with a knife.

That explains why, just 16 days after Leslie Jr. was born, Dorothy took her baby and fled for the safety of her parents' home in Grand Rapids,

Michigan. Leslie Sr. didn't pursue her; nor, before or after the subsequent divorce—and despite his family's great wealth—did he ever support his child or the boy's mother.

The resulting scandal not only engulfed Leslie Sr., but also his parents, who had been pillars of Omaha society. In their shame, they sold out and moved to California. But always, until his death in 1930, little Leslie's grandfather sent his ex-daughter-in-law money in support of the boy. Unlike his son, Charles Henry King had remained a man of honor and integrity through the entire mess—yet, he would never see his name attached to that of his famous grandson.

Three years later, Dorothy Gardner King married Grand Rapids businessman Gerald Rudolff Ford. Severing all links to her terrible past, Dorothy named her son, now three, Gerald Rudolff Ford Jr. The boy didn't officially change his name, to **Gerald R. Ford,** until he was 22—and he did so then to honor the man he considered his real father. In this close-knit family (He would have three younger brothers.), Jerry Ford learned the decency and integrity that characterized his adult career—and taught him to control the fiery temper he had inherited from his natural father.

Jerry Ford only learned his real family history when he was 17—and, by coincidence, that same year, while he was waiting tables in a restaurant, he first encountered Leslie King Sr., who had sought him out. Ford would later describe his father as a "carefree, well-to-do man who didn't really give a damn about the hopes and dreams of his firstborn son."[21] They would only be in contact a few more times before King's death.

By then, Jerry Ford had grown to be a large, hugely athletic young man—captain of his high school football team and headed for college as a star varsity athlete. Even more than sports, the single-most important activity in young Jerry's life was Boy Scouting. He seemed to take to the outdoors, the skills, the ranks, and leadership responsibilities like few before or since. Whereas for many famous old Eagles there is often little more than a date and a memory, for Gerald Ford there is a wealth of photographs of him as a Scout: visiting the governor of Michigan, serving on camp staff, standing with his troop . . . and in each shot, he is unmistakable: burly, blonde, and radiating confidence like a Rockwell painting. Ford seems the ultimate Eagle Scout—which he was, earning the rank at age 14 in 1927, then staying involved in the program until he left for college.

It would hard to exaggerate just how important Scouting was to Jerry Ford. He often treated it—as much as the presidency of the United States—as the emblematic achievement of his life. Interviewed during his time in the White House about his Scouting experiences, Ford said, "One of the proudest moments of my life came in the court of honor when I was awarded the Eagle Scout badge. I still have that badge. It is a treasured possession."[22]

He would show that love not only throughout his long life, but also even in death.

As high school graduation approached, Jerry Ford was approached by numerous college recruiters. In the end, he chose the University of Michigan, where, playing center and linebacker in his sophomore and junior years, he helped lead the football to back-to-back undefeated seasons and national championships.

Ford was a superb football player—but not a great one. And, in his senior year, all of his efforts weren't enough to keep the team from suffering a miserable season in which it won only a single game. However, it was, in retrospect, Jerry Ford's most important season. Besides unwittingly making a bit of historic trivia—in a game against the University of Chicago, he became the only future president to tackle a future Heisman trophy winner (Jay Berwanger, and Ford carried a scar from that tackle for the rest of his life)—the long, frustrating run of games tested his character far more than any of the winning seasons. So inspiring was Ford and teammate Cedric Sweet's performance in one lost-cause game that their coach wept at halftime.

Ford would later recall about that effort: "Remembering [that game] has helped me many times to face a tough situation, take action, and make every effort possible despite adverse odds."[23] At the end of the season, Ford's teammates voted him Most Valuable Player—because, said one assistant coach, "They felt Jerry was one guy who would stay and fight in a losing cause."[24] Ford was selected for the East-West Shrine game and was named to the Collegiate All-Star team.

That spring, Jerry was recruited by the Detroit Lions and Green Bay Packers, but turned them down for a coaching job at Yale in hopes of also being accepted to the Law School there. Unfortunately, the plan backfired, as the Law School concluded that Ford would be too busy with his coaching work—so instead he spent a summer at the University of Michigan Law School . . . and then in the spring of 1938 transferred at last to Yale.

He earned his law degree in 1941. By then, Ford had already had his first taste of politics by working on the Wendell Willkie presidential campaign. He even signed an antiwar/neutrality petition. But, after Pearl Harbor, Ford left his newly created law partnership and enlisted in the navy.

Commissioned as an ensign, Jerry Ford spent the war in the Pacific as assistant navigator and anti-aircraft battery officer on the carrier USS *Monterey.* He saw considerable combat, including the Battle of the Philippine Sea, the landings at Leyte, and the fighting in the Marshall Islands. But the most dangerous moment for the young officer came during a devastating typhoon (named Cobra) that battered the Third Fleet in December 1944. Ford was racing to his battle station on the *Monterey*'s bridge when the ship rolled 25 degrees, sending him sliding across the deck. Only his athletic skills saved him; Jerry caught the lip of the deck and swung himself down to the catwalk below—instead of being flung overboard.

Like many young men of the era, Lt. Commander Jerry Ford left the war as a man in a hurry to make up for lost time. In 1948, he not only decided to run for Congress, but also to marry to Elizabeth Warren. Worried about possible bad publicity—Betty was both divorced and a former dancer—the two postponed their wedding to just before the election. In the end, Jerry won on both counts: he would go on to serve 13 terms in Congress, and Betty, to whom he would be married for 58 years, would prove to be among the most admired of all First Ladies.

So it might have remained, with the couple raising their four children, and Jerry serving out a long and comparatively undistinguished career as a middle-of-the-road congressman slowly working his way up into the Republican Party leadership—perhaps even fulfilling his dream of becoming Speaker of the House. Indeed, if there was anything in Ford's long House career that was memorable it was, first, his participation as a junior member on the Warren Commission; second, the general opinion (driven by an angry Lyndon Johnson) that Ford was merely a dumb jock; and, finally, his reputation for honor and integrity. Congresswoman Martha Griffiths would say of him, "In all the years I sat in the House, I never knew Mr. Ford to make a dishonest statement nor a statement part-true and part-false. He never attempted to shade a statement, and I never heard him utter an unkind word."[25]

Then, in October 1973, destiny called on Gerald Ford, who was happily ensconced in his eighth year as House Minority Leader. Vice President Spiro Agnew resigned in scandal, and his position needed to be filled. President Richard Nixon called on the Republican leadership to offer candidates. The recommendations were unanimous. "We gave Nixon no choice but Ford," recalled House Speaker Carl Albert.[26]

In December 1973, Gerald R. Ford became the first vice president to assume the job under the vacancy provisions of the 25th amendment. He barely had time to settle into his new role when, nine months later, buried in the Watergate scandals, Richard Nixon became the first person to resign from the U.S. presidency.

Taking the oath of office, President Gerald Ford said that he was "acutely aware that you have not elected me as your president by your ballots, and so I ask you to confirm me as your president with your prayers."[27] He knew that his task was to heal a nation torn by scandal, an unfinished war, racial strife, and cultural divisions . . . and with that first speech, President Ford made a memorable start: "My fellow Americans," he announced, "our long national nightmare is over. Our constitution *works*. Our great republic is a government of laws and not of men. Here, the people rule."[28]

For the next three years, Ford presided over one of the most tumultuous periods in modern American history. Despite Ford's last-ditch attempt to help South Vietnam, he was overruled by Congress, and the Vietnam War was lost. At home, the country suffered the economic body-blows of rampant inflation, a potential swine flu epidemic, and the near-bankrupcy of New York City. Internationally, Cambodian collapsed into genocide and the United States and the Soviet Union signed the Helsinki Accords.

Ford himself was the target of two failed assassination attempts, occurring within three weeks of each other.

But in terms of scandal and public debate, all of these events paled in comparison to one single act of President Ford's: the pardoning of Richard Nixon. Though he would be accused of numerous underhanded motives in making the pardon, Ford would always claim that he did it to heal the nation's open wound and put Watergate behind them. The decision likely lost Ford re-election in 1976.

But as the years passed, Ford's greatest opponents eventually came to believe that he had made the right decision. Even Senator Edward Kennedy, who had excoriated Ford at the time, admitted—as he honored his old enemy with the John F. Kennedy Profile in Courage Award in 2001—that history had shown that Ford had made the right decision.

But his successor understood immediately. In his inaugural address, President Carter said, "For myself and for our Nation, I want to thank my predecessor for all he has done to heal our land."[29]

In the long aftermath—Jerry Ford would live to age 93, the longest life of any president—the ex-president filled his life with speeches, commissions, occasional acts of diplomacy . . . and golf. In the intervening years, all of the controversies had fallen away, and what remained was the memory of those bitter years, and how President Ford had healed the nation even at the cost of his own career. He finished his life among the most beloved of modern presidents.

Thanks to his long life, Jerry Ford had time to design his own funeral. It, of course, included his casket lying in state in the Capitol rotunda—but the rest, including the ceremonies in Michigan, would be the former president's choice. Looking back on his life, choosing the experience that most defined him, Gerald Ford chose the Boy Scouts.

He died on December 26, 2006. In both Washington, DC and in Grand Rapids, Michigan, calls went out for Scouts. For former President Ford's funeral service at Washington's National Cathedral, 125 Scouts helped with the preparations . . . and Eagle Scouts served as ushers for the honored guests.

In Michigan, the scene was even more extraordinary. Fulfilling Eagle Scout Gerald Ford's final wishes, 200 Eagle Scouts were requested to serve in the honor guard for his casket. It was an easy request to fulfill. "I could have had a thousand Eagle Scouts there," said Scout Executive Michael D. Sulgrove of the Gerald R. Ford BSA Council.[30]

It was an indelible sight—and among the most moving in the history of American Scouting. Four hundred Eagle Scouts, aged 15 to 85, some having driven hundreds of miles, lined the Grand Rapids road leading to the Presidential Museum & Library and saluted as the funeral cortege passed.

That night at the Gerald R. Ford Library, the chosen 200 Eagles served as the President's honor guard. In the single most affecting image of the funeral ceremonies, the Eagles, without prompting, lined up in three columns and, in turn, marched up to the flag covered casket and silently saluted their fallen brother.

"I can say without hesitation," Gerald Ford once stated, "because of Scouting principles, I know I was a better athlete, I was a better naval officer, I was a better congressman, and I was a better prepared president."[31]

BOOMER EAGLES

In 1966, the first of the baby boom Boy Scouts, along with hundreds of thousands of other 18-year-old American boys, signed up with the U.S. Selective Service. Within months, many were fighting in the Vietnam War.

A classic Army brat, **Phil Gioia** joined Cub Scouts while his father was an instructor at West Point, and became a Boy Scout when his father was transferred to Italy. In Livorno, he joined Troop 76 of the Transatlantic Council, along with other sons of Cold Warriors from around Europe, North Africa, and the Middle East. Every summer, Troop 76 would go to Camp "Passalaqua" (Camp Waterfall) in Northern Italy, at a beautiful old chalet near Lake Garda—and there, would compete against the Scouts from the other American Scout Troops in Italy from Verona and Vicenza.

When his father was again transferred, to Fort Rucker, Alabama, Life Scout Phil Gioia joined Troop 49. He joined the Order of the Arrow, earned the *Ad Altare Dei* Catholic religious medal, and taught in the NRA marksmanship program for Scouts. And, in early 1961, he completed his Eagle Scout.

When Phil Gioia entered the Virginia Military Institute (VMI) in September 1963, it was still a time of optimism—but just three months later, Gioia found himself part of the VMI honor guard at the funeral of John F. Kennedy. When he graduated four years later, the Vietnam War was in full force—"a gigantic engine pulling millions into it, and dividing the nation,"[32] he recalled. After a year of airborne and ranger training, in February 1968 he was sent to Vietnam.

He arrived in the middle of the Tet Offensive and was immediately sent to fight in the siege of Hue, one of the most savage battles of the entire war. His unit discovered the mass graves of the local citizenry slaughtered by the Viet Cong—an experience that haunted him for decades.

That April, Gioia was wounded and was sent back to the United States for surgery and recuperation. A year later, he was back in Vietnam, commanding an infantry company patrolling near the Cambodian border and regularly clashing with North Vietnamese Army units. "The NVA were good soldiers," he says, "We were better."[33]

In November 1969, now a captain and unit commander, Gioia was wounded again, this time by shrapnel. It was the end of his war. He returned to the United States "a wiser and more experienced man," wearing two Silver Stars, a Bronze Star with a V for valor, and two Purple Hearts. He went on to become a successful investment banker and noted military historian. But he has never fully shaken off the memories of combat—nor ever stopped being thankful for Scouting:

Scouting stood me in good stead—I had slept on the ground as a Scout, hiked and camped in unfamiliar terrain, knew how to use a map and compass before I ever saw one at VMI or in the Army. I could build a fire. I could endure rain and snow without complaining. The self-confidence I gained as a Scout was priceless. And the friends I made in Scouting were terrific. I still know the Twelve Points of the Scout Law; I still have all my handbooks and all my uniforms, from Cub through Explorer, right down to the hand-carved neckerchief slides. I wouldn't have swapped it for anything.[34]

Phil Gioia, along with all of the other Fighting Eagles of the Vietnam era, came home to an America torn in two by Vietnam, a cultural war between young and old, and assassinations and race riots. The late 1960s was a time of choosing sides—and many American boys found themselves on the opposite side from the Boy Scouts of America. The BSA had, from the beginning, tied itself to patriotism, the military, and the American way of life—and it had paid off handsomely both for Scouting and the country.

But now all of those beliefs were under attack . . . and an organization of boys and adults in "paramilitary" uniforms, saluting the flag, and advocating traditional values—that produced military officers like General **William Westmoreland** (Eagle Scout, 1930), an army commander in Vietnam, and that had the reviled Presidents Johnson and Nixon as its honorary head— seemed to many young Americans to be not only anachronistic, but an outright enemy.

As in WWII, the Vietnam War produced its own Eagle Scout heroes— none of them more famous than **Thomas R. Norris.** In April 1972, Lt. JG Norris, one of the last remaining Navy Seals in Vietnam, in one of the most harrowing missions of the war, led a team of Vietnamese Navy commandos behind enemy lines to rescue a downed Air Force officer Lt. Col. Iceal Hambleton.

The desperate rescue attempt to keep Hambleton, an intelligence officer, out of enemy hands, had already cost five aircraft and 11 lives. Now Norris led his team in on the ground, hoping to rescue both Hambleton and any surviving downed airmen. The successful rescue of the colonel and one of the airmen has become part of Seals' legend and was the subject of the popular movie *Bat 21*.

Six months later, while protecting the evacuation of troops to his rear, Lt. Norris suffered such a grievous head wound that he was left for dead. But a fellow Seal, Michael E. Thornton, refused to accept that news, went back under fire, and found Norris, now barely alive, and rescued him.

For the Bat 21 mission, Norris initially refused the Medal of Honor, but eventually accepted it from fellow Eagle, President Gerald Ford, in 1975. For his rescue of Norris, Michael Thornton also was awarded the Medal of Honor—the only time in an American history that one Medal of Honor recipient was honored for saving another Medal of Honor recipient.

Despite the loss of an eye and part of his skull, Norris not only recovered from his wounds but went on to a distinguished 20-year career with the FBI, where, appropriately, he was a founding member of the agency's Hostage Rescue Team.

Eagle Scouting's other Medal of Honor recipient during the Vietnam War was Major (later Colonel) **Leo K. Thorsness**. On April 19, 1967, Thorsness led four F-105 fighters on an attack on surface-to-air missile installations outside Hanoi, North Vietnam. Dividing his forces to confuse the enemy, Thorsness found his plane and his wingman under attack. The second plane was hit and the two crewmen parachuted out. Thorsness circled the drifting parachutes to spot their landing—not knowing that the other two fighters had been attacked and returned to base. This left Thorsness' plane alone over Hanoi.

Spotting a North Vietnamese MIG-17 heading toward the parachutes, and though the F-105 wasn't designed for air-to-air combat, he attacked, shooting down the enemy plane with his cannon. Now, Thorsness and his crewman, Captain Harold Johnson, came under attack both from ground missiles and two more MIGs coming up on their tail. Thorsness went to afterburner, dove to treetop level, and outran the two attackers through narrow canyons.

By now, the pair had called in a rescue on the downed fliers and were heading for a tanker refueling, when Thorsness learned that the rescue team of slow-flying planes and helicopters was under attack. With less than 500 rounds of ammunition left, Thorsness and Johnson raced back to try to draw off the attackers. Finally, after 50 minutes of aerial combat, Thorsness and Johnson were relieved by other fighters and left the combat zone. Then, as they approached the tanker once again, the pair learned that a lost U.S. fighter, nearly without fuel, had spotted the tanker and was limping in. Thorsness decided to give away and, though his own plane was also low on fuel, attempt a dangerous trip to a ground base at Udorn, nearly 200 miles away. Sixty miles out, and in growing darkness, Thorsness cut the engines on the F-105 to idle and glided to the runway, landing on empty tanks.

Just eleven days later, Thorsness was shot down and taken prisoner by the North Vietnamese. Despite continuous pain from a back injured on ejection, as well as torture by his captors, Thorsness refused to cooperate— an act of heroism that earned him a year in solitary confinement. Six years later, in 1973, Colonel Thorsness was released from captivity—and learned for the first time that he had been awarded the Medal of Honor.

Like many institutions, Scouting had thrived on the fickle attentions of the baby boom; now it would wither as those attentions turned elsewhere. After 60 years of working to find its place at the heart of American culture, Scouting now found itself facing a counterculture for which it seemed to have nothing to offer. The BSA continued to produce more Eagles than ever, but that was a trailing indicator, drawn from the ranks of boys who had joined Scouting early in the decade. The real measure was further down in the ranks—and there, membership was falling. The seventh national jamboree drew just 35,000 Scouts and leaders—a 40 percent drop in attendance[35] that was blamed in part on the site's isolation. But it was, in fact, an omen.

Even as Boy Scouts of America rushed to hire outside consultants to produce reports with titles (in psychedelic font) like *Is Scouting in Tune with the Times?* Scouting lost 65,000 members in 1969.[36] And the numbers looked even worse indefinitely into the future, as the culture wars combined with the end of the baby boom to continuously shrink the pool of available new Scouts.

In just five years, Scouting had fallen from the zenith of the most successful era in its history into a nightmare of declining membership, with a society that seemed to be turning against it, and worst of all, it seemed to have serious doubt about its own mission and core philosophy. It would take most of the next decade for the Boy Scouts of America to regain its confidence and footing.

In the meantime, it would fall to the Eagles, even as they struggled to understand the dimensions of the Service Project now facing them, to maintain Scouting's image in the public eye until Scouting once again rediscovered itself.

THE EAGLE HAS LANDED

Though it didn't seem so at the time, with the nation wracked by protests, riots, war, and domestic terrorism, 1969 was, in retrospect, an *annus mirabilis* in modern American history. Scouting, like many other established American institutions, may have seemed to be sliding into the abyss, but elsewhere miracles were taking place that would give new meaning and purpose to everything. The microprocessor was being invented in a laboratory at Intel

Corporation in Northern California. Meanwhile, just up the road in Menlo Park the first network connection that would lead to the Internet was under construction. In New York, a vast crowd gathered for a rock concert on the Yasgur farm in Woodstock.

And, on July 21, the entire world—including the Scouts at the national jamboree in Idaho—watched as, on the moon, Neil Armstrong and Edwin "Buzz" Aldrin prepared for the extravehicular activity (EVA)—humanity's first steps on another world. After landing on the evening of July 20, the two astronauts were supposed to sleep for five hours, as they had already been up for more than 15. But they were too excited and decided to spend the time preparing.

At the 2½ hour mark during this interval, Aldrin, an elder in his Presbyterian Church, radioed down to Houston and fellow astronaut/ chief communicator **Charlie Duke** (Eagle Scout, 1946) to say, "This is the LM pilot. I'd like to take this opportunity to ask every person listening in, whoever and wherever they may be, to pause for a moment and contemplate the events of the past few hours and to give thanks in his or her own way." Then, turning off the microphone, he performed a quiet communion with a kit he'd brought with him.

At 2:39 UTC on Monday, July 21, 1969, Armstrong opened the hatch of the lunar excursion module and slowly made his way down the ladder attached to one of the LEM's legs. Because of the remote control device on his chest, he couldn't see his own feet, so he made the descent very slowly, using the low-gravity to help him "feel" his way to the next rung. Along the way, he reached out and pulled a D-ring, which activated the external television camera and beamed the now-historic images to Earth.

Pausing on the LEM's footpad, Armstrong described the dust on the moon's surface as "fine grained. . .almost like a powder."[37] Then, as a billion people collectively caught their breaths, Neil Armstrong stepped off the footpad onto the lunar surface—the first human being to step on to another world. As he did, Armstrong, the most famous person—the most famous Eagle Scout—in the world, said over the crackling radio the immortal words, "That's one small step for [a] man, one giant leap for mankind."[38]

The author thanks Dr. Armstrong for his assistance in correcting many long-standing factual errors in his standard biography.

CHAPTER SIX

LOST AND FOUND

IN THE 1970S, BOY SCOUTING EXPERIENCED A
CRISIS THAT SHOOK IT TO ITS FOUNDATION. AT THE
SAME TIME, EAGLE SCOUTING EMBARKED ON THE
GREATEST YOUTH COMMUNITY SERVICE INITIATIVE
IN HISTORY.

I n 1965, as part of that milestone year, the BSA set out to address an
underserved segment of American youth—and in the process make
amends for past sins. As the stories of the Tuskegee Eagles tell, poverty
had been a limiting factor to the Scouting experience from the beginning.
Any poor boy could join Scouting, and some communities and sponsoring
organizations even helped with the comparatively low BSA annual dues—but
real-life Scouting was also about uniforms and patches, camping equipment,
and summer camp . . . and they all cost money.

Poor boys, even if they were able to obtain the funds for uniforms
and events, also typically faced a shortage of leaders—dads often held
multiple jobs or were looking for work—and a lack of sponsoring groups
and places to meet. This was true in low-income communities from the

hills of West Virginia, to migrant worker camps in the Southwest to the inner-city neighborhoods of Northeastern cities.

But, it also went deeper than that. Like many venerable organizations, and despite considerable vigilance, Scouting had not entirely escaped the subtle threat of de facto segregation. The BSA had shown admirable inclusiveness in its early years, allowing African American, Native, and Jewish boys, among other minorities, to join the organization even as Jim Crow, reservations, and quotas still ruled in the rest of American life. Indeed, black and Jewish Scouts were part of Scouting almost from the start, and one of the very first Scout troops in the Midwest was founded on an Oklahoma Indian reservation. Santee Sioux Charles Eastman (nee Ohiyesa), a physician, advised both Seton and Beard in the early days of the BSA.

But Scouting headquarters couldn't control the day-to-day operations of individual troops. As the organization spread across the country, some troops, especially in South, were unofficially segregated. Unfortunately, this trend continued well into the 1950s . . . and beyond.

And so, in 1965, enjoying a level of success it had never before known (and never would again), Scouting set out to make amends. It embarked on a major new initiative it called The Inner-City Rural Program (ICRP). Though this project was presented to the public as an update to the previously racially oriented programs of the BSA—the Inter-Racial Service (1927) and the Urban Relationship Service (1961)—it represented a very different level of commitment. And though ostensibly it was targeted at all low-income boys in America, its primary target was inner-city minorities, especially African American boys, whose participation in Scouting was near zero.

This time the BSA went all out. It essentially gave the ICRP carte blanche to change whatever it needed to in Scouting to successfully recruit and keep low-income boys in 18 urban and rural locations. In practice, this often meant bypassing traditional troop meeting sites such as churches and schools, and instead gathering in private homes, or (in the case of Cincinnati) aboard a van that moved through the city. Where there weren't traditional sponsors, some troops tried "Block Scouting," in which they were supported by neighborhoods in exchange for community service projects. And, where camping trips to the countryside were all but impossible, ICRP substituted tree planting, sidewalk hiking, street or park camping, and other alternative activities.

The biggest supporter of the Inner-City Rural Program was Alden G. Barber, who assumed the title of chief Scout executive in 1967. Barber, whom the reader will remember as the young leader of the Knights of Dunamis a quarter century before, was a man of his time—confident, media savvy, and eternally optimistic—and he saw the ICRP not only as a way to reach "at risk" boys in America, but also as a superb promotion for Scouting. As time passed, and Scouting's membership began to fall, Barber also saw in the program a source of new recruits to the organization. Said Barber at the time, "The boy in the ghetto had no real basis for many of the things we [the BSA] talked about . . . so we had to make the program acceptable to him."[1]

But dedicated and brave as were both its volunteers and Scouts—and it often took real heroism to wear a Scout uniform on the same streets as urban gang members who saw Scouting as a threat—the ICRP ultimately proved to be little more than a *succès d'estime.* While hundreds of young men in America's inner cities, and to a lesser degree in impoverished rural areas, did enjoy an experience they might never have known otherwise, in terms of results, the time, energy, and money spent by the BSA on this initiative probably could have been better invested elsewhere.

Unfortunately, the lesson Scouting learned from the ICRP was the wrong one. It saw a noble failure in the face of almost intractable social and economic obstacles. But on closer inspection, the real lesson of the ICRP was that even boys trapped in the depths of ghetto life were drawn to Scouting for the same reason as their middle-class suburban and country brothers: camping, ranks, leadership experience, and skills training. Scouting's real strength and appeal lay in its traditions dating back to Seton, Beard, and Baden-Powell, not in its attempts to stay relevant to the latest cultural fads.

Scouting was hardly alone. Across the country, organizations and institutions walked away from long-standing practices and traditions in a desperate attempt to adapt themselves to the reigning youth culture. And the desperation only grew greater as the vast youth population bulge reached adulthood and the ranks of youth organizations began to fall.

It is a tragic, but widespread, behavior pattern of mature and especially of successful enterprises that, when faced with a cultural shift and declining numbers (i.e., in membership, customers, revenues, profits, and market share), they will almost always choose to change their operations, even abandon their core philosophy, in an attempt to shore up those numbers in the short term, even at the cost of the long term. It almost never works.

What *does* usually work is also usually counterintuitive: fall back on your core business, participants, and philosophy, take the hit in the numbers while you regroup, and then implement your comeback strategy when the marketplace is ready. The primary reason most institutions don't take this path, even when the evidence is right before their eyes, is that careers are short and nobody gets rewarded for presiding over decline.

And so, as the 1960s ended and Scouting found itself both on the far side of the cultural divide from many of its prospective members *and* with falling membership numbers—and with an entrepreneurial character in charge—it decided to roll the dice.

The result, seemingly appropriate for those radical times, was a radical, top-to-bottom reorganization of Scouting—the most sweeping in its history—called the Improved Scouting Program.

The final catalyst for this initiative was a 1969 report by market researcher Daniel Yankelovich, Inc. investigating why—and why not—boys joined and stayed in Scouting. The results were both sobering and, ultimately, compelling. What Yankelovich found was that a growing number of teenaged boys found Scouting to be out-of-date, overly structured, and even socially embarrassing. This was particularly true with older Scouts.[2]

None of these results were in dispute. But what was missing from the Yankelovich report was *context*. Scouting after all, had always been anachronistic—those city boys heading out into the woods in 1908 with the Woodcraft Indians and Sons of Daniel Boone were already living out an experience whose age had passed. And older Scouts had always chafed at the same structured experience in which younger Scouts thrived—that was why they had filled the ranks of Exploring, the Order of the Arrow, and the Knights of Dunamis; and why many Scouts left the program after earning their Eagle. As for wearing the uniform in public places . . . that had been at least a mild embarrassment for many boys since Armistice Day, 1918.

Still, Scouting had thrived in spite of—and in important ways *because* of—these "weaknesses" for 62 years. But now after its first real setback, the BSA felt it needed to be saved from itself.

NEW AND IMPROVED

The official launch of Improved Scouting, as was usually the case with a revision in the program, came with the publication of a new *Handbook*, the eighth edition, in 1972. And it was literally the *Scouting Handbook*, because the BSA even decided to drop the word "Boy" from the title.

And that was only the start. Inside, the text about camping, first aid, and woodcraft that had changed the lives of 27 million readers over the previous six decades was now almost entirely thrown out, and was replaced by a new narrative that emphasized more "modern" and largely urban and suburban topics. As one commentator later wrote: "Gone were signaling, map-making, canoeing, tracking and fire by friction. In their place were sections on drug abuse, family finances, child care, community problems, and current events."[3]

The first aid section of this new edition dealt with urban problems such as rat bites, bringing along money for pay toilets, and the proper etiquette for long-distance hikes on city streets.

Troops themselves were also reorganized. Older Scouts, who had traditionally made up a quasi-patrol of "Senior Scouts," were now divided into multiple groups. Fourteen- and 15-year-olds, who had traditionally led the troops' patrols, were now placed into a "Leadership Corps" with their own forest-green uniforms and separate activities. Sixteen- and 17-year-olds, who had traditionally run the troops and provided their institutional continuity, were now expected to either move up to a title called "Junior Assistant Scoutmaster" or to leave the troop entirely and join an Explorer post. It was an inspired strategy for keeping Scouting relevant to individual boys at each age level, but was hugely destructive to the long-standing principle of the "boy-run troop": the boys who were supposed be running the troop were now busy elsewhere.

That now put the onus on the adults: the Scoutmasters and assistant Scoutmasters. But here the incentives were changed as well. In the words of the BSA's own official history:

> Scoutmasters were now expected to be "managers of learning" and to hold "personal growth agreement conferences" with Scouts before they moved up a rank, and they were encouraged to master a 'Cornerstone' leadership program based on eleven "competencies." Many Scoutmasters felt that they hadn't volunteered to become 'counselors' instead of leaders, and they weren't comfortable with their new responsibilities.[4]

Thus, at a time of enormous change, Scouting managed to alienate much of its unit leadership—the heart of the organization, and the very people it depended on to execute its new philosophy.

But that was only the beginning. The biggest change in the new *Handbook* dealt with that most defining feature of Scouting: the ranks and their requirements. Here, in an effort to clarify the process of advancement, Scouting managed only to sow confusion.

The starting point for this confusion was the establishment of a whole new set of "skill awards"—camping, citizenship, communications, community living, conservation, cooking, environment, family living, first aid, hiking, physical fitness, and swimming . . . essentially all the things that used to be the stuff of Scouting—that a young Scout had to earn as part of the trail from Tenderfoot to First Class. Painted brass loops worn on the Scout's web belt showed attainment of these skills. The notion behind these skill awards was that they provided more immediate recognition of a Scout's advancement in competence—but the reality, wrote Scouting historian Robert W. Petersen trenchantly, was that during the years before the skill awards were abandoned in 1989: "[It] was possible to become a First Class Scout without ever going hiking or camping or cooking over an open fire."[5]

It got only stranger with the higher ranks. In terms of requirements, the Eagle award looked about the same, notably in continuing the new service project concept. But now to become an Eagle, a Scout had to earn 24 merit badges—three more than ever before in Scouting history—but with only 10, instead of 11, actually required.

The good news in this was that Scouting also expanded the number of optional merit badges to include the likes of Environmental Science and Computers. The bad news was that, once again, the actual experience for the individual Scout on his Trail to Eagle was now a long away from the original vision of Scout craft. The official history records the complaint of one veteran Scoutmaster from New York:

> [The Eagle] rank, respected throughout the country as a top-notch achievement for youth, has been cheapened drastically. By the elimination of Camping, Cooking, Nature and other [merit] badges heretofore required, a Scout may become an Eagle virtually without ever setting foot past his city line.[6]

As if to drive home this notion of the new "Pop" Eagle, even the historic Eagle Scout uniform badge was radically changed. Though it had gone through some minor modifications over the years, mostly to take advantage of improved embroidery equipment, the badge had always consisted of an Eagle, in the upward wing formulation of the medal, clutching the Be Prepared scroll from the Boy Scout Insignia, atop red, white, and blue stripes, within a red ring bearing the words "Eagle Scout Boy Scouts of America in silvery-white thread.

The new badge featured simply a small, silver Eagle silhouette against two broad red and blue stripes, and a narrow white stripe in the center. No detailing. No words. No hint of the meaning of the image. It was, in almost every way, a cruder image than the Tenderfoot badge—as if recognizing that the Eagle Scout, spending much of his time in the public eye, might not want to be associated with the Boy Scouts of America. Not surprisingly, there were soon reports from around the country that troops and new Eagles were custom-ordering the previous, 1956-version, of the badge from private vendors.

The new Eagle patch, shocking as it may have seemed, was in fact a part of the overall new "look" of Scouting: Oscar de la Renta-designed uniforms, skill awards on the belt, streamlined and simplified badges, and most infamously, red berets.

These last came to symbolize this era of Scouting. Scouts had long worn very American headgear, from Army campaign caps to WWII-type garrison flat caps. Now, reflecting its own identity crisis as it was torn between the two sides of divided nation, Scouts were asked to wear a piece of European headwear, impractical against the sun and weather while camping, that was most associated with two groups on opposites sides of the ideological spectrum: United States Army special forces and the Black Panther party.

By the mid-1970s, the Boy Scouts of America had lost an estimated one-third of its membership. Ironically, even as Scouting had scrambled to keep up with the cultural changes taking place around it, those changes had already begun to come full circle. The vanguard of the New Age had left the cities, psychedelia, and revolution and had now gone back to the land and to traditional skills. Even as the new *Handbook* diminished the role of Scout craft, *The Whole Earth Catalog*—dubbed "the Boy Scout Handbook of the counterculture" by *Time* magazine—was extolling its earlier edition as a key text of the back-to-earth movement.[7]

AGAINST THE FLOW

Remarkably, in the face of all of this confusion, radical change, and obstruction, the one part of Boy Scouting that continued to grow was Eagle Scouts. Though the total number of new Eagles per year fell in the 1970s—to an average of 29,306—the ratio of Eagles to total Scouts maintained its climb: from the historic 2 percent of all Scouts who joined the organization, to 4 percent—and climbing starting in 1991.

In other words, Scouts were continuing to pursue their Eagles as they always had, accepting whatever new obstacles as merely a new set of requirements to overcome. Even the service project, whose unwritten demands seem to grow by the decade, wasn't enough to slow their progress.

For some, even the Eagle wasn't enough. Over the years the BSA had created a number of other top awards for Scouts to earn if their interests took them in a different direction from Eagle—or, more commonly, if they were looking for new challenges in Scouting *after* becoming Eagles.

For example, there were the religious medals: more than three score medals and emblems representing more than 30 different religious groups, from Roman Catholicism (Ad Altare Dei, the first such medal, created in 1926 for the Archdiocese of Los Angeles) to Buddhism to Zoroastrianism, each with a difficult set of requirements that often took years to earn. And there was the Hornaday Medal, one of the nation's most respected conservation awards—awarded at the highest levels to only a few Scouts and Scouters each year for extraordinary contribution to the field. Exploring also had its own top medal, the GOLD (Growth Opportunity in Leadership Development) Award.

The most popular pathway for ambitious Scouts to compete and continue their accomplishments after earning their Eagles was through the earning of merit badge palms. A sizable percentage of Eagles earned at least a bronze, gold, or silver palm device to pin to their Eagle ribbon for 5, 10, or 15 extra merit badges, respectively, beyond the required 21. This often happened because most Scouts accumulated extra optional merit badges while working on their required ones. It was also much easier when palms were awarded for earning increments of five badges; once a three-month service requirement was added in September 1965, many Eagles ran out of time before their 18th birthday . . . and were denied the one-upmanship of festooning their medal's ribbon with an array of shiny silver palms.[8] But throughout the history of Scouting there has always been a small subgroup of Eagles for whom only the ultimate achievement—earning *every single merit badge*—is acceptable. Then and now, such an accomplishment has almost always guaranteed local (and sometimes national) media coverage, endless looks of awe at a merit sash covered front and back (and sometimes on a second, crossing, sash) with an impossible number of merit badges, an impressive resume entry in later life—and, in theory, proof of highly-developed skills in organization and time management.

Over the last century there have been enough of these ultimate merit badge earners to actually produce category winners within the group. Thus, the youngest all-merit badge winner is likely **Christopher Haskell** of Elk Ridge, Utah, who did it in 2003 at the tender age of 13. And then there are the brother all-merit badge winners **Chad and Craig Carson** of Ogden,

Utah, who had earned 127 each by 1975—which, not coincidentally, also happened to be the year that the most merit badges were ever offered.

But among all the Eagle Scouts who have earned every available merit badge—and the entire group would probably just fill an average high school classroom—only one Eagle can claim to have earned the *most* merit badges. As already noted, Scouting began with just a handful of merit badges and climbed to more than 100 during the Second World War. In the 1950s and 1960s—and again today—the number has hovered around 120 badges, give or take about five . . . and the BSA has been vigilant about retiring obsolete badges as often as it creates them.

But, thanks to the distortion created by the Improved Scouting program, there was a seam that briefly opened between 1970 and 1972 in which a Scout might earn one group of merit badges . . . and then also earn the second set of the badges that replaced them, often merely with the substitution of a new name (e.g., Textile and Textiles). And that appears to be what Eagle Scout **John Stanford** from Limestone, New York, did. By his 18th birthday, he had earned his 142nd merit badge and eighth silver palm—the most ever. Unless the BSA decides to upend itself a second time, his is likely to be a Scouting record that stands forever.[9]

At various times in its history, Scouting had contemplated answering this hyper-competitiveness with an award *above* the Eagle. Happily none of those plans came to fruition because it would likely have resulted in an open-ended Scout rank arms race. And for most Scouts, the Eagle medal, much less a palm or two, was more than enough of a challenge.

Still, in 1969, the BSA—largely for promotional reasons (that is, to show the importance of adult Eagles in American life) and to maintain contact with its most successful alumni, created what is Scouting's highest, most exclusive—and least known—rank. The award derives, at least officially, from a special one-time-only gold Eagle medal awarded to Dan Beard in 1922.

It is called the Distinguished Eagle Scout Award (DESA) and consists of the BSA Eagle, now in gold, suspended from a red, white, and blue neck ribbon. It is not a rank you can earn—at least not intentionally—but rather, it is awarded only to adult Eagles after at least 25 years of distinguished service in their lives, profession, or avocation field. Most of the Eagle Scouts named in this book, if they were still alive in 1969, have been recipients. So exclusive is this award that most Scouts, much less non-Scouts, have never heard of the DESA. Of the 2 million Eagle Scouts in the BSA's history, less than 2,000—that is, 1 in 1,000—have been honored with the Distinguished Eagle Scout Award.[10]

GREEN BAR BILL

The man who saved American Scouting in the late 1970s was an elderly gentleman who had recently retired from the BSA after 60 years as the most important Scouter in the organization's history.

The climax of Improved Scouting came in 1976, which was also the same year it died. Chief Scout Executive Alden Barber had done what mavericks always do: he had shaken up the organization and made the BSA rethink all of its assumptions and revisit every one of its long-standing practices.

Many of the results had been restorative. Scouting was now fairer than it had ever been in its history: disabled boys, minority boys in the inner city, poor boys living in rural areas—all now had an equal chance to fully experience Scouting. The BSA now, at last, lived up to what it had always claimed to be: the ultimate experience for *all* boys.

And if the Boy Scouts was seeing declining membership, Barber could point to the huge success of Exploring, which was not only thriving, but also creating such enduring initiatives as the High Adventure program— an outdoor program that had all of the exciting characteristics that Boy Scouting now seemed to lack.

At the same time, Scouting was now more engaged with the communities it served than at any previous time (other than during war). Part of this was the massive expansion—and greater delineation—of the community and environmental service requirements at each rank, especially so for Eagle Scout. But beyond that, Scouting also embarked on a series of high-profile service initiatives during this era, most notably *Operation REACH*, an anti-drug campaign; and *Project SOAR,* a National Good Turn event, held on June 5, 1971, that engaged 2 million Scouts and Scouters cleaning up an estimated 1 million tons of litter across the country.[11]

After the dark days of the late 1960s, America began to see Scouting in a new, and more positive, light—an opinion that continued to improve when the nation elected its first Eagle president. It was a timely coincidence that 750 Scouts camped on the U.S. Capitol Mall to celebrate the nation's Bicentennial.[12] But for all of the extraordinary accomplishments of Scouting under Alden Barber, the BSA ultimately paid for that other side of mavericks: their indifference to tradition. Not only was the Boy Scouts continuing to lose members, but also many troops were in open revolt: wearing older uniforms and patches, teaching Scout craft, and even bending requirements.

Scouts themselves chafed at the increasing aggrandizement of troop leadership by the adults; while the adults, who had little choice but to lead in the face of the new national initiatives and rules, wondered how they had become neighbor organizers and child counselors when they had signed on to lead campouts.

There were no real objections to the cultural changes made by national headquarters—Scouting's widespread acceptance and support of disabled, disadvantaged, and minority Scouts was one of the greatest achievements of its long story. But Scouts and Scouters wanted Scouting's *soul* back. They just wanted to go camping again. At first these dissidents were dismissed as a reactionary minority obsessed with an imagined better past; but in time, they became the majority—at least among scouting veterans.

In 1973, the BSA held its eighth national jamboree, this time at *two* different sites: Moraine State Park in Pennsylvania and Farragut State Park in Idaho. The combined attendance of 73,610 Scouts and Scouters disguised the fact that each individual event drew less than 37,000 attendees, fewer than any before.[13]

However, at the 1973 jamborees, an announcement was made that would point toward the future of Scouting. At public gatherings of hundreds of Eagles, fellow young Eagles—several of them until recently Knights of Dunamis—took the stage and announced the creation of a new entity designed to bring together all Eagles, new and old: the National Eagle Scout Association (NESA).

In 1976, even as Scouting was putting on a good face for the U.S. Bicentennial and preparing for the next year's ninth jamboree, the BSA's leadership decided to cut its losses. Alden Barber, the great innovator of Scouting's modern era, was quietly pushed into retirement before the normal age. Scouting, after nearly a decade of experimentation, had decided to hit the "reset" switch—and it turned to the one person who knew how to lead the BSA back to its core principles.

That person was **William "Green Bar Bill" Hillcourt**. He was 77 years old and happily retired with his wife, Grace Brown, former secretary of Chief Executive Scout James E. West, in their home just outside the Schiff Scout Reservation in Mendham Borough, New Jersey.

Hillcourt had already enjoyed a fabled Scouting career—one that was, in the words of the noted newspaperman and historian Robert W. Peterson, "the foremost influence on development of the Boy Scouting program."[14] Now, he would be given his greatest challenge.

He was born Vilhelm Hans Bjerregaard Jensen in Aarhus, Denmark, in 1900. When he was 10, Vilhelm's older brother gave him a copy of the newly printed Danish language version of Baden-Powell's *Scouting for Boys*—and the boy found his life's work. Joining Danish Scouting two years later, Vilhelm earned his Knight-Scout award—the equivalent of Eagle—at age 18.

Three years later, in 1920, he attended the first World Jamboree, in Olympia, Greece . . . and there met his hero, Lord Baden-Powell, for the first time.

By this point, Vilhelm was studying to become a pharmacist. But he was also getting more deeply involved in Scouting as well—serving as a Scoutmaster, national instructor, and the editor of the *Danish Scouting Journal*. He even published a book about his early Scouting experiences.

While preparing his troop to attend the second World Jamboree, this one in their own backyard of Ermelunden, Denmark, Vilhelm managed to also obtain press credentials to cover the event. This led to a journalism career—and in time a decision by Vilhelm, probably for a book, to tour the world studying the best Scouting practices in different countries. Toward that end, he traveled throughout Europe, then visited the UK, and finally in February 1926, he arrived in New York City at the offices of the Boy Scouts of America. He stayed for the rest of his life.

Thanks to a friendship he'd made at the World Jamboree in Ermelunden with an American Scouter (and future head of Cub Scouting), William Wessel, Vilhelm soon found a job at the National Scout Headquarters—and, in a foreshadowing of the future, he soon found himself teaching American Indian dances to a group of American Boy Scouts from Brooklyn.

After working briefly at a Scout camp, Vilhelm landed a job at Scout headquarters in the Supply Division. There, in a fortuitous turn of events, his leg was broken by a falling crate. A week after this accident, he hobbled on crutches into headquarters. As he recalled, "I was walking into the elevator when an astonishing coincidence changed my life completely"—he ran into Chief Scout Executive James E. West. Here is his account of that meeting:

> He knew of my accident. He stopped to greet me, then said, 'Well, my young man, what do you think of American Scouting?' The elevator came. We went down together, chatting.
>
> His words may have been just a casual remark. But I took them seriously. I wrote an eighteen-page report and sent it to him. It was complimentary in spots, critical in others. But for each criticism I offered a suggestion for remedying the situation.[15]

Within days, Vilhelm was called to West's office. "While I don't agree with everything in your report," West said, "I am interested in what you have to say about the Boy Scouts of America not using the patrol method effectively. You suggest that we should have a *Handbook for Patrol Leaders*. What should it contain?"[16]

As he did throughout his life, Vilhelm answered with the written word. With West's blessing, and despite deep doubts about his facility with English, he set to writing the BSA's *Handbook for Patrol Leaders*. First published in 1929, and now having gone through numerous editions (three of them by Vilhelm himself) it remains the classic text on small unit organization and leadership—not just for Boy Scouts, but adults as well.

The *Handbook for Patrol Leaders* changed Scouting. It also represented a turning point in Vilhelm's own life. In 1930, he Anglicized his name to Bill Hillcourt, an almost direct translation. Two years later, he began working for *Boys' Life*—and for the next 33 years, each issue carried a page dedicated to Scout craft, advancement, and outdoor skills, written by and signed by

Hillcourt. The signature, superimposed over the two green bars of the Patrol Leader badge, quickly earned Hillcourt the nickname "Green Bar Bill."

In 1934, the newly-wed Hillcourt was asked by E. Urner Goodman—the BSA National Scouting Director and founder of the Order of the Arrow—to write the new version of the *Boy Scout Handbook*. With his typical attention to detail, Bill moved with Grace to a renovated barn on the grounds of the 500-acre Mortimer L. Schiff Scout Reservation in Mendham. There, he formed and served as Scoutmaster to Troop 1—a troop of local boys that was uniquely chartered by the BSA National Council—and set about discovering how Scouting *really* worked.

With the run of the entire camp, the boys of Troop 1 would remember it as one of the greatest experiences of their lives. But for Bill Hillcourt, it was the ultimate test bed, his beta site, for his theories about Scouting. Over time, this research became increasingly sophisticated and codified. Even the family of IBM founder Thomas J. Watson donated a complete film studio at Schiff to help create training materials for Scouting. Meanwhile, Hillcourt reported on his discoveries both in *Boys' Life* and in other Scouting publications.

Hillcourt's most important finding—and one for which he became the passionate advocate—was that Baden-Powell had, intuitively, been right from the start: the heart of all Scouting was the *patrol*. Everything great about Scouting—teamwork, camaraderie, learning to follow and to lead, mastering new skills, a sense of duty and responsibility—all emanated from those small groups of six or seven boys, Hillcourt came to believe. Everything else, he concluded, from adult leadership to jamborees to the BSA itself, merely existed to empower and enrich these tens of thousands of patrols and their young leaders.

The "patrol method" was a vision of Scouting that, though often observed in the breach, has defined the BSA ever since—not least because "Green Bar Bill" (the name had proven prophetic) expounded it on the pages of *Boys' Life* every month. It also colored every Scouting text Hillcourt wrote . . . which happened to be every important Scout book in the middle years of the twentieth century: three editions of the *Handbook for Patrol Leaders* (1929, 1952, and 1967), the *Scout Fieldbook* (1948, with West;

generally acknowledged as the greatest text on outdoor craft ever written), the *Handbook for Scoutmasters* (1936), and three editions of the *Boy Scout Handbook* (most famously, the 1959 sixth edition, which Hillcourt considered his masterpiece and one of the best-selling children's books of all time; the 1965 seventh edition; and the 1979 ninth edition). The patrol method also lay at the philosophical heart of the adult BSA Wood Badge training program, which Hillcourt created at Philmont in 1948.

Hillcourt retired from Scouting in 1965, having earned every honor and award that U.S. and World Scouting could give. Green Bar Bill was even unofficially designated "Scoutmaster to the World." The first thing he did after retiring was to travel with Grace to the World Jamboree in Japan—thus, 40 years later, finishing the Scouting tour he had begun years before.

Bill Hillcourt was a dozen years retired, and a widower, when Scouting called on him one final time. Improved Scouting was now generally acknowledged as a failure, the BSA was in crisis, the 1977 national jamboree had drawn less than 29,000 attendees[17]—and there was no solution to which everyone agreed. What was obvious though was that many Scout troops were reverting to older uniforms, a renewed focus on patrols, and most visibly, to dog-eared old *Scout Handbooks*, with Norman Rockwell's smiling, striding Eagle Scout on its cover.

The new Chief Scout Executive Harvey Price approached Hillcourt and asked him to come out of retirement to write a new edition of the *Handbook*—one that retained the best of Improved Scouting, but that still restored "the 'outing' to Scouting."[18]

Hillcourt agreed. Perhaps sensing the BSA's desperation, he delivered the ninth edition (1979) of the *Boy Scout Handbook*, complete with a (1970) cover painting by his old friend Norman Rockwell, showing a Scoutmaster and group of Scouts camping, cooking, and canoeing in the woods. Inside, with a deftness unexpected from an octogenarian author, Hillcourt brilliantly wove together the two great threads of Scouting at the end of the twentieth century: the power of traditional camp craft and outdoor skills, with the lure of modern life and technology.

If the ninth edition of the *Handbook* didn't quite rank with Hillcourt's other masterworks, this valedictory may have been the single most important contribution of his distinguished career with the BSA. This version of the *Handbook* was universally acclaimed as Scouting's return to its roots; and as a timely reassertion of the patrol method. It pulled Scouting back from the brink—and set it again on a path to health. In the words of the BSA in promoting the new *Handbook*:

> This edition places greater emphasis on fun and adventure and uses Scout skills as a method to achieve the aims of Scouting. Strengthening the family and broadening the outdoor experience also are major objectives of th[is] new handbook.[19]

Green Bar Bill Hillcourt lived to age 92, long enough to see the profound impact of his last work. He died as he lived, while on a Scouting trip to Stockholm, Sweden, in 1992. And his work is still widely read: his columns are regularly reprinted in *Boys' Life*, his editions of the *Handbook* have sold more than 12 million copies,[20] and his immortal *Fieldbook* will likely remain the standard text for outdoorsmen—and outdoorswomen—for generations to come. The Danish "Eagle" who saved Scouting is buried alongside his wife Grace near the Schiff Scout Training Center.

THE LIST

Very little survived the transition from the Improved Scouting eighth edition *Handbook* to the restorative ninth edition *Scouting Handbook*.

But Green Bar Bill Hillcourt, in exorcising the BSA's brief fling with trendiness, decided to retain one piece of the old book in the new. It was the section on the Eagle Scout service project—and in keeping it, Hillcourt unconsciously established one of the most enduring and influential documents in Scouting history.

The section had just three pages of large print in the eighth edition—and even less in Hillcourt's ninth edition—but it was read by tens of thousands of Scouts who dreamed of earning their Eagle. Indeed it quickly became *the* text for Eagle project planners. It remained so for almost 40 years: not the text itself, but the attached list of model Eagle service projects.

There are just nine projects on The List; two more were quietly added in later years. But, after it was perpetuated in the ninth edition of the *Handbook,*

The List took on a life of its own. That same list of Eagle projects has not only appeared in subsequent issues of the *Handbook,* but eventually became enshrined in the official *Eagle Scout Workbook* that twenty-first century Eagle candidates used to organize and track their progress.

Whether The List was recycled on its own merit, or was merely the result of a lazy copy editor, it proved so venerable and so influential as the gold standard to more than a million Eagle Scout candidates—half of all of them in Scouting history—that it too is now an important chapter in the Scouting story.

Here is The List of exemplary Eagle service projects:

- *Made trays to fasten to wheelchairs for veterans with disabilities at a Veterans Administration hospital.*

- *Collected used books and distributed them to people in the community who wanted and needed, but could not afford, books.*

- *Built a sturdy footbridge across a brook to make a safe shortcut for children between their homes and school.*

- *Collected and repaired used toys and gave them to a home for children with disabilities.*

- *Organized and operated a bicycle safety campaign. This involved a written safety test, equipment safety check, and a skills contest in a bike rodeo.*

- *Surveyed the remains of an old Spanish mission and prepared an accurate map relating it to the present church.*

- *Built a "tot lot" in a big city neighborhood and set up a schedule for Boy Scouts to help run it.*

- *Set up a community study center for children who needed a place to do schoolwork.*

- *Trained fellow students as audiovisual aides for their school. Arranged for more than 200 hours of audiovisual work.*

- *Prepared plans for a footbridge on a trail in a national forest. Worked with rangers to learn the skills necessary to build the structure, gathered materials and tools, and then directed a Scout work group to do the construction.*[21]

Why were these particular activities (the first nine at least) chosen to be the exemplary Eagle projects of the early years of the new service requirement?

And why did they remain as the touchstone for thousands of Eagle projects and millions of hours of service in the subsequent four decades?

One answer is that they do a pretty serviceable job of setting both boundary conditions and acceptable complexity for a good Eagle service project. On closer inspection, certain themes emerge. One is need: several of the projects deal with improving the lives of the disabled, the impoverished, and the at-risk. Others—such as the "tot lot," the footbridge to school, and the bicycle rodeo—deal with issues of safety. One, the footbridge at the park (the double appearance of footbridges was probably appealing because of the use of knots, lashings, and other Scouting skills) represents an improvement in a community's quality of life.

As for the audiovisual training, it suggests opportunities for a boy, within his daily milieu of school life, to make an important contribution. And the last, the most unusual of the group, the mapping of the mission, points not only to contributions to religious organizations, but also to Scouting's long-standing commitment to history and preservation.

If, in some ways, it is an odd list because it ignores 99 percent of all Eagle projects of that era—which typically consisted of cleaning up a schoolyard or vacant lot, painting a neighborhood building, or working on a trail—it is also an interesting list because its very oddness forced Scouts to think beyond the usual prosaic projects . . . and to ponder the real definition of "service." Each of The List's projects also, if only implicitly, showed that a true Eagle service project required not only heavy participation (planning, execution, and follow up) by the Eagle candidate himself, but also extensive interaction with adults and institutions, and the management of other people.

At a time when the still-new Eagle project requirement was largely seen as an extended solo effort by a Life Scout, The List pointed toward something much more sophisticated in its scope and purpose—the next step beyond the career and management training of the merit badges and troop leadership roles. Seen in this light, the Eagle project was to be not only a boy's last great act in Scouting, but also his first real experience of adult life He was to devise, plan, and execute a major project for a nonprofit "customer," and then assemble and manage the project team needed to pull it off. Finally (as later refinements of the project required), he was to conduct a postmortem on the project, reporting on what worked and what did not, how he coped with unanticipated events, and what he had learned from the experience.

The List shows all of these things. And ultimately, that may be why it still endures after the Scouts who performed these projects have grown middle aged and gray haired; it lasted because it works. It is telling that when The List first appeared, its examples were considered to be model service projects that Eagle Scouts should aspire to; while today, largely because they helped propel 40 years of service projects to become ever-more ambitious, The List now represents a baseline for all good Eagle projects. The best modern projects *start* with The List—and then set the bar far higher than any Eagle Scout in 1972 could ever have imagined.

LEGEND AND REALITY

There is a second reason The List is important. Until 2005, when NESA took on the job, the national BSA office did not keep records of Eagle service projects. (The name of the Eagle project and number of hours spent was only added to the application in August 2008.)

Until then, any record keeping of this kind occurred at the local council office, where most Eagle boards of review took place as well. And, whereas all Eagle applications eventually were sent to the national office, any reports and other documentation about the projects themselves were typically treated as ephemera—and either returned to the new Eagle or trashed. Of what little remained, much would be soon lost to a conflagration.

As a result, other than anecdote and the occasional line in a newspaper story of the era, we have little record of what it was like to be a Life Scout pioneering the Eagle service project in the late 1960s and early 1970s. Through sheer serendipity, we *do* have a complete record of two of the projects enumerated in The List. That's because I happened to participate in one of those projects—the bicycle rodeo. And the other—the mission mapping and exploration project—was my own Eagle project.

The fact that I was involved in two of the most famous Eagle projects of all time is a mystery of its own. Both projects took place within weeks of each other in the early spring of 1967, and both were the work of two Life Scouts from a single troop: Troop 480, based at Mango Junior High School (now Sunnyvale Middle School) in Sunnyvale, California.

How these two projects, from the same troop, taking place almost simultaneously at a local public school in a suburban city in the San Francisco Bay Area, managed to join The List—the bicycle rodeo was even illustrated in the 1972 *Handbook*—and become a mainstay of Scouting for decades, is a question that may never be answered. Perhaps some anonymous copywriter, desperate for some case studies for the *Handbook*'s new Eagle Service Project section, stumbled across a cache of aging reports from the Santa Clara County Council, and grabbed the two that best fit his narrative.

What I do know is that the now-famous Bicycle Rodeo was the project of Fremont High School student **Mark Habermeyer**, now a respected dentist nearing retirement in Southern California. Mark's father, John Habermeyer, was our Scoutmaster—and had inspired the troop's older boys to strive for what would ultimately become more than a dozen Eagles. John was also director of safety at NASA's Ames Research Center—where in the early 1970s an electronics-dedicated Explorer post was formed that would ultimately provide many members to the Homebrew Computer Club . . . and spark both the birth of Apple Computers and the personal computer revolution.

Mark's bicycle rodeo took place on the asphalt basketball courts and exercise area at the back of Mango Junior High. Mark had met with the Sunnyvale Safety Department and together with a police officer there had come up with a plan for the riding events to teach bicycle safety, a quiz, and even some awards.

The event took place early one Saturday afternoon. It was a small affair—subsequent generations of Scouts who read the description and imagined an arena complete with crowds, flags, and professional bicyclists would have been disappointed. In fact, the illustrator of the *Handbook* got it about right: a bunch of little kids on Schwinn Stingrays riding a small course complete with traffic signs, being monitored by Boy Scouts with clipboards and stopwatches. We older Scouts had arrived early to set things up, do some test runs on the course (which led to a lot of good-natured competition), and then safety-checked the bikes and managed the courses when the kids started to arrive. We were done before dinner.

In retrospect, it was a perfect Eagle project: carefully prepared, organized, and executed; it served an important purpose; and it educated a bunch of children, Scouts, and even adults about an important life skill. But I suspect few of those hundreds of thousands of prospective Eagles who read its entry on The List quite imagined the reality of Mark Habermeyer's Bicycle Rodeo.

But if the gap between reality and the mental image produced by the text was wide for Mark's project, it surely was a vast gulf for mine, the most exotic project on the list.

SUBURBAN EXPLORER

Over the years, I've often imagined what a 16-year-old Life Scout must have imagined as he read: *Surveyed the remains of an old Spanish mission and prepared an accurate map relating it to the present church.* Did he picture me in some crumbling desert village in the Southwest, dressed in khakis, and directing a crew of surveyors armed with transits and levels as they marked out the ruins of some long-abandoned eighteenth century Franciscan mission? Did they imagine some young Howard Carter ordering around the workers in an archaeological dig for golden artifacts from the age of conquistadors? And if so, did they wonder how I ever managed to find such a project? Or did they simply conclude that such an unusual project was impossible for them—and move on to the more realistic "tot lot" and footbridge?

They might have thought differently had they known just how prosaic my Eagle project really was. I did survey the remains of an old Spanish mission—but it was Mission Santa Clara, at the center of Santa Clara University and in the heart of busy Santa Clara (soon to be Silicon) Valley, just a few miles from my home. And I did prepare a map—though it was a far more complicated process than the description presented . . . while the surveying was simple, and almost an afterthought.

Here's what really happened. I was just 13 years old, young for an Eagle candidate even then, when I heard (from whom I can't remember) that there might be a potential Eagle project idea available from the venerable archivist at Santa Clara—Father Arthur Spearman, SJ. I made a nervous telephone call. Being a suburban Presbyterian boy I had never had an extended conversation before with a Catholic priest, much less a Jesuit academic. But Father Spearman was pleasant enough, patient with my obvious nerves, and invited me down to the university.

A week later my father drove me down to Santa Clara, helped me find my way to the Jesuit residence building, and then left me in the lobby. The dark lobby and ringing marble floor combined for an intimidating experience, but I managed to find the telephone and call upstairs.

In time, Fr. Spearman came down to meet me. He was an elderly man wearing very thick glasses, in black trousers, shirt, and collar. I didn't even know what to call him—but eventually settled on "Father."

I didn't know at the time that Fr. Spearman had a reputation for being a crusty and difficult man. He had once been something of a firebrand, and his stubbornness was only now being credited for having saved many of the mission's greatest artifacts. But he was kind enough to take me over to the basement of the nearby campus museum and show me some of those artifacts, some dating to the eighteenth century.

But what Fr. Spearman really wanted to show me was a small stack of old maps, some of them on vellum, which he carefully pulled from a drawer. "This is how you can help me if you are interested," he said. "These maps are of each of the five different Missions of Santa Clara, beginning with the first one in 1777, all of the way up to the present one built in 1928 after the previous one burned.

"No one," he continued, "has ever combined all of these missions into a single map. And that is because none of them are drawn in the same scale. Perhaps you'd like to try to put them all together?"

I didn't know enough to say no. And so, for the next three months, to my family's growing chagrin, I taped a large sheet of paper, covered with maps and smaller sheets of paper, to one end of our dining room table. This being well before the personal computer age, my father, who also worked at NASA Ames, arranged for me to visit the art department there and get some rudimentary instruction in using a rapidograph pen, overlay transparencies, and handling an Exacto knife to cut out forms in red mylar.

My goal was to create five overlaying transparencies, each showing the buildings of one of the missions, and each in the same scale and in the proper location.

But I quickly ran into a major problem: not only were the maps not in the same scale, as Fr. Spearman had said, they weren't even in the same *units of measurement.* The modern ones were in yards and meters, but the older ones were in such obsolete measures as rods, chains, and links . . . and in one, they were actually indecipherable.

The result was weeks spent in a nightmare of pocket calculator and hand calculations, followed by a clumsy attempt to act like a professional graphic artist and cartographer. Eventually, 80 hours into the project, I hit a wall: I simply couldn't reconcile one of the older maps to the modern city of Santa Clara.

Desperate, I went back to the men in the NASA art department. Being right in the middle of the transition from the Gemini to Apollo programs, they no doubt had better things to do—but they still found time to both show me how to improve my work to date . . . and, more important, suggested I visit a blueprinter and see if they would blow up portions of the two maps until one or two key features could be made congruent.

That led me to yet another meeting with an adult professional, the manager of a Sunnyvale blueprint firm. He managed to puzzle out my confused request, nodded brusquely, and told me to come back in a couple days.

I did as I was told—and found that the man had created a series of blow-ups, both on paper and transparencies, that put all of my missions and their outbuildings in common scale. He had saved my project.

It had not been a simple job, or an inexpensive one. I pulled out the blank check, signed by my mother (who waited in the car outside), and asked how much it would be. The man never smiled. Instead, he handed me the big prints and said, "There's no charge, son. Just remember today. And when you grow up, I want you to do the same thing for some young man working on his Eagle project."

I thanked him quickly and, clutching the prints, raced home to get back to work.

Twelve weeks after I began, I finished the five maps, all of them properly aligned atop one another.

It looked great, especially considering that it had been created by rookie mapmaker. But was it accurate? There was only one way to know for sure. And so, late one Saturday afternoon that spring, I led of group of a half-dozen fellow Scouts from Troop 480 down to Santa Clara University and the bright green lawns around the Mission.

There, armed with hammers, we drove three stainless steel rods into the ground at scores of different locations, testing to see if they hit buried foundation rocks and stone floor, or just compressed dirt. We used stakes and strings to delineate the overall dimensions of the long-lost buildings.

We must have been an incongruous sight: seven young boys in Scout uniforms inching across a wide lawn beneath a tall campus dormitory building which, from almost every window—many of them draped with peace symbols and North Vietnamese and Cuban flags—blared acid rock. Certainly the students passing by found us amusing—when they weren't dismissing us as tools of the military industrial complex. We tried to ignore them by focusing on our work.

In the end, we confirmed as best we could that my maps were accurate. I wrote up the report on my project and delivered the results to a pleased Father Spearman, who took the maps and immediately stuck them in a drawer. I never saw them again.

A month later, I survived an Eagle board of review before adult strangers held in one of the chambers of a courthouse in San Jose (today's Eagle boards are typically held by the troops themselves). Finally, in July 1967, in the gymnasium of a local elementary school, I was part of a triple Eagle Court of Honor, along with Mark Habermeyer and **Chris Henry**, now a Silicon Valley senior executive.

It goes without saying that the reality of my Eagle service project was a long way from the mental image created by the description of that same project on The List. And yet, looking back over more than 40 years, I am struck that my real project was just as remarkable as any imagined one.

Four years later, I came limping home from the Air Force Academy with pneumonia and needing surgery on both knees. I had less than a week to find a college before classes started. Among those that I had turned down months before was Santa Clara—and so, armed with a recommendation letter from the mayor of Sunnyvale—I raced down to SCU and met with the academic vice president. I was accepted, thanks in part to his remembering my Eagle project. (This is my own version of the old adage that an Eagle is the ultimate college application tie-breaker.) I went on to earn two degrees from SCU, teach in its law school and English department, sit on numerous boards, and deliver the President's Lecture—all at a university I first visited for my Eagle project.

Meanwhile, Father Spearman, after a few years, took my map out of the drawer . . . and it became the basis for all subsequent maps of the university in brochures, tour guides, and other publications. I often passed a sign bearing a descendent of my map as I raced to teach one of my classes—one of which I taught in a temporary building atop one of the lawns where my little team had traced out old foundations.

But, membership on The List aside, the most enduring impact of my Eagle service project was on my own life. I long ago forgot the name of the man at the blueprint company, and the shop itself is long gone. But I never forgot what he said to me. And four decades after he told me to pass on his contribution, I did just that: taking on the job of assistant Scoutmaster, mentoring the next generation of Eagles. As I write this, there have now been more than 25 of these Scouts. All have read The List, of course, but few know of their historic connection to it . . . or of the anonymous businessman of early a half-century ago who still plays a role in helping them earn their Eagle.

A NEW GENERATION

Scouting had begun the 1970s convinced it had found a radical solution to both its declining rolls and its alienation from large segments of American society. It ended the decade turning to an octogenarian in a last-ditch effort to save itself. Green Bar Bill had delivered—more than anyone could ever have expected.

But it would take more than a new *Handbook* to turn Scouting around. And even then, the iron rule of demographics almost guaranteed that

Scouting would likely not see a return to its membership levels of the 1950s and 1960s for decades. And though in 1980 the BSA cheered as it showed its first membership growth—to 4.3 million youth members—in nearly a decade; it was obvious that most of that growth had come from member retention due to the restoration of traditional Scouting, not from a sudden burst of brand new members. That was good news, of course, but it hadn't changed the reality of a declining pool of potential new members.

So the challenge now was one that the BSA had never faced before: could it make Scouting a dynamic, engaging experience for American boys without depending on the built-in advantages of continuous growth?

Here too, Bill Hillcourt pointed the way: go small, go local, and go back to the patrol model. And, to drive that message home, for his final great contribution to Scouting he prepared a third edition of the Handbook for Patrol Leaders—*The Official Patrol Leader Handbook*—in 1980.

The old guard had now done all it could. It was time for a new generation of Scouting leaders to take Boy Scouting into its next era—one defined by fewer young people; a technology and communications revolution that would soon deliver the personal computer, Internet and wireless telephony; a greater emphasis on awards and other college application assets; a complete transformation in outdoor equipment; an explosion in immigration; the greatest period of wealth creation in U.S. history; and a return to more traditional values.

Scouting now had a new look, new texts, and a new/old philosophy with which to meet this new world and to complete its own renaissance. And, on the eve of the 1990s, Scouting took one final step to show its commitment to the future: it moved BSA headquarters from New Jersey to Irving, Texas, into the heart of the fast-growing Sunbelt.

But if Scouting was going to become more traditional *and* diminished in size, how would it continue to gain the attention of the general public it needed to continue to recruit young Cub and Boy Scouts? Scouting had managed, in 1980, to mobilize millions of its Cubs, Boy Scouts, and Explorers to assist in making the U.S. Census that year the most accurate on record.[22] But the great national BSA initiatives would now be few and far between. How would Scouting continue to maintain its hard-earned role as an American institution, as a vital part of American boyhood, and as a critical part of the American way of life?

The answer would come, as if often had over the years, from Eagle Scouts.

By the 1980s a new generation of Eagles, boys who had earned the rank in the 1950s and 1960s, were now coming into their own on the national stage.

An extraordinary number of these postwar Eagles were astronauts. Including Neil Armstrong and Charlie Duke, two of the 12 Apollo astronauts who walked on the moon were Eagles (with 11 of the 12 having been former Scouts). In total, as this book is being written, *40* Mercury, Gemini, Apollo, Skylab, and Shuttle astronauts have been Eagles—an extraordinary percentage that seems to underscore the unique balance of physical and mental acumen that is almost unique to the process of earning the Eagle rank.

Several of these Space Eagles are of particular note. Tragically, the best known is **Lt. Col. Ellison Onizuka**. Onizuka, the first Asian-American in space was born in Kealakekua, Hawaii, and earned his Eagle with a Scout troop there. A veteran test pilot, he was selected for the NASA Space Shuttle program in January 1978. His first space flight was aboard the Shuttle *Discovery* six years later.

On January 28, 1986, Onizuka was a member of the crew of the Shuttle *Challenger*—and was killed when the ship exploded soon after takeoff. An investigation after the disaster found that Onizuka had likely survived the explosion and had fought to save the *Challenger* until it crashed into the ocean. He was posthumously promoted to Colonel and the U.S. satellite facility in Sunnyvale, California—near where he trained at NASA Ames Research Center—now bears his name, as do a number of sites in Hawaii.

In late 1986, Colonel **Guion Bluford**, who participated in four Shuttle flights, and was the first African-American in space, was tasked by the federal government to visit Troop 514 of Monument, Colorado. The troop had successfully submitted the flag, which had flown over the U.S. Capitol, to be flown on the *Challenger* flight . . . and when the wreckage of the shuttle was finally recovered, it was found that the flag was miraculously still intact while the medallions with which it had been stowed had melted. Col. Bluford returned "the Challenger flag," as it was now called, to the troop in an emotional ceremony at nearby Falcon Air Station.

A year later, Chief Justice Earl Warren designated the Challenger flag as the official flag of the U.S. Constitution Bicentennial celebration. It has since been reflown over the Capitol (the first flag to ever fly twice there), at the 2002 Winter Olympics in Salt Lake City, and at the 25th anniversary memorial ceremonies for the *Challenger* crew.

Other notable Space Eagles include **Sonny Carter**, who had a singular career as an astronaut, a doctor, a test pilot, and a professional soccer player; **Lt. Col. Roger Chaffee**, who died in the Apollo 1 fire during a ground test; **Col. Richard O. Covey** helped lead the commission that led NASA back into space after the *Challenger* disaster. He then piloted *Discovery*, the first Shuttle mission in NASA's "Return to Space" program in September 1988. **General Robert T. Herres** was slated to be an astronaut aboard the Manned Orbiting Laboratory—but when it was cancelled, he became the first commander-in-chief of the Air Force Space Command, then the first vice chairman of the Joint Chiefs of Staff. Upon retirement from the USAF, he served as BSA's president as well as the chairman and CEO of the USAA Group, where he took the insurance giant into the Internet age. **Vice Admiral Richard Truly**, who flew twice on Space Shuttles. His first flight into space in 1981 was as pilot of the Space Shuttle *Columbia*, which was significant because it was the first manned spacecraft to be reflown in space. His second flight in 1983 was as commander of the Space Shuttle *Challenger*, which was the first night launch and landing in the Shuttle program. He became the first former astronaut to lead NASA and served as NASA Administrator from 1989–1992.[23]

James Lovell, who earned his Eagle in 1943, had one of the most memorable of all careers as an astronaut, flying on Gemini 7 and 12, Apollo 8, and as commander of Apollo 13 (the role played by actor Tom Hanks in the movie)—one of the great human adventure stories of the twentieth century. After retirement, Lovell served as president of the National Eagles Scout Association in the 1990s.

Baby boom Eagles were also showing up in leadership roles across American society. Medical doctor and biologist **Peter Agre** (Eagle 1964—

Northfield, Minnesota) shared the 2003 Nobel Prize in Chemistry for his discovery of aquaporins, the proteins that channel water into cells. His two physician brothers, as well as Agre's son, are also Eagles. **Lamar Alexander** (Eagle 1954) served as U.S. senator and governor of Tennessee, as well as secretary of education. **Norman Augustine** was CEO of Martin-Marietta Corporation and led its acquisition of Lockheed Corp. He also was under secretary of the army and the president of numerous nonprofit organizations, including the Red Cross and Boy Scouts of America (1994–1996). **John W. Creighton Jr.** was president of Weyerhauser and Boeing, and served as president of the BSA from 1996–1998.

Academia also saw it share of Eagles during this era, including **Lawrence Bacow**, chancellor of MIT; **Charles Bayless**, president of West Virginia Tech; paleoanthropologist **Lee Berger**; **John Caldwell**, chancellor of North Carolina State; **Kim Clark**, dean of faculty at Harvard Business School and president of Brigham Young; **James Daughdrill Jr.**, president of Rhodes College for 26 years; **Richard Herman**, chancellor of the University of Illinois, Urbana-Champaign; and **David Leebron,** president of Rice University. Noted oceanic engineer **J. Kim Vandiver** was dean of undergraduate research at MIT.

Famed investigative reporter **Michael Dunne** of the *Baton Rouge Morning Advocate* also volunteered with his local Scouting council. Brothers **Roy** and **Walter Menninger**, both Eagles, would start the Foundation that bears their family name. **James Rogers** was CEO of Kampgrounds of America; while his brother **Gary** was CEO of Dreyer's Ice Cream. **Chuck Smith** became chairman of AT&T West. **Rex Tillerson** served as chairman and CEO of ExxonMobil beginning in 2006; he is also the current president of the BSA. **Howard Lincoln**, CEO of the Seattle Mariners and of Nintendo America, was also one of the sleeping boys who posed for Norman Rockwell's famous painting "The Scoutmaster."

Among the most famous adventurers of modern times was **Steve Fossett**, who as aviator, sailor, and balloonist, set 116 records in five different sports—60 of which still stood at the time of Fossett's untimely death in a plane crash in September 2007.

Fossett grew up in Garden Grove, California. His father was an Eagle Scout, and Steve joined Troop 170 in the city of Orange, where he earned his Eagle at age 13. He later credited the trips he took with Scouts into the nearby San Jacinto Mountains as having changed his life: "When I was 12 years old I climbed my first mountain, and I just kept going, taking on more diverse and grander projects."[24] Fossett eventually joined the Order of the Arrow and served on the staff at Philmont Ranch. As an adult, he credited Scouting with having the most impact on his youth.

After a short corporate career, Fossett made his fortune as a commodities trader and later, renting floor trading privileges to new traders. This freed him to pursue a life as an adventurer and explorer. He trained himself to become perhaps the finest glider, small plane, and balloon pilot of his generation, as well as a world-class sailor . . . then Fossett set out to break every record possible.

Thanks to his skill, technological acumen, and careful preparation, he did just that. In 1992, on his sixth attempt, he became the first person to fly a balloon solo around the world. In 2005, piloting the single engine jet *Virgin Atlantic Global Flyer,* he became the first person to circumnavigate the world solo, nonstop, and unrefueled. A year later, he did it again, setting the record for the longest plane flight in history. That same year, Fossett set the world altitude record for gliders. Meanwhile, between 1993 and 2004, Fossett was also the world's greatest speed sailor, breaking every known record—including, in 2004, the faster circumnavigation of the world by water.

In his amazing career, Fossett also ran in the Boston Marathon, drove a dog team in the Alaskan Iditarod, raced cars in Le Mans and in the Paris to Dakar Rally, and swam the English Channel. Along the way, he earned every award for adventure and achievement possible—but the one he continued to cherish the most was his Eagle. He remained deeply involved with Scouting his entire life—and at his death was president of the National Eagle Scout Association.

The number of baby boom-era Eagles who entered politics and government would overwhelm this chapter. But here is a brief selection: Rep. **Gary Ackerman**, New York; Rep. **William Alexander**, Arkansas; Sen.

Jeff Bingamen, New Mexico; Rep. **Sanford Bishop**, Georgia; Mayor (and noted businessman) **Michael Bloomberg** of New York City; Sen. **Sherrod Brown**, Ohio; Rep. **Russ Carnahan**, Missouri; Sen. **Thad Cochran**, Mississippi; Rep. **Jim Cooper**, Tennessee; Sen. **Mike Crapo**, Idaho; Sen. **Mike Enzi**, Wyoming; Rep. **Mike Fitzpatrick**, Pennsylvania; **Louis Freeh**, FBI director; Rep. **Daniel Frisa**, New York; Lt. Gov. **John Garamendi**, California; Majority Leader Rep. **Dick Gephardt**, Missouri; Rep. **Louie Gohmert**, Texas; Rep. **J.D. Hayworth**, Arizona; Rep. **Jed Hensarling**, Texas; Lt. Gov. **Peter Kinder**, Missouri; Gov. **Gary Locke**, Washington; Rep. **Michael McNulty**, New York; Gov. and Sen. **Ben Nelson**, Nebraska; Gov. **Jay Nixon**, Missouri; Sen. **Sam Nunn**, Georgia; Rep. **Edward A. Pease**, Indiana (also chairman of the Order of the Arrow); Gov. **Rick Perry**, Texas; Rep. **J.J. Pickle**, Texas; Rep. **Dana Rohrabacher**, California; Sen. **Warren Rudman**, New Hampshire; Rep. and Gov. **Mark Sanford**, South Carolina; White House Chief of Staff **Samuel Skinner**; Rep. **Steve Stivers**, Ohio; Rep. **Bart Stupak**, Michigan; and Gov. **John Waihee**, first Native Hawaiian governor of Hawaii.

Whatever the stereotypes attached to Scouting, you would be hard-pressed to find a common political position among all of these Eagle-politicians. The same is true in the judiciary, where hundreds of Eagles have achieved important positions as state supreme court justices, federal judges, and state attorneys general. Of this legal-Eagles generation, the best known is **Stephen Breyer**, associate justice of the United States Supreme Court. Breyer earned his Eagle with Troop 14 in San Francisco. Before his nomination to the Supreme Court, Breyer served as United States assistant attorney general and as an assistant special prosecutor during the Watergate investigation.

What may be surprising is the number of Eagle Scouts from this era involved in sports. Most of them were head coaches: **Chan Gailey**, Dallas Cowboys and Georgia Tech Yellow Jackets; **Ray Malavasi**, Denver Broncos and Los Angeles Rams; **Jim Mora**, Baltimore Stars, New Orleans Saints, and Indianapolis Colts; and **Ken Whisenhunt**, Arizona Cardinals. There were also a number of Eagles who became professional athletes, the best known probably **Albert Belle**, the hard-slugging (and often combative) outfielder for the Cleveland Indians, Chicago White Sox, and Baltimore Orioles.

But perhaps no athlete Eagle has ever had a more remarkable career than **Bill Bradley.** Exactly how he managed to earn his Eagle in the middle of his famously rigorous basketball training schedule is a measure of both his intelligence and discipline. The most famous high school basketball player of his era, Bradley was offered 75 college scholarships. He chose Princeton, was NCAA player of the year, and earned an Olympic gold medal. Then, after spending two years at Oxford as a Rhodes scholar, Bradley returned to the United States and joined the NBA's New York Knicks. He spent his decade-long career with the Knicks, which retired his number with him.

Bradley was elected to the basketball hall of fame in 1982. By then, he had been elected to the U.S. Senate (D-NJ), an office he held for three terms. In 1997, he retired from politics—but then returned in 2000 with an unsuccessful run for president of the United States. He still holds the NCAA free throw percentage record, which he set between 1962 and 1965.

On April 29, 1975, in a tragic postscript to a painful era, Marine Lance Corporal **Darwin Judge**, who had earned his Eagle just four years before, became one of the last two U.S. servicemen to die in the Vietnam War. A member of the Marine security guard at the U.S. Embassy in Saigon he was killed by a North Vietnamese rocket attack. A year later, Senator Edward Kennedy used diplomatic channels to secure the return of Judge's remains to the United States—but it would be 25 more years, until 2000, before he would receive a full military funeral. The Fall of Saigon Marines Association sponsors two scholarships each year for Eagle Scouts attending Iowa's Marshalltown High School, Judge's alma mater.

Needless to say given the times, this generation of Eagle Scouts produced more than its share of outsiders and controversial figures.

Probably the most notorious was **Marion Barry**. Born in Leflore, Mississippi, the third of 10 children, Barry's father died when he was a child, forcing him to take work as a cotton picker, grocery bagger, and American Legion hall waiter. Despite this, he joined a Boy Scout troop and earned his Eagle just before his 18th birthday. Barry earned degrees from LeMoyne and Fisk University—and in 1978 he was elected as the second mayor of Washington, DC.

Barry's first tenure in office as one of the most powerful African American mayors in the country was controversial, but largely successful. However, in 1990, at the end of his third term, his widely reported drug arrest (with accompanying video) shocked the nation. He chose not to run for re-election and served one year in a federal penitentiary.

But if his behavior appalled the rest of America, Marion Barry the politician was still beloved by minority voters in Washington, DC. And, within two years, he was again elected mayor. This fourth and final term was more contentious than controversial because the mayor and city council fought over a shrinking budget and and chafed under federal oversight. Barry officially retired in 1999, explaining (probably correctly) that DC would never earn statehood as long as he was mayor. In 2005, despite another drug incident, Barry ran for DC City Council and won—a position, as of this writing, he still holds.

White House Press Secretary **James Brady**, who barely survived being shot in the head during the 1981 assassination attempt on President Ronald Reagan, became, along with his wife, the most passionate and successful gun control advocate in the country. **William DeVries**, the famous cardiothoracic surgeon, implanted the first artificial heart in a human being (Barney Clark) in 1982. Nixon's Assistant to the President for Domestic Affairs **John Ehrlichman** and White House Chief of Staff **H.R. Haldeman**, were central figures who had their careers destroyed in the Watergate scandal. **Andy Looney** became a cult figure among video game designers. **Henry Nicols**, a hemophiliac who contracted AIDS from one of thousands of blood transfusions, became an internationally known AIDS activist in 1991 when he announced that he would use educating others about his illness as his Eagle service project. In 2000, he died at age 26 after a car crash on the way to a Scouting event.

David Lynch directed some of the most surreal and disturbing films ever to emerge from Hollywood. As an Eagle candidate, Lynch joined an honor guard outside the White House during the Kennedy inauguration. **Michael Moore** earned his Eagle in Flint, Michigan, at age 16, two years before he was elected to the local school board and embarked on a his Academy

Award-winning career of social activism and radical politics in film making. **George Moore** became writer and producer of *The Simpsons;* while **Bill Amend** created the comic strip *Fox Trot.* Actor **Mike Rowe** became host of the popular cable series *Dirty Jobs.* Journalist **Ray Suarez** became a long-time news correspondent on the *PBS Newshour.*

Paul Theroux, who earned his Eagle with a Medford, Massachusetts, troop in 1955 became a novelist and one of America's most celebrated travel writers. **Leonard Tower** was a computer hacker before helping found the Free Software Foundation. **David Foreman** was co-founder of the environmental activist group Earth First!

In 1982, symbolically closing the door on Scouting's recently troubled past, and open a new one on a more stable and optimistic future, a young, 13-year-old Life Scout named **Alexander Holsinger**, from the unlikely named city of Normal, Illinois, become the 1 millionth Boy Scout to earn his Eagle award.[25]

The year before, 30,000 Scouts had poured into the 11th national jamboree at its new location at Fort A.P. Hill, Virginia—the first increase in attendance in nearly a decade. By the time Scouting celebrated its 75th anniversary in 1985—the theme: "The Spirit Lives On"—the missteps of the previous decade had been all but forgotten. The next two jamborees would continue to see increases in attendance. In 1988, showing its renewed prowess, Scouting successfully attempted a new national initiative, "Scouting for Food." The program, designed to gather food and clothing for the homeless and poor, drew headlines when it collected more than 60 million food items.[26]

Boy Scouting was back.

EAGLE SCOUT, SUPERSTAR

On May 24, 1989, crowds formed long lines in front of theaters across America in anticipation of the opening of the third installment of one of the most popular movie series in history.

Early reviews were strong. Not only did the film have a fast-moving and entertaining plot, it also had an impeccable pedigree: the producer and director were the most successful ever in their respective professions and to the cast had been added an older, legendary movie idol and the hottest new teen star.

The rapt audiences, in hundreds of movie palaces and strip mall multiplexes cheered as the opening scene—a vista of Arches National Park in Moab, Utah—unfolded across the screen and the title appeared:

INDIANA JONES and THE LAST CRUSADE

As the names of the lead actors—Harrison Ford, River Phoenix, Sean Connery—appeared one after another in the foreground, the background filled with a line of figures on horseback in wide-brimmed campaign hats, yellow neckerchiefs, dark khaki uniforms, and puttees. They are wearing backpacks, and the second horseman—the guidon bearer—holds a staff with a pennant.

These aren't the modern Boy Scouts of iPhones and rules about rope bridges being no taller than five feet because of legal fears—this is the Scout troop of myth—riding horses into the wilderness, and led by a mustachioed Scoutmaster.

Beneath a tall rock arch, that Scoutmaster, Mr. Havelock, who wears a high-collared uniform, binoculars slung over his shoulder, and a whistle dangling from his left pocket, orders a halt. As he commands, "Dismount" everyone climbs out of the saddle crisply and in unison . . . except for the inevitable chunky Scout who catches a foot in his stirrup and tumbles into the dust.

The next shot shows the Scouts climbing a jumble of rocks to enter the vast mouth of a cave. Inside the cave, one of the Scouts, apparently the senior patrol leader, hears a noise emanating from a side chamber. He pauses as the other Scouts pass on and, his face still in shadows, listens. Joined by the chunky, disheveled Scout, Herman, he heads into the side chamber.

He sees an opening to a chamber below, then a rope, and then the silhouette of a figure wearing a leather jacket, khakis, and a wide-brimmed fedora. The figure—whom the audience instantly assumes is Indiana Jones—is leading a work party . . . and as the Scouts look on, one of the workers brings over an old wooden box. As the rest of the crew watches, the Jones figure sits at a table and carefully opens the lid. He pulls out an old golden crucifix: the Cross of Coronado. As the leader lifts his head to look at the dazzling artifact, the audience is stunned to discover that he isn't Jones, but some other person in identical dress.

The camera cuts to the two Scouts, who sit back in amazement at what they've just seen. The senior Scout takes off his campaign hat and leans forward—his face caught in the lantern light for the first time: he resembles nothing less than a cross between a Leyendecker Apollo and Norman Rockwell's third edition *Boy Scout Handbook* cover painting.

"Indiana," pleads Herman, "Indiana."

The audience suddenly realizes that the senior patrol leader is in fact, the young Indiana Jones. And in light of all that it has learned about Jones from the first two movies, it is instantly appropriate that his younger self should be a Boy Scout.

The caption reads "Utah 1912." The chubby Scout wants to run, but young Indiana will have none of it. "That cross is an important artifact," he tells Herman. "It belongs in a museum." And that means, left unsaid, is that he will have to steal it . . .

The idea to open *Indiana Jones and the Last Crusade* with the creation of the Jones persona came from the film's producer, George Lucas. But the execution was in the hands of two Eagle Scouts: film editor **Michael Kahn** and, most of all, director **Steven Spielberg**.

Spielberg was born in 1946 Cincinnati to an orthodox Jewish family. During his childhood, his family moved first to Haddon Heights, New Jersey, then to Scottsdale, Arizona. Young Steven entertained his friends by making Super 8 movies and charging them 25¢ to watch while his sister made popcorn.

Steven joined Scouting at age 12 and progressed through the ranks. And, like an estimated 40 percent of all Eagle Scouts, he found his adult career while working on a merit badge. In this case it was, not suprisingly, photography. As he later recalled, "My dad's still-camera was broken, so I asked the scoutmaster if I could tell a story with my father's movie camera. He said yes, and I got an idea to do a Western. I made it and got my merit badge. That was how it all started."[27]

Spielberg earned his Eagle in 1961 at age 15. By then he was busy making movies, even showing one at a local theater for a profit of $1.

When his parents divorced, Steven moved with his father to Saratoga, California, while his mother and sisters remained in Arizona. It was a difficult time—Steven later said he experienced anti-Semitic attacks during his single, senior year at Saratoga High. Nevertheless, this connection to the emerging Silicon Valley would prove to be fruitful to his future.

After graduation, Spielberg applied three times to the famous film school at USC, but was turned down each time (it later gave him an honorary degree). Instead, he attended Cal State Long Beach . . . and more importantly, interned at Universal Studios. Soon, the internship eclipsed school—and it would be a quarter century before Spielberg finally finished his degree at Long Beach State.

After making a short film whose name (*Amblin'*) would become that of his production company, Spielberg became the youngest director ever signed to long-term deal by a major movie production company. He was 22.

The rest, of course, is movie history. Spielberg's adventure films (the *Indiana Jones* tetralogy, the *Jurassic Park* trilogy, and *Jaws*) and science fiction films (*Close Encounters of the Third Kind, E.T., A.I.,* and so on) are among the most successful movies ever made—most becoming, each in turn, the highest-grossing films of all time. His "serious" films, from the TV movie *Duel* to *Schindler's List* and *Saving Private Ryan*, are among the most honored.

Both Spielberg and his films are regularly listed among the top 10 directors and movies in film industry. In 1996, *Life* magazine named him the most important figure of his generation.

In 1989, when he was making *The Last Crusade*, Steven Spielberg was 43 years old, with a son of his own. Scouting was also at the forefront of his mind because he would be attending the national jamboree and introducing the new Cinematography merit badge he had helped to develop. And so, when the time came to shoot the "early Indiana Jones" opening of the film, Spielberg publicly announced that he had decided to make Young Indy a Boy Scout in honor of his own Scouting experience.

In part because of the BSA's long-standing wariness of representations of Scouting on the silver screen—and in part because of the social upheavals of the previous two decades—Boy Scouts had not appeared prominently in a movie since at least the 1966 Fred MacMurray/Kurt Russell comedy *Follow Me, Boys!* and not in a serious role since long before that. And now, thanks to a middle-aged Eagle, the most famous action hero in movie history was appearing in a blockbuster film dressed in a Scout uniform—not for laughs, but as part of the explanation for how he had *become* such a hero.

And as the millions of audience members watched, River Phoenix as the Young Indian Jones crept down into the chamber and stole the cross, bent on returning it to the right authorities.

But he is soon spotted and takes off running into what would be the most expensive allegory of the Trail to Eagle ever made.

Emerging from the cave at full speed, Indiana looks around desperately for his fellow Scouts, he shouts for his Scoutmaster. There's nobody. With the perspective of the true hero, Indy mutters, "Is everyone lost but me?"

He looks back to see that he is still being chased by the men, so he runs to a rock ledge, whistles, and leaps to the back of his horse . . . and misses. Finally, he manages to mount and takes off at a gallop across the desert, the tomb raiders in hot pursuit in a car and truck. Ahead is a passing steam locomotive—pulling a circus train. Indy rides up and leaps aboard, the pursuers just behind him.

What follows is five minutes of classic Spielberg set-piece action, as young Indiana races from car to car, the others in hot pursuit, facing one outrageous situation after another: an anaconda emerging from a basin of water, a rhinoceros trying to impale him, a lion, a tank full of snakes. Spielberg makes this action even more engaging and entertaining by having each of these encounters serve as the obvious source of one piece or another of the fully formed Indiana Jones persona. Thus, the snakes are the source of his pathological fear of the creatures. The whip he grabs to hold off the lion—with which he manages to cut his own chin—becomes not only the inept beginnings of Indiana's later mastery of the bullwhip, but also the fictional source of actor Harrison Ford's real-life chin scar.

The opening ends with young Indiana, having escaped his pursuers, arriving in town, and rushing into his father's study—only to discover that the man in the fedora and leather coat is right behind him, with the sheriff. The man takes the crucifix. As he does, we see the heart shape of the Life rank on the chest of Indy's Scout uniform. The man gives Indiana a look of admiration and says, "You lost today, kid, but that doesn't mean you have to like it." Then he takes off his fedora and places it on Indiana's head, hiding the boy's face.

When Indiana Jones lifts his face again—he is the middle-aged hero known to all.

Having passed a series of challenges, each of which in some way changes him forever; having, in the course of this, encountered the profession that will one day be his own; and having been almost invisibly guided towards this future by men who have served as his mentors, Life Scout Indiana Jones surely will earn his Eagle.

It is a path that Steven Spielberg knew well—one that he had once taken himself. And if his Trail to Eagle hadn't been quite as cinematic that of young Indian Jones, it had affected Spielberg's adulthood just as deeply. Now, with his unequalled talent, he transformed that memory into an unforgettable fictional experience to be shared by the world . . . putting the cap on Scouting's return.

CHAPTER SEVEN

GOLDEN EAGLES

SERGEY'S LIFE HAD THE MOST DIFFICULT START IMAGINABLE. BORN IN 1994 AT L.S. BERZON CITY CLINICAL HOSPITAL NO. 20 IN THE SIBERIAN CITY OF KRASNOYARSK, RUSSIA, LITTLE SERGEY WAS BOTH PREMATURE—HE WEIGHED LESS THAN 2 POUNDS—AND SUFFERED FROM CEREBRAL PALSY.[1]

Sergey's parents, faced with huge costs and an uncertain future, abandoned the baby to what they assumed would be a life of perpetual care and institutionalization. But the hospital didn't give up on the baby boy . . . and thanks to the heroic efforts of doctors and nurses—and a well-used incubator—little Sergey survived. And, as he neared his first birthday, it was apparent that not only would Sergey, though still very ill, make it—but that even his cerebral palsy was minor in severity.

That's when little Sergey got his second chance. L.S. Berzon City Clinical Hospital No. 20, like many Russian hospitals after the fall of the Soviet Union, was overwhelmed with orphans—and was regularly visited by childless Western married couples hoping to adopt and give those orphans an unimaginably better life.

Dwight and Jenny Griffith of the Baltimore suburb of Forest Hill, Maryland were just such a couple. And when they toured the hospital in Krasnoyarsk, they spotted tiny Sergey and fell in love.

They knew what they were getting into. Little Sergey, whom they would soon rename "Alexander," was now 11 months old, but still in very bad shape. Recalled Dwight Griffith, "The first time we saw Alex, he had rickets and he was malnourished. At first Alex did not smile and hardly moved."[2]

But the Griffiths—Dwight is a successful home builder—were prepared to do whatever it took to give Alex a happy and healthy life . . . and soon the little boy found himself with a new name—**Alex Griffith**—living with a new family, in new home, and on the other side of the world. And thanks to a loving family and world-class medical care, Alex grew into a healthy and typical suburban American boy, his days filled with school, life with his four adopted siblings, riding his dirt bike, and playing video games. Russia, of which Alex had no memory, existed only as anecdotes told by his parents and a few snapshots taken by them during their visit.

Still, Alex hadn't fully escaped his nightmarish beginnings. The symptoms of the cerebral palsy eventually disappeared, but there proved to be other aftereffects—including attention deficit/hyperactivity disorder and impulsivity—that were likely the result of the limited medical care the hospital could give baby Sergey. So too, Alex's small size and fragile frame were a reminder of the rickets and other signs of malnutrition the Griffiths saw that first day.

By nature a plucky kid, Alex didn't let these limitations slow him down—and when he turned 11 in 2005, Alex joined Boy Scout Troop 809 in Forest Hill. A clever and committed kid, he quickly rose through the ranks, and at the comparatively young age of 13, Alex had reached the point that comes in the career of every successful Scout, when he began to ponder the ultimate challenge that lay ahead: the Eagle Scout service project.

Most Scouts, when faced with their Eagle project, look to local institutions—church, school, the local parks & recreation department—for potential project ideas. A small fraction—probably no more than a few percent—have greater ambitions: they want to leave their mark on the world.

Alex Griffith was one of this group. And unlike most other Eagle candidates, especially the ambitious ones, Alex didn't have to look far. He knew exactly whom he wanted to help with his project: the boys and girls who were now what Alex had once been: pediatric patients at L.S. Berzon City Clinical Hospital No. 20 in Krasnoyarsk, Russia.

"Russia is part of me and this hospital is part of me," said Alex, "They gave me life, so I [wanted] to give back to them, to give them a fun place to play."[3]

But how? All Alex had to work from was his parent's limited memories of their brief visit to the hospital more than a dozen years before—and they had been looking for a child, not running an inspection—as well as a handful of quick, barely composed, snapshots of the place.

It was one of those photographs, easily overlooked by an uninvolved viewer, that had long haunted young Alex. It showed a sad and dreary "playground" at the hospital that consisted of little more than a rusted swing set with a single rotting wooden seat, and a sandbox that Alex characterized as "a mud pit because of all of the rain." The image captured a world so very different from the one that fortune had allowed Alex to grow up in.

Studying the photograph once more, now with a different eye, Alex Griffith knew what he had to do: he would build a new, state-of-the-art playground at the hospital where he was born.

The "Krasnoyarsk Playground Project," as it came to be called, consumed the next two-and-a-half years of Alex's life. During that time, he took advantage of his father's membership in the Rotary Club to convince that organization to mobilize in support of the project—an operation that eventually engaged 500 volunteers in five countries, including more than 100 in Russia. At the same time, Alex organized Scouts in the Baltimore area to conduct fund-raising through barbecues, car washes, and candy sales.

In the end, these many efforts raised $60,000—enough to enable Alex, who had also been doing extensive research on playground equipment, to purchase exactly the setup he wanted for the hospital. It was also enough money to ship the heavy parcels to Russia. Alex, his parents, and a small group of volunteers followed, arriving in early August 2009.

On August 12th—Alex's 16th birthday—at a dedication ceremony, the playground was unveiled. Hospital 20's young patients and their families were awestruck by the sight: swings, a rock wall, a climbing bridge, zip lines . . . and, of course, a new sandbox. To capture the international spirit of the project, the entire playground was painted with a red, white, and blue motif. And, flanking the entrance, stood two carved wooden statues, one of the Russian bear and the other the American eagle.

As Alex told CNN, which named him one of its annual "Heroes," "It makes me feel awesome opening the playground on my 16th birthday. It's just made me really happy just being here."[4]

For Alex, as it is for many Scouts working toward the ultimate rank, the Krasnoyarsk Playground Eagle service project was a life-changing experience. During his visit, he and his father toured the hospital . . . including the pediatric intensive care ward. There they saw, still in use, the ancient incubator that had been Alex's home for the first months of his life. "It kept you alive," his tearful father told him.

It goes without saying that the children of Hospital 20 were thrilled by their new playground—a feeling made even richer by the knowledge that Alex Griffith was one of their own. Said 11-year-old Sonja Sultanova, a patient at the hospital, "I like this playground, because when you slide on it all the sadness goes away . . . I think that Alex is a noble person."[5]

NESA REDUX

In January 2010, almost 60 years after it began, the largest youth community service project in history finally found its voice.

Like many important events in the story of Scouting, this announcement was made almost as a whisper, with considerable confusion, and it was destined to be heard—at least at first—by only a few.

The news announcement first appeared on the website of the National Eagle Scout Association (NESA), the BSA operation that manages all communications with Eagle Scouts new and old.

After its big launch at the two national jamboree sites (as well as the National Order of the Arrow conference) in 1973, NESA had experienced a slow start—if not in membership, but in content. This was in large part because Scouting did not really know what to with it, other than use NESA as a giant mailing list/database it could someday tap as needed for local, regional, and national fund-raising, talent, and political support. But for the hundreds of thousands of Eagles across America who allowed their connection to Scouting to lapse, NESA at first seemed little more than yet another alumni fund. And for older Eagles, especially those who had seen the lively, albeit small-scale, efforts of the Knights of Dunamis, its replacement seemed pretty short on either action or ambition.

Indeed, for the first two decades of NESA, the only contact most Eagles had with the organization occurred every few months with their receipt of the *Eagletter*, a three-times-per-year newsletter of the organization. A low-budget production, the *Eagletter* nevertheless became the de facto bulletin board for Eagles of every age.

Before the *Eagletter*, the BSA had always tried to sublimate Eagle Scouting into the larger Scouting universe. The Boy Scouts had always attempted to maintain a balance between celebrating the Eagle as the zenith of the Scouting experience; while at the same time, for fear of losing those same Eagles too early, never labeling Eagles as *different* from the rest of Scouting. The half-century experiment of the Knights of Dunamis may have proven the desire of Eagles to stay engaged with Scouting; but it also warned the BSA that any such organization, if not tightly constrained, would eventually go renegade and set its own terms for that engagement.

The *Eagletter,* designed essentially as a newsletter for dues-paying NESA members, inadvertently proved a valuable touchstone for the Eagle brotherhood, reminding its members that they were still part of a great, if almost invisible, movement.

Subscribers (i.e., current and lifetime NESA members) would quickly skip to the middle pages to read about Eagles around the United States who had earned recent honors and promotions. Some were young men who had just earned their medal a year or two before and were now joining the military, heading off to a service academy, or graduating with honors from college; others were elderly men reaching the highest levels of government, the corporate world, or their professions. Not until Wikipedia and other websites began publishing lists of famous Eagles a quarter-century later, would there be another location where older Eagles could revel in the success of their peers.

Less obvious, but perhaps even more engaging was the page or two in each issue filled with photographs of "Eagle Families": two, three, even four generations of men in a single family, all of whom had earned their Eagles, sometimes a half-century apart. If the member achievement pages were a reminder of the extraordinary career successes of Eagle Scouts, the "Families" page was the first real celebration of Eagle Scouting as a living tradition, and an enduring presence, in American life.

Finally, more solemnly, there was a page or more dedicated to Eagle Scouts who had recently died. It was a standard obituary page—with an important exception: along with the men of great age and accomplishment, there were also a surprising number of young men. Achievers are also often risk takers, or young men and women in a hurry before their clock runs out. And to read these memorials to young men killed in battle or in a high adventure or from a fatal illness was to take consolation in the knowledge that, because of their Eagle, even their short lives had contained at least one enduring achievement.

Each Spring issue of the *Eagletter* would also carry news of that year's newest crop of Eagle scholarship winners. A careful reader would notice that the number and size of these scholarships seemed to grow by the year. In time, NESA would manage a score of such scholarships, offered to as many as 100 finalists, and ranging in awards from $500 from the Epsilon Tau Pi Alpha Chapter of the University of Dayton to the $48,000 ($12,000 per year) Mabel and Lawrence S. Cooke Scholarship. In between were numerous scholarships from NESA and the BSA at the regional and national level, from religious institutions (with the most coming from the National Jewish Committee on Scouting), to academic institutions (from small regional bible colleges to giants such as Stanford University and Texas A&M), to nonprofit associations such as the American Legion, VFW, and Sons of the American Revolution.

By the mid-1990s, these scholarships had become so numerous and large that they became their own source of identity—even the defining purpose— for NESA itself. Before the advent of the Web, many young Eagles joined

NESA just for the *Eagletter* and its access to scholarship information (as well for the distinctive neckerchief).

But beyond the scholarships, the newsletter (which slowly metamorphosed into a real magazine) and the neckerchiefs and other swag, NESA had little impact in the lives of America's Eagles. At the quadrennial national jamboree, the National Eagle Scout Association inevitably set up a tent to serve as a meeting place for visiting Eagles. The Association also held its own convention every four years, largely as an exercise in solidarity. In all, for its many achievements, in the 1990s NESA largely remained a giant organization without a greater purpose than to stand and wait, as the BSA's de facto reserves, for a call to action.

RETHINKING THE MODEL

As Eagle Scouting inched its way forward toward an independent purpose and identity, Scouting continued on its own hike home. The retrenchment begun with Green Bar Bill's landmark 1979 *Handbook* had by the early 1990s pervaded all of Scouting, with a new generation of Scouts and leaders who had never known the Improved Scouting era. The baby boomers, who had swelled the ranks of Scouting in the 1950s and 1960s, and had been largely absent now for two decades, began to return with their own sons— causing a secondary membership boomlet across the BSA, as well as a jump in adult Scouter volunteers.

Through these years, Scouting seemed content to keep its core operations, while fine-tuning its specialty programs on the margins. The BSA opened the 1990s with the establishment of a new classroom program called "Learning for Life." Learning for Life, open to students from kindergarten through high school, evolved out of the inner-city programs first created in the 1970s by Improved Scouting. At that time, a number of schools in low-income neighborhoods had asked if Scouting could be integrated into the curriculum rather than be an after-school program.

At the end of the 1970s, as Scouting returned to its traditional philosophy, the In-School Scouting programs (often organized with the Girl Scouts and Campfire Girls) slowly evolved into Learning for Life, which was formally instituted in 1991. Learning for Life was distinctly different from Scouting not just because it eschewed such BSA stalwarts as the Oath and Law—but in a concession to the changing larger culture, one that would soon prove very important—Learning for Life didn't restrict membership by gender, residence, or sexual orientation.

Still, one legacy matter did prove to be vexing: Exploring. This third major program of the Scouting triumvirate, designed for older teen boys, and focusing on both high adventure and career training, had become increasingly schizophrenic. There had always been "Scouting" Explorer posts that camped and hiked and focused on helping young men reach Eagle (if they were under 18) or the Silver Award (if they were beyond that birthday). At the same time, by the mid-1960s, a second and even more celebrated type of Explorer post—this one affiliated with law enforcement, law, medicine, or other professional careers and serving as a kind of apprenticeship program—had begun to appear.

With the arrival of Learning for Life, these "worksite-related" Explorer posts migrated to that program—and kept the Exploring name. Meanwhile, the traditional posts, now orphaned, founded a new organization in 1998 with "Venturing." Exploring now largely focused on a new set of awards, notably the Young American medal, while Venturing retained the Eagle and Silver awards.

One obvious effect of this reorganization was that Scouting's rolls instantly lost a couple hundred thousand members. Given the BSA's still depressed numbers in the post-baby boom era, this kind of drop was dispiriting—even if it was easily explainable. After all, strictly speaking, this wasn't just a bookkeeping entry transfer: those Learning for Life Explorers were no longer on the Trail to Eagle, or even the Silver Medal; they were gone from Scouting forever. Not surprisingly, jamboree attendance in the 1990s still hovered down around 30,000. Meanwhile, Learning for Life, which saw 700,000 members in its first year alone, was by any measure a huge success.[6]

But once again, Eagle Scouting—with its uniquely ambitious and disciplined aspirants—ran counter to expectations. At the dawn of the 1990s, the number of Scouts each year earning their Eagle once again crossed the 30,000 threshold—a number not seen since the early 1970s at the peak of the baby boom (where it peaked, in 1973, at 46,966). One might have predicted a long-term slump in these numbers as Learning for Life drew away a sizable pool of potential Eagles. But, in fact, other than a brief dip in 1995, the number of new Eagles continued to advance year-by-year right through into the new century. In 1997, the number broke the 40,000 threshold for new Eagles, crossing that barrier for the first time in a quarter century.[7]

And it just kept going—despite the fact that the total membership of Scouting had continued to hover around 3 million, as it had for 20 years. In 2004, another barrier was broken: 50,377 Scouts earned their Eagle.[8] The legendary "2-percent" ratio of the number of Eagle Scouts to the overall total of all Scouts still held—but only because (thanks to recessions, depressions, war, and the Bird Study merit badge) the ratios were even lower in Scouting's first half century. Now, in a given year, that ratio was more like 6 percent—and in some competitive areas, where an Eagle was seen as an especially valuable line item on a university application, it was even higher than that.

It wasn't surprising, then, that in 2009, Scouting saw its 2 millionth Eagle Scout: **Anthony Thomas**, a 16-year-old Scout from Troop 471 of Burnsville, Minnesota. Thomas had been born just about the time Alexander Holsinger had earned the 1 millionth Eagle medal. In 2010, the centennial year of American Scouting, 56,176 Scouts earned their Eagle medal—the greatest single year number ever.[9]

Why this sudden increase in the percentage of new Eagles? One answer, as already noted, was the restored worth of the award, after the devaluation of the 1960s and 1970s, on college applications and in job interviews. For large sections of the population—both educated professionals and upwardly mobile blue collar families—earning the Eagle was seen as just as much a teenage ticket to adult success as a high SAT score or a transcript full of AP courses.

A second reason was the growing systematization of the Trail to Eagle. A Boy Scout working toward his Eagle in 1925, 1945, or 1965 faced a truly difficult uphill path. For one thing, for those past Eagle candidates, each merit badge was major challenge: the Scout not only had to fulfill the requirements of the badge (many of which had heavier writing requirements than for modern Scouts), but also had to locate, contact, visit, and work with an adult who was usually a stranger. And then, having earned the requisite 11 required and 10 optional merit badges, the Eagle candidate then typically had to submit to the grilling of a council board of review, again by adult strangers, in some distant courtroom or office building.

But, by 1985, and especially by 2005, the process had radically changed. Because of the new BSA Youth Protection Rules, Scouts now typically earned their merit badges with at least one other Scout or adult nearby—and from a merit badge counselor who was most likely a familiar parent from his troop. And there was an even easier way than that: week-long summer camps geared to enable dedicated Scouts to earn a half-dozen merit badges or more in just a matter of days . . . or even more extreme: day-long local merit badge "midways" that typically made the merit-badge-earning process so systematic and easy that many troops banned their Scouts from attending them.

It wasn't surprising then to see Scouts going into their Eagle board of reviews—now typically manned by a couple troop parents and a district representative—with a once unheard-of 30 or more merit badges.

A third reason was the changing nature of the Scouts themselves. It is not a coincidence that Alex Griffith, whose story began this chapter, was a Russian baby adopted by American parents—or that Anthony Thomas, the 2 millionth Eagle, was adopted from South Korea. Early Scouting was almost exclusively white European- and black African- and a small percentage of Native-American boys. But, beginning with the end of the Second World War and accelerating in the decades that followed, the United States absorbed one wave after another of new immigrants—Mexican, Southeast Asian, Russian, Saharan African, Indian and Pakistani, Latin American, Chinese and Korean, and South Sea Islander.

Like immigrants everywhere, most of these new Americans were anxious to dive into the daily life of their new country, to assimilate and succeed. And, as in the past, many of these immigrants focused on making sure their children participated fully in the life of the new culture—including Scouting. The BSA, which a generation before had been reviled for its perceived connection to the nation's establishment, its patriotism, and its traditional values, now saw that liability turn into an asset with millions of new immigrant families.

As a result, Scouting, which had always prided itself on ecumenicalism and tolerance, now found itself living out those ideals to a degree it had never before imagined. It wasn't surprising to find a twenty-first century Scout troop with parents speaking both English and a dozen different languages and dialects, and with the Scouts themselves professing to a score of different religious faiths and denominations. Those changes were dealt with through training, changes in official imagery, and new programs (such as "Interpreter" badges, changes in the required Citizenship in the World merit badge, and special adult awards for work with minority communities), and ultimately, with an ease that belied the conventional view of a "traditionalist" BSA.

Immigrant families answered Scouting's hospitality and easy assimilation by making it a popular doorway into American life. Many troops, especially on the two coasts, found themselves with new Scouts whose parents spoke little or no English, but who saw in troop meetings and campouts a way for their sons to enter daily life in the United States that wasn't possible in the increasingly immigrant-dominated public schools. Just as important, they saw the Eagle Scout award as the most American of childhood achievements—the ticket to adult success in the New World.

Though there is no official BSA record of the ethnic background of new Eagle Scouts in the 1990s and 2000s, even a brief glance at the names on the annual lists—or, better yet, attendance at a council annual awards dinner in, say, California, Florida, or Texas—suggests a sizable and growing presence of first-generation American Eagles. It is from these ranks that much of the annual growth of new Eagles likely came during those two decades. And that in turn argues that not just Scouting, but the lure of the Eagle rank, played a significant role in the assimilation of new Americans at the turn of the twenty-first century.

BEYOND ACCEPTANCE

Ironically, even as these forces were at work restoring Scouting to its old glory, and swelling the rolls of new Eagles in the process, two other forces were at work consciously trying to slow this growth and undermine the organization's newfound success.

Though complex in their nature, these forces did have both common adherents and equally simple demands, so it is not surprising they soon came to be nicknamed together under the sobriquet: *God and Gays.*

But as simple as these two debates may have seemed to both the media and the general public, they were in fact very different, and Scouting's response to these challenges followed very different tracks.

In the public eye, the debate over God and Boy Scouts seemed very straightforward. Simply put, you couldn't be a Boy Scout unless you professed a belief in God Almighty. The BSA had always used the term "God" in its publications; every Scout knew that the twelfth part of the Scout Law was "A Scout is Reverent"; and every Scouting event from a local troop meeting to a national convention, began by reciting the "Pledge of Allegiance," with its statutory phrase ". . .under God . . ."

The official Boy Scout position as of 1970 on the subject was "The recognition of God as the ruling and leading power in the universe and the grateful acknowledgment of His favors and blessings are necessary to the best type of citizenship . . ." The official Scouting membership form said, "The Boy Scouts of America maintain that no member can grow into the best kind of citizen without recognizing his obligation to God."

This would seem to make it an open-and-shut case: you could not be a Boy Scout unless you believed in God. Period. And indeed, in the 1970s there were reports of Eagle candidates being turned down by local boards of review because they professed to be atheists.

But, as always, Scouting's real-life relationship to the divine was much more complicated than that.

Religious faith was not really a problem for Scouting during its first half-century. The United States was almost a purely Judeo-Christian nation, appeals and prayers to the Almighty were part of everyday political discourse, most new immigrants were Catholic, Eastern Orthodox, or Jewish, and atheism was a fringe philosophy shared by European Communists and anarchists. Indeed, two of the founders of Scouting, notably Beard and Seton, expressed naturalist views of God that didn't fit with Christian ontology.[10]

But all of that changed in the postwar world. Religious skepticism was on the rise even in the United States, that most religious of developed nations. And it wasn't long before boys, raised as atheists and agnostics, arrived in Scouting—and forced the organization to take a look at itself.

On the one hand, this led to a retrenchment by the organization, as exemplified by that 1970 statement. On the other hand, Scouting had always been flexible when it came to its definition of the meaning of "God." After all, from the beginning, Scouting had never questioned Hindu, Buddhist, Confucian, or Shintoist Scouts (the last three seeing considerable growth in the 1920s and 1930s), despite the fact that none featured a monotheistic "God"—and Buddhism, strictly speaking, had no God at all. In fact, Scouting more than tolerated these faiths; it *honored* them: the 1948 edition of the *Handbook*, which official began the BSA religious medal program, listed a Buddhist medal alongside Roman Catholic, Jewish, Mormon, Lutheran, and Protestant medals.[11]

Beginning in the 1980s, the situation became even more complicated. Former Scouts who believed they'd been discriminated against for their lack of religious faith filed the initial lawsuits. The first of these, filed in the summer of 1985 and backed by the ACLU, claimed that 15-year-old Scout, Paul Trout of Charlottesville, Virginia, had been asked to leave Scouting because he admitted to atheism during his Life board of review. Trout was readmitted to Scouting that October, after an investigation by the BSA National Council concluded that the events of that board of review had led to a miscommunication.[12]

A far greater challenge came six years later, when three Cub Scouts, including a pair of twins, from Chicago and Anaheim, respectively. This time, the twins' father won the case in superior court, in large part because he argued from the Buddhist example. When the California State Supreme Court refused to hear the case, the challenge slowly made its way through the appellate system to the United States Supreme Court.

There was no little irony in all of this. After all, even as Scouting rules about its members' relationship to a Supreme Being was challenged in the courts, on the ground, Scout troops were happily admitting members, including those legions of new immigrants whose religious views ranged from agnosticism to (in the case of African Scouts) animism and ancestor reverence, to Wiccanism and Gaia worship . . . and most of all to a kind of scientific "faith" (derived from sources as diverse as Newton, Einstein, quantum physics, and the Heisenberg uncertainty principle) that believed in some kind of underlying order, first mover, or purpose that was currently beyond human ken but might someday, through science, be discovered.

The BSA continued to hold to its traditional definition of reverence (though even that was rewritten to "belief in a Supreme Being" after the Trout case. But in practice, at millions of boards of review—especially the all-important Eagle boards—across the country, small groups of adults bent over backward to understand the slightest nuances and turns of phrase of self-professed "unbeliever" Scouts. In the end, most came to the same conclusion: only if a Scout professed to pure nihilism and held that the universe was purely random and without purpose, could that belief be grounds for disqualification.

Since few pure sociopaths ever join Scouting, much less reach Eagle, it was unlikely that there'd be many legal challenges to this new position. But as every great institution knows, there is a big difference between de facto and de jure—and so, even as local Scouting units reached their separate peace over Scouting and the Almighty, the Boy Scouts of America continued with its quest for a legal solution. This search would soon gain added impetus from a second and even more highly publicized challenge to Scouting.

HIGHER JUDGMENT

Tim Curran was an 18-year-old Eagle who had just aged out of his troop in Northern California's Mount Diablo Council and wanted to rejoin that organization as an adult assistant Scoutmaster. However, the Council learned that Curran had been interviewed for an article in the *Oakland Tribune* for an article on gay youth—and refused Curran's application. Curran filed suit for discrimination. The case wasn't decided until 1998, and then by the California State Supreme Court. It found in favor of the BSA because it was not a "business organization" and could not, under the state's civil rights act, be made to change its membership requirements.

It was a Pyrrhic victory for Scouting. It may have won the case in legal court, but it lost in the court of public opinion. Much of that had to do, once again, with confusion about the facts of the case. Because Curran was still a teenager, the general public assumed he was still a Boy Scout—that he was an Eagle only added to the power of his argument—and was being thrown out of Scouting solely because he was gay, not because he had made a public profession of that fact.

Though America had become less squeamish about such matters after the sexual revolution of the 1960s, it was a topic that Scouting never wanted to address—especially not publicly.

One important reason for this was that Scouting, at its philosophical core, was not about sexuality. Intentionally so: from the beginning, Baden-Powell and the founders of both international and U.S. Scouting had wanted Boy Scouting to be an oasis away from the sexual confusions and compulsions of adolescent boyhood. It was to be a place where boys could be their true selves without the preening, posing, and competition for girls that characterized the other parts of their lives. The sexuality of Boy Scouts was rarely discussed, because sexuality was not a part of Boy Scouting.

The sexuality of adult Scouting volunteers was a different story. Like all youth organizations, the BSA tried to be vigilant against predators using the organization to stalk children. Like every other youth organization in the early years of the twentieth century, it was naïve about the nature of the threat and the magnitude of its own responsibility. But, propelled by a few tragic cases, the BSA learned its lesson—and over the decades continuously improved its child protection programs through training, rules about boys being alone with adults, and increasingly sophisticated background checks.

Nevertheless, in an organization with 3 million boys and a million adults, no filter was perfect, as the public regularly learned from the media. For Scouting, the rule against gay leaders may have been sweeping, but it was also seen as the ultimate protection. Now, the Curran case had brought this previously low-key matter to the surface. And it would be just the beginning.

In the end, as everyone knew, because it sat at the nexus of public and private organizations, religion, and the liberal and conservative sides of American culture, the matter would have to be adjudicated by the highest court in the land. The case that would be chosen to run this gauntlet was filed by yet another Eagle Scout, **James Dale**, a New Jersey assistant Scoutmaster. As with Curran, this was a case of an Eagle Scout not being stripped of his medal, rather trying to remain *with* Scouting.

Dale, who had been dismissed from his duties as an assistant Scoutmaster after it was learned that he had been co-president of the Gay/Lesbian Student Alliance while at Rutgers University, filed suit in superior court in 1990—and through the rest of the decade the case worked its way up to the New Jersey Supreme Court, which found for Dale, saying that the BSA's decision had violated the state's public accommodations law.

The Boy Scouts appealed, and in 2000, the U.S. Supreme Court took up the case. The case was argued on April 26 of that year, and decided on June 28 . . . *for* the Boy Scouts of America. The landmark decision, decided 5-4 largely on ideological lines, ruled that the BSA and similar organizations had the right, under the freedom of assembly guaranteed by the First Amendment to establish its own rules of membership. Chief Justice William Rehnquist wrote the majority opinion. The majority made no opinion on the worthiness of those rules.

It was a victory for Boy Scouts, but once again a Pyrrhic one. Now, and for all time, no outside individual or group could force the BSA to accept it for membership. And Scouting now had one more bulwark against adults who might target its young members for nefarious purposes.

But once more, Scouting had lost in the court of public opinion—at least among that vast population of American liberals and progressives upon whom the BSA had been built in its first half-century, then had lost in the 1960s and had only just begun to win back. Once again, much of this was a communications breakdown—millions of average Americans were now convinced that Scouting was, willy-nilly, throwing out Cub Scouts and 11-year-old Boy Scouts for acting gay. At the same time, councils across the country watched in dismay as some of their largest, and most dependable, supporters and donors broke off contact because they couldn't risk being connected to an organization that was antigay. Others lost the support of that powerful local legitimizer of nonprofit groups, the United Way, or saw their access to public facilities—some built by Scouts themselves decades before—now denied.

Most of these cases were eventually settled. But they had the secondary chilling effect of making local governments and public schools much less willing to partner with Scouting in any way. And that in turn had the ironic impact of driving Scouting even deeper into the religious institutions that the gay and atheist activists objected to—and stripping away available Scout troops from the communities that most needed them.

AT ANOTHER LEVEL

But there was one aspect of Scouting that seemed to float above all the changes and controversies of the BSA and America at the turn of the twenty-first century: Eagle Scouts, and in particular, the Eagle Scout service project.

Those thousands of stories about local Eagle projects continued to appear in small newspapers and local weeklies—and now on websites, in blogs, and even on local television—year after year. And, despite whatever was going on in the larger world, the projects were almost always met with uniform approval across the political spectrum.

After all, what was there not to like? A Scout leading a dozen other Scouts painting a city building, cleaning up a polluted local stream, taking children from a battered women's shelter camping, collecting cell phones for troops at war, or racing to help in the cleanup after Hurricane Katrina—just to give a brief sampling of typical Eagle projects of the era—this kind of community service, done without any hidden agenda or for pay, appealed to everyone: business people, environmentalists, community activists, politicians, and working folks.

And they made for great copy. In a cynical and ironic age, the image of a teenage boy putting down his videogame player and temporarily turning off his Facebook page to help his community or country by tackling a project at the very limit of his abilities . . . and seeing his confident and sincere excitement at having succeeded, warmed even the coldest heart with hope for the younger generation.

And some of these projects truly pulled at the heartstrings. Alex Griffith's story of his Krasnoyarsk Playground Project was just one example. Thanks to Scouting's willingness to modify the requirements for Eagle in special cases, every year saw numerous stories of the estimated 100,000 mentally or physically disabled Scouts overcoming unusual obstacles on their Trail to Eagle. For example, in 2008, **Mathew McClain**, a 41-year-old Scout with special-needs Troop 216 in Anne Arundel County, Maryland, earned his Eagle after 23 years of regular attendance with his troop. McClain had not been expected to survive long after his birth—now at an age when many of his contemporaries were returning to Scouting as middle-aged parents, McClain, the new Eagle medal pinned to his chest, stood before a large crowd (including a state senator) and proudly thanked all of them for their help.[13]

In the coastal city of Bandon, Oregon, **Kyle Lawrence** completed his Eagle while attending a local junior college and preparing to transfer to Oregon State. A high school track, cross-country, and soccer athlete, Lawrence had been hit by a car in 2010 while walking home on Highway 101. He sustained life-threatening injuries and spent months in the hospital. He was still recovering from his injuries when he received his Eagle.

Said his Scoutmaster Jim Proehl to an audience that included many of Kyle's old high school classmates, "There are some things that, because of the accident, Kyle will never have a do-over." For example, his first day of senior year, playing soccer, or running cross-country. "But this was one of the things that he did get a second chance at—and we were glad the Boy Scouts of America [was] able to give him that."[14]

Eagles run in the family of Philadelphia Scout **Brian Miller**, whose grandfather, father, and brother had earned the award. But there was some question that Brian, a student at the Overbrook School for the Blind, could complete the requirements even with Scouting's alternate requirements for the rank.

But Miller persevered, and against all odds, managed to earn his Eagle before his 18th birthday and using the standard requirements. With one exception: in earning the Bird Study merit badge (that once-required badge that had ended the dreams of generations of potential Eagles), Miller was allowed to identify species of birds by their calls rather than by sight.

At one point along the trail, Miller came close to giving up. But, while working one summer at his council's Camp Ockanickon, Miller had an epiphany: "I could finally see the mountaintop," he recalled. "It would take serious devotion, but I could do it, and I did."[15] He earned his Eagle in January 2010.

A SEARCH FOR PURPOSE

The turn of the century also represented a turning point in the story of the National Eagle Scout Association.

After 30 years of adding to its membership rolls, handing out Scholarships and waiting for Scouting's call, NESA suddenly seemed impatient to make something happen. This transformation was most visibly exemplified by the three high-profile presidents who ran the organization over the next decade.

Robert Gates, who became president of NESA in 1998, was unquestionably the most prominent figure to date to lead America's Eagles. Gates, who had earned his own Eagle in 1958, had remained engaged with Scouting, whenever possible, for his entire adult life. And it had been a very busy life. By the time Gates accepted the NESA presidency he had already served for a quarter-century at the Central Intelligence Agency—where ultimately, under President George H.W. Bush, he became its director and a member of the National Security Council.

Following his retirement from the CIA, Gates accepted the presidency of Texas A&M University. He later turned down an offer to become the first Director of National Intelligence in order to stay at the university and to serve on the board of a number of major corporations. It was during this period that Gates also agreed to serve as the president of NESA. There, his reputation and connections at the highest levels of government and industry, gave NESA a high profile and image it had never before known.

A Distinguished Eagle who publicly credited Scouting with giving him his first training in leadership, Gates certainly understood the influence of

Eagles; and it was during his tenure that NESA for the first time set out to measure the magnitude of this influence. It proved to be a hugely difficult task. For one thing, thanks to the records being lost in a fire at national headquarters in the late 1980s, the BSA didn't even know the names of America's Eagles before that date. Records of these individuals that still survived were held at the local councils. In other words, to even *begin* to understand the nature of being an Eagle Scout in the twenty-first century, much less measure the total impact of Eagle Scouts over the previous 90 years, NESA first had to figure out just who these Eagles were.

In a speech in 1998, Gates announced that his time as president of the National Eagle Scout Association would be dedicated to three initiatives: 1) To locate America's Eagle Scouts—mostly by comparing local council lists with what had survived at the national level—and then to get that information digitized; 2) To establish NESA committees in councils that currently lacked them; and 3) To create an "Eagles Helping Eagles" mentoring program.

Gates' speech was met with yawns and some criticism. Where were the great initiatives expected from an organization composed of Scouting's elite? Where was NESA's *purpose*—especially as compared to the now-legendary days of the Knights of Dunamis? To most observers, Gates' strategy just seemed more of the same thing that had already kept NESA largely inconsequential for 25 years.

But in retrospect, Gates' plan proved to be more influential than it seemed at the time. Eagles Helping Eagles was pretty much a bust; but the two other programs ultimately gave Eagle Scouting and NESA an empirical platform and a national infrastructure it had never before enjoyed. And it would be a combination of these two factors that, by the end of the next decade, would help NESA find its way. Moreover, in the short term, by locating and then contacting lost Eagles, NESA suddenly saw an explosion in its membership—which by 2008 would reach 250,000 members in 175 local chapters.

When Robert Gates received the call in 2006 from President George W. Bush to serve as the U.S. Secretary of Defense at the height of the Iraq War, he resigned both the NESA and Texas A&M presidencies as the law required. At the time he left NESA, it had become one of the most dynamic and fastest-growing operations in the BSA.

Remarkably, Gates was replaced as NESA president by a figure of equal, but very different, prominence. If Gates had represented the *achievement* side of Eagle Scouting, his replacement, Steve Fossett, was the ultimate embodiment of its maverick, *high adventure* side.[16]

Fossett was not only the greatest adventurer of his generation—he continued to set aeronautical records throughout his tenure at NESA—but, like Gates before him, he was anything but reticent about his love for Scouting and for being an Eagle. As he told CNN when he accepted the NESA presidency, "When I was 12 years old, I climbed my first mountain, and I just kept going, taking on more diverse and grander projects."[17]

"As a Scout, I learned how to set goals and achieve them," he said in another interview. "Being a Scout also taught me leadership at a young age when there are few opportunities to be a leader. Scouting values have remained with me throughout my life, in my business career, and now as I take on new challenges."[18]

Fossett even went out of his way to credit his old Scoutmaster. As he told a Scouting gathering in 2005, "The words of my Scoutmaster, Al Lucic, have never left me, and I think about him whenever I take on a new challenge. His presence is always with me in those quiet moments of reflection and thanks."[19]

Simply put, Fossett was the ultimate spokesman for America's Eagle Scouts, as well as for NESA. But, tragically, his tenure would be a brief. On September 3, 2007, Steve Fossett, whose life had been spent taking enormous risks, resetting the limits of human achievement, and cheating death, disappeared while piloting his small plane on a routine flight across the Sierra Nevada Mountains near the Nevada border. A massive month-long search yielded nothing—and Fossett was declared dead. It would be another year before the crash site and Fossett's remains were discovered.

The world's greatest adventurer—holder of 115 world records, almost half of which still stood at his death, was gone.

The National Eagle Scout Association, like the rest of the world, mourned Fossett's loss. Now, it faced a serious challenge: After so much national attention had been directed at the organization over the previous eight years, who could NESA now find to become the face of Eagle Scouting? Who would have the courage to step into Steve Fossett's shoes?

The answer came from the third characteristic trait of Eagle Scouts: *entrepreneurship.*

Before his 30th birthday, **Glenn A. Adams** was already one of the world's best-known names in the ferociously competitive world of independent oil and gas exploration. Adams had barreled out of Southwestern University in 1978, briefly tried an MBA at the University of Texas, Austin, but was impatient to get out into the business world and make his mark in the energy industry.

By age 29, he was among the youngest executives of a publicly traded energy company in the United States. Four years later, he was CEO of that company and led it through a life-saving restructuring. For the next seven years, Adams led an energy development partnership for large New York investment bank. But like all good entrepreneurs, he craved getting back to the day-to-day struggle to build a new company.

He found that chance at last in December 2001 when he teamed with his brother Craig and founded Adexco Production Co. Adexco, which Adams led as CEO, shrewdly pioneered the exploration of the Barnett Shale Field, the 5,000-square mile geologic formation centered under Fort Worth that may ultimately prove to be the largest onshore source of natural gas in the United States—and the largest such discovery in the continental United States in 40 years.

Despite the unceasing demands of his volatile profession, Adams still found time to raise a large family, collect vintage muscle cars, stay deeply involved in his church, serve on numerous energy industry committees, ski, fly fish, collect rocks and minerals . . . and most of all, participate in Boy Scouting at every level from local Scoutmaster in Fort Worth to the presidency of the BSA National Eagle Scout Association.

In other words, Glenn Adams was a classic American entrepreneur. And the chance to take on a national organization of overachievers that was currently in disarray after the loss of a charismatic president was just the kind of challenge he lived for. In October 2007, as the death of Steve Fossett was made official, Adams accepted the job as his replacement.

The NESA Adams inherited was very different from the one encountered by Robert Gates eight years before. With a quarter-million members and a recent and gigantic (if ultimately tragic) burst of publicity, NESA, long a sleeping giant in the BSA, had now become something of a Scouting superstar. Thousands of new applications were rolling into NESA's offices each month; and in many councils, joining the association had become a pro forma part of earning the Eagle rank.

But NESA still largely remained what it had always been: an organization with little purpose beyond its own perpetuation. There was still the *Eagletter*, with its parade of Eagle career promotions and Eagle families, and there were still the growing number of scholarships; but Adams knew that wasn't, nor would ever be, enough. And being an entrepreneur, Adams instinctively understood that while his organization might be growing now, if it didn't soon provide its members with a spectacular new product—or at least a galvanizing common purpose—the good times and the rapid growth would soon come to an end.

But where to look for that solution? As a Scoutmaster who had mentored his share of young Eagles, Adams instinctively knew the answer: the Eagle service project.

A WORLD-CHANGING DISCOVERY

The data-gathering initiative first begun under Robert Gates had yielded a considerable quantity of information about America's Eagle Scouts. It had also identified and located more than 1 million living Eagles. But there was still one block of information missing—the one dealing with the magnitude and impact of the service project.

So, almost from the day he stepped into the job, Adams—working with NESA director (i.e., its dedicated professional Scouter) **Bill Steele**—set out to find those missing statistics. In their efforts, they enjoyed the strong support of yet another Eagle, the new Chief Scout Executive **Robert Mazzuca**. Mazzuca, born and raised in Northern California, had the entrepreneurial attitude of that region and the goal of restoring Scouting's image and support inside the Beltway. Reanimating Eagle Scouting fit both those goals neatly.

But almost immediately, Adams and Steele hit a wall. As already noted, the national office had never retained records of Eagle projects. That just left anecdotal data—letters, aging newspaper clippings, memories—all of it either limited, unreliable, or self-promotional . . . and The List. Even building off of that limited database was almost impossible because the fire had destroyed much of the files on the Eagles themselves.

The only solution was to abandon the reconstruction of the past and focus on making a new start, gathering and collating information on each year's cohort of new Eagles as they appeared. The vehicle for this quiet relaunch of the Eagle would be the new *Eagle Scout Service Project Workbook.* The *Workbook*, a 16-page manual for Life Scouts, not only served as both guidebook for the service project (including The List), but also as the reporting form for its execution. This latter feature—page after page of sections in which the Scout was to list the volunteers on the project and the hours worked, provide an accounting of materials and their costs, and include photographs and approval signatures—was how NESA could at last obtain material and empirical data on each of the 50,000+ Eagle service projects completed each year in the United States. Needless to say, it also had the added value of finally systematizing the Eagle reporting process—finally, after more than 90 years, Eagle candidates at last knew what was expected of them.

In early 2009, as the final tallies came in on this first real census of Eagle Scouting, it was generally assumed that most Eagles put in about 40–60 total hours on their projects. And though Scouting had always gone to great pains to never put any expectations on these projects beyond their requirement for service and leadership—in fact, Eagle projects didn't even have to *succeed* if they were noble failures—every generation of Scouts had its own scuttlebutt about just how many hours national and local BSA and boards of review expected a typical project to be.

In the 1960s, this mythical time requirement was 40 hours; in the 1990s, 80 hours. And so, as the hours were added up on the thousands of incoming Eagle workbooks, the folks at NESA expected that America's Eagles perhaps contributed 200,000 hours each year in their communities . . . a spectacular figure in itself.

But when the final numbers came in, their jaws dropped. In 2009, the total number of Eagle Scout project service contribution was: *10½ million hours*. Recalled Bill Steele: "When we first saw that number, we were literally dumbstruck. We knew that Eagle projects were an important part of American life. But that figure was just . . . astonishing. It suddenly hit us that we weren't just looking at something remarkable, but actually historic."

And it wasn't just that one figure that was stunning. On closer inspection, NESA found that, while the central, northeastern and southern regions of the BSA had generated about 2.25 million hours each, the western region—America's traditional bellwether of the future—had produced 50 percent more: 3.75 million hours. This suggested that the "hours" race there was as strong as the merit badge race had been in years past.

A second number that astonished NESA was just how far this race had come—simple division showed that the average Eagle project at the end of the first decade of the twenty-first century consumed more than *200 hours.*

And this was no anomaly: in 2010, Scouting's centennial year, Eagles would once again contribute 10 million hours of service.

The obvious next question was: how long had Scouts been maintaining this level of service? "It suddenly hit us," said Steele, "that Eagles had been doing this for a long time. Perhaps a decade or more. And that was just staggering."

If Eagle Scouts since the late 1980s had indeed performed 200 hours per service project, and there was no reason now to assume they hadn't, Eagle Scout projects during those years had accounted for *200 million hours*—22,000 man-years—of service to the nation. Add a low-ball estimate of another 50 million hours for the Eagle projects performed in the years between 1952 and 1989, and the total hours contributed by all Eagle Scout projects likely exceeded a *quarter-billion* hours.

This last figure not only made the Eagle Scout service project the largest voluntary youth service initiative in American history . . . but probably the greatest in human history. For that matter, it belonged in the ranks of the greatest feats of voluntary service at any age, ever.

For a comparison, in 2006, Muhammad Yunus of Bangladesh was the worthy recipient of the Nobel Peace Prize for pioneering microloans to the poor in the developing world through his Grameen Bank. Grameen, which has had 7 million borrowers (95 percent of them women), serves 80,000 villages with 25,000 paid employees. Grameen is generally considered to be the largest and most successful "social enterprise" ever attempted.

By contrast, in the last half century, 2 million Eagle Scouts have performed, without pay, that estimated 250 million hours of direct service, involving a total of about 15 million other volunteers, to help other nonprofit organizations in the United States with projects ranging from helping the poor, to improving community infrastructure, to preserving local history.

Seen in this light, surely the BSA Eagle service project must be considered in at least the same category as Yunus' magnificent achievement as one of the greatest feats of social entrepreneurship ever attempted.

And it is more than that. With the *Workbook*, NESA now, with no fanfare, embarked as well on one of the largest "intellectual capital" projects ever undertaken. That's because each of those booklets, when completed, represented the latest addition to a growing library of thousands of "best practices" in community service. Want to know what it takes—cost, number of volunteers, materials, and time—to replace a flagpole, to clean up and reorganize a Pop Warner equipment room, or to distribute and collect 500 samples of standing water for a mosquito abatement program? The NESA database now has that data—and 20 years from now, it will have a million such case studies on file. That will be hugely useful body of information for anyone (including future new Eagle candidates) who needs it.

Why had no one noticed? Why were there no congressional decrees in support of the Eagle service project? Why had none of the big foundations dedicated to supporting social entrepreneurship around the world not noticed the giant example in their own backyard? One reason was Scouting itself certainly wasn't trumpeting the news. And, of course, politics had a lot to do with it. But perhaps, most of all, it was the fact that the Eagle project was not a great, monolithic effort, but a million small programs incrementally improving the communities in which they took place.

With these revelations, the National Eagle Scout Association was not only rocked on its heels—but, as the realization sunk in, the organization also seemed energized. NESA had always been an association in search of purpose. And now it had one: managing, nurturing, and directing the Eagle Scout project to even greater glory.

One effect of that new understanding and pride was that NESA could finally see itself in a historic context. After all the intervening years, the organization finally began to embrace its past. The Knights of Dunamis, from which NESA had spent more than 30 years trying to distance itself, now was properly presented in NESA publications and website as its true precursor. What Raymond Hanson had begun in his office that afternoon in April 1925, had changed American life in a million different ways. And thanks to a succession of high-achieving, maverick, and entrepreneur leaders that followed—Barber, Steig, Gates, Fossett, Adams—Eagle Scouting had found the destiny that had always resided within it.

What had begun nearly a century before as little more than a final, capstone, rank for Boy Scouts—a rank that was expected to be so rarely awarded that its official requirements and medal design weren't even completed at the time it was announced—had morphed into an honor that served as the ultimate bridge between youth and adulthood, which was pursued by millions of boys and earned by tens of thousands of them each year, and that, ultimately, had transformed America in uncounted ways.

The Eagle had long been called the "PhD of Boyhood," but that never seemed more true than when its "dissertation," the service project, served the same role as its academic counterpart. Just as the doctoral dissertation was required to contribute to the overall knowledge of its intellectual discipline, the Eagle project was now expected to improve, if only in a small way, the overall quality of American life . . . and more.

Now it was time to recognize that contribution. And to give it a voice.

THE FINALISTS

In January 2010, the National Eagle Scout Association announced the creation of the first *Glenn A. and Melinda W. Adams National Eagle Scout Service Project of the Year Award.*

As was often the case with twenty-first century Scouting, the announcement was lowkey—little more than an announcement on the NESA website and in some other Scouting publications. It had been many years since the traditional media had covered anything Scouting other than various lawsuits and the quadrennial jamboree.

Even those Scouts and Scouters who read the announcement probably only saw it as yet one more Eagle scholarship program. But the nation's new Eagle Scouts, almost alone, had a glimmering that something fundamental had changed in the nature of being an Eagle . . . one that could prove to be turning point in the BSA—and that ultimately might even have a material impact on the world.

When the figures came in about the total number of Eagle service hours per year, Glenn Adams had been as thunderstruck as everybody else: "I remember looking at those figures in disbelief. Like every middle-aged Eagle, I assumed that today's Eagle projects were pretty much the same as my own and others I remembered from the 1970s. Even as a Scoutmaster, it hadn't registered with me that many of the new generation of Life Scouts were taking on Eagle projects far beyond anything we had ever imagined.

"When I saw those figures, especially the 200-hours-per-project average, and then as I read the workbooks and saw some of the amazing projects being done by these boys, I was staggered. It suddenly struck me that what I was seeing was not only the biggest untold story in Scouting, but also of American boyhood. Here was a leadership, management and entrepreneurship program for teenage boys that was the equal of any MBA or executive development program offered anywhere. And because no one had ever seen the Big Picture before, no one had noticed."

For Adams, it was an epiphany. "It struck me that we were seeing, for the first time, the ultimate purpose of Scouting in the modern world—

and that anything we could do to support the advancement of this purpose would benefit everyone on the planet. It also struck me that the best way to accomplish this would be to create a competition—Scouts love competition—for the best Eagle project of the year."

Adams was so convinced of the value of such a competition that, after conferring with his wife, he decided that the two of them would endow the annual competition with their own money.

The nature of this competition had yet to be finalized. Being Eagles themselves, the troika of Adams, Steele and Chief Scout Executive Mazzuca, had a unique understanding of what motivated Eagles. And all agreed that while college scholarships would be a good start, the kind of Eagles likely to win such a competition would probably already be top students loaded up with scholarships from top schools. No, they agreed, what was needed for this competition was a new kind of award, one that would figuratively and literally attach to a Scout's Eagle award for the rest of his life. The new Adams Award, they decided, would combine a scholarship and a special device that would be pinned to the Eagle medal ribbon.

That couldn't fail to capture the attention of every new Eagle in the country. After all, the last time the BSA had allowed anything to be pinned to the Eagle medal ribbon, it was the Eagle palms—and that was in 1927. So, this addition of the Adams Award device—it too would be in bronze, gold, and silver for the council, regional, and national levels—would, by Scouting standards, be a momentous event. With just a few dozen council, four regional, and one national award each year, the "Adams" would quickly become among the rarest and most desirable of all Scouting awards.

In an unconscious, and ironic, tribute to the creation of the original Eagle medal, NESA didn't actually have a design for the device when it announced the Adams Award. But it didn't need to: as with Arthur Eldred a century before, Eagle Scouts only needed to know that such an award *would* exist for thousands to begin pursuing it.

The January 2010 announcement made eligible for the competition all 52,470 Eagles who had earned the rank in 2009. This group of applicants were made doubly unique: not only would the winners be the first to ever receive the Adams Award, but they would be the very last to conduct their Eagle service projects outside the influence of that award. There was no doubt in anyone's mind, especially after they saw the applications flowing in, that the lure of the Adams Award would take the Eagle project to a whole new level of achievement . . . and thus, the 2009 finalists would represent the last "pure" Eagle projects done entirely for the sake of earning the Eagle, and not with one eye on an even higher glittering prize.

As such, these finalists, as they might be called, represented a new baseline of achievement for those Eagle candidates aspiring to do something great with their service projects. The finalists were now the new version of The List for the Adams Award generation. And, like The List before them, the impact of the finalist might well last for generations. For that reason, they deserve closer scrutiny. The table that follows lists the council and regional winners by region.

NORTHEAST REGION		
KEITH EDMUND BROWN	*Patriots' Path Council* Florham Park, NJ	Built a 40-foot bridge across a stream on the Middle Brook Trail in Bridgewater Township, New Jersey. He did much of the work in mid-winter to be able to work on frozen ground, rather than mud.
BRIAN HONG-SUI CHING	*Monmouth Council* Morganville, NJ	Built swimming pool cubbies for YMCA Camp Topanemus in Millstone, New Jersey.
JAMES E. COLLINS JR.	*Narragansett Council* Providence, RI	Made knotted rosary beads for men and women in the armed forces. His original goal was 200 beads, but thanks to community help, made a total of 700.

JOHN A. HECK	*Greater Niagara Frontier Council* Buffalo, NY	Restored the German Evangelical Church Cemetery in West Seneca, New York.
AARON E. KREIMER	*Greater Pittsburgh Council* Pittsburgh, PA	Built a memorial walkway for the Charles Morris Nursing Facility in Pittsburgh.
J. COLIN MCCORMICK	*Chester County Council* West Chester, PA	Provided school equipment for 405 students at Sixth Ward Elementary School in Pearl River, Louisiana.
THOMAS R. RITTERHOFF	*Southern New Jersey Council* Millville, NJ	Designed, built, and installed artificial fish reefs in Union Lake, Millville, New Jersey to create habitat for local fish.
BENJAMIN SHAVITZ	*Greater New York Council* New York, NY	Conducted a book drive benefiting the Metropolitan Hospital Center in East Harlem, New York.
TYLER L. SIBLEY	*Connecticut Rivers Council* East Hartford, CT	Built a one-acre public dog park for the town of Middlefield, Connecticut. The park featured fenced areas for large and small dogs.
BRIAN ELLIOTT SLATKY	*Suffolk County Council* Medford, NY	Built a Holocaust memorial garden, using "green" materials, at Congregation Sholom in Babylon, New York.
ZECHARIAH D. SPARROW	*Transatlantic Council* Livomo, Italy	Refurbished the memorial to a crashed and killed Berlin Airlift pilot in Heroldishausen, Germany. Sparrow and his crew traveled 400 km to complete the project.

CENTRAL REGION		
Joshua Broze	*Blackhawk Area Council* Rockford, IL	Built a memorial garden for VFW Post 1461 in Belvidere, Illinois.
Derrick L. Gregg	*Lewis & Clark Council* Belleville, IL	Built an emergency helipad for the city of Highland, Illinois.
Timothy Crosby Judge Jr.	*Miami Valley Council* Dayton, OH	Organized a Memorial Day recognition event at the Dayton National Cemetery in Dayton, Ohio. Judge led 65 volunteers for three months sorting through 40,000 American flags to repair or retire damaged ones.
Christopher LaMarche	*Hiawathaland Council* Marquette, MI	A diver, LaMarche worked with the Coast Guard to replace the navigational buoys on a historical shipwreck, the "E.R. Williams," in Lake Michigan.
Charles J. Livesay III	*Greater St. Louis Area Council* St. Louis, MO	Organized an awareness event for the National Alopecia Areata Foundation in San Rafael, California.
Jacob Paul Edward Music	*Sagamore Council* Kokomo, IN	Renovated the playground at the St. James Lutheran Church and School in Lafayette, Indiana.
Thomas Geoffrey Reuter	*Samoset Council* Weston, WI	Created diagrams with safe-landing zones for medical helicopters serving Taylor County, Wisconsin.

BRYAN ROTHMEIER	*Northern Star Council* St. Paul, MN	Organized a send off for the local National Guard unit deploying to Iraq.
JACOB PETER SCHOWALTER	*Bay-Lakes Council* Appleton, WI	Built a bell tower for the St. Peter of Alcantara Church in Port Washington, Wisconsin.
JOHN SEWELL	*Northeast Iowa Council* Dubuque, IA	Removed one mile of barbed-wire fencing from the Lost Canyon Wildlife Area near Cascade, Iowa. The project restored ancient animal movement patterns in the region.
SOUTHERN REGION		
PRESTON F. BOYLES	*Cherokee Area Council* Bartlesville, OK	Beautified two public parks in Nowata, Oklahoma.
RICHARD DENSON	*Alabama-Florida Council* Dothan, AL	Upgraded access for those with disabilities to a playground at St. Columbia Catholic Church in Dothan, Alabama.
ALEXANDER SCOTT HUTCHINS	*Piedmont Council* Gastonia, NC	Built an honorarium to Floyd's Creek veterans in Forest City, North Carolina.
JOHN ANDERSON MORSE	*Daniel Boone Council* Asheville, NC	Created four murals for ABCCM Veterans Restoration Quarters in Asheville, North Carolina.
CHRISTOPHER A. PYLE	*Stonewall Jackson Area Council* Waynesboro, VA	Installed a memorial garden at the Emmanuel Episcopal Church in Harrisonburg, Virginia.

ZACHARY WRIGHT	*Lincoln Heritage Council* Louisville, KY	Constructed a team-building course at the Pleasant Valley Youth Camp in New Albany, Indiana.
JUSTIN AARON YOURMAN	*Tukabatchee Area Council* Montgomery, AL	Built accessible shooting platforms for those with disabilities for the Alabama Department of Conservation.
WESTERN REGION		
JOHNATHAN DOUGLAS BAIRD	*Los Padres Council* Santa Barbara, CA	Organized a multiphase organ and tissue donor awareness campaign.
EISEN CLARK GROSS	*Denver Area Council* Denver, CO	Replaced a 255-foot boardwalk over a wetland area along Bear Creek Greenbelt in Lakewood, Colorado. The 1,300-hour project required replacing hundreds of boards with new pressure-treated ones, as well as building handicap-safe areas.
MICHAEL STEPHEN POLOWSKI	*Grand Canyon Council* Phoenix, AZ	Designed and built a rosary garden for the Good Shepherd Center in Mesa, Arizona.

Each of these Eagles was the first to earn the bronze Adams Award device for their medals. Here are the first four regional winners of the gold Adams Award device (they were also council winners). In these four can be found a glimpse of what the best service projects will look like for at least the next generation of Eagles.

NORTHEASTERN REGION

Alex Griffith
Baltimore Area Council—Baltimore, MD

Alex Griffith's story, of building a playground for a children's hospital in which he was born in Krasnoyarsk, Russia began this chapter. Alex's project, which consumed nearly 2,000 hours, was carried by CNN, and was the cover of *Eagle Scout* magazine (the much-upgraded successor to the NESA *Eagletter*).

CENTRAL REGION

Justin Lee Mengon
Buckeye Council—Canton, OH
Justin Mengon renovated the Canal Fulton Heritage Society Museum building in Canal Fulton, Ohio. The tiny museum, housed in a two-century-old historic home, was once called the "smallest museum in America." Combined with an additional structure, it now holds one of the country's largest collections of canal-era artifacts. Justin and his team cleaned up the interior of the museum, restored parts of the damaged structure, and then gave the facility a new paint job—creating a regional showpiece.

SOUTHERN REGION

Torey McCleskey
Central Florida Council—Apopka, FL
Torey McCleskey, an avid diver, working with as many as 20 fellow Scouts at a time, as well as members of the local Lockheed Martin dive club, fabricated a dozen "reef balls"—sophisticated four-foot diameter, multichambered and perforated concrete domes designed to serve as the foundation of an artificial reef. Torey first had to constructed the complex molds out of fiberglass (with removable metal inserts for the perforations), then carefully fill those models with the rough liquid concrete. Meanwhile, he raised enough money to pay for the transport by truck of these heavy structures to the Reef Ball Foundation in Sarasota, where they became part of a local artificial reef construction. An interesting side note is that McCleskey, like Arthur Eldred before him, earned the Boy Scout Honor Medal for saving a life—while he was working on his Eagle.

WESTERN REGION

Patrick Talmadge Malone
Santa Clara County Council—San Jose, CA
"Tad" Malone, who had no idea his father was represented on The List in his Eagle workbook, convinced a famous Silicon Valley venture capitalist to purchase a 40-foot shipping container for him, which Tad then filled to the brim with thousands of textbooks, hundreds of used school uniforms, desks, computers, pianos, and school supplies donated from a half-dozen local public and private schools. Dubbed a "classroom in a box," Tad then convinced other Silicon Valley executives to fund the shipping of the container to Children's Town AIDS orphanage and school in Zambia, Africa—a process that took more than a year. The Zambian Minister of Education officially opened the container at a regional gathering—and the container was emptied and, converted, is now used as the school library. Tad's project, which took three years and consumed more than 3,000 hours, earned local and national network news coverage in the United States and a documentary on Zambian television.

On May 28, 2010, during the Boy Scouts of America's centennial year, at the Americanism Breakfast during the BSA National Meeting in Dallas, Texas, NESA committee member and Distinguished Eagle **Thomas Owsley** was joined on stage by Glenn and Melinda Adams to announce the first-ever national winner of the Adams Award: Alex Griffith of Baltimore's Troop 809.And as, to great applause, Alex—now much taller and lankier than the boy who had returned to L.S. Berzon City Clinical Hospital No. 20 in Krasnoyarsk, Russia—took the stage to receive his award, it was apparent that not only had he changed since completing his Eagle project, but so had Eagle Scouting itself. As he reached out to take the award box from Glenn Adams, Alex was symbolically leading his fellow Scouts out of the second great epoch of Eagle Scouting—the Service Project Era—into something new and as yet unknown.

What was already evident was that this new era, defined by the Adams Award and the finalists for the award, and coincidentally beginning on the eve of Eagle Scouting's own centennial, would have an even greater impact on Scouting and American life than the two that preceded it. And that the Eagle Scout project, the greatest youth volunteer community service initiative in history, was only just beginning.

A GATHERING OF EAGLES

WASHINGTON, DC, JULY 2010—WHEN IT IS 95 DEGREES, THE TWO GUYS YOU DON'T ENVY ARE SANTA CLAUS AND THE MAN IN THE BOMB DISPOSAL HELMET AND GEAR.[1]

There were a couple hundred of them, mostly old guys, hiding from the heat by standing under the trees on the Capitol Mall. What distinguished them from the 10,000 or so other marchers resting under the trees beside us was that the others were all under 18 years old and wearing Boy Scout uniforms, while the men hiding under the trees ranged in age up to 71 and were mostly wearing white shirts and khaki trousers.

They were the Eagles, designated as the closing contingent/grand finale of the 100th anniversary parade of the Boy Scouts of America—and their task was to march with the parade down Madison, turn right on 7th, then left for about a mile down Constitution Avenue . . . all the while trying to look like exemplars of that most famous of boyhood achievements: Eagle Scout.

Toward that end, other than the white shirt/khakis ensemble, the men were asked to wear symbols of their professions. Hence the heavily sweating, white-bearded guy in the Santa outfit. "It's all velvet," he said with dismay, holding an ice pack to his neck. And miserable as he was, it must have been nothing compared to the military officer in full camouflage fatigues who, just before the Eagles formed up, put on his thick, heavy "Hurt Locker" ensemble, complete with massive helmet.

There were others. An Army colonel in full dress uniform and ribbons. A doctor in his white smock. A couple younger guys in their old Scout uniforms, both with more than 100 merit badges each on their sashes. An old Scout in a uniform that must have been from the 1940s. Even the Bermudan diplomat, with his blazer, tie, red shorts, and knee socks, looked visibly uncomfortable. I stood by as a veteran journalist with a satchel over my shoulder and a MEDIA identification card around my neck. Several of the older men were among the last surviving Knights of Dunamis. And a few of the old-timers had been New Deal babies the last time Scouts had marched from the Capitol Mall.

Many of the men had come thousands of miles to be here and planned to head down into Virginia, to Fort A.P. Hill, after this to attend the Centennial Scout Jamboree. But, before everything else, they had to survive this parade.

After a couple hours of waiting, a young man with a bullhorn got the old Eagles to their feet and into formation on the street. The heat and humidity was overwhelming—and in the few minutes the men waited there, the hot asphalt had already begun to burn through the soles of their shoes.

Finally, with a cheer, they began to move, taking their place in the parade between an Eagle float and a big, helium-filled Eagle balloon. Somehow, the bomb disposal guy—everyone was worrying how he was managing inside his personal sauna—remained upright and moving forward. He was probably thinking that this was a cakewalk after Fallujah.

In the front row, Santa looked like he was melting. The merit badge boys seemed fresh; but some of the elderly guys in the back of the cohort already appeared soaked.

But the men held their heads high, sipped on water bottles, and tried to keep their ranks straight as they marched. That task became easier when, after the asphalt blast furnace of the intersection of 7th and Constitution, the roar of the crowd met the men.

The reviewing stand announced their arrival: "Ladies and Gentlemen, America's Eagle Scouts!"

A roar went up from the thousands lining the route. People cheered, waved, pointed out the men to their children, even saluted as the men—many now with eyes filled with tears—marched past. After all of the controversies and changes, America had never forgotten its Eagles.

Here in the twenty-first century, after more than a decade of controversy, Scouting was something many of these men rarely spoke of with their more sophisticated, right-minded friends and neighbors. And so, to now find themselves marching with legions of Scouts, representing its pinnacle of achievement, before thousands of people cheering their childhood accomplishment, was far more dumbfounding than even the heat.

At the beginning of the parade, each of the Eagles had been given a small America flag. Now, with the crowds cheering, the men held those flags just a little higher. For each of them, becoming an Eagle was one of the defining events of their lives—their first truly important achievement—and now they had been allowed to honor that award by representing it before the world.

Or at least a large part of the world. What was equally striking about the parade, besides how many people were there, was just who *wasn't* there. Unlike 1937, when a Progressive president had embraced Scouting as an ally against Depression and war, the new Progressive president (and much of Congress) during a time of Recession and war—had decided to stay away. It was a stunning, even appalling, disconnect at a time of unprecedented numbers of fatherless boys and unemployed teenagers, when the United States had an unequaled need for trained young leaders. The unspoken message at the front of Sunday's parade was: *Here is the bright young future of America*. And at the back of the parade, the message of the Eagle ranks was: *Here's what Scouting can do*. But many people were no longer listening. Perhaps one day their children would.

The Eagles understood that. And still, as they started to drip with sweat and the older guys started to limp on their bad hips and arthritic knees,

218 · MICHAEL S. MALONE

the men who had once conquered 50-mile hikes and Philmont's Tooth of Time, kept their pace and their chins up and acknowledged every cheer. Even Santa and Bomb Disposal Guy maintained their stride. Once an Eagle, always an Eagle.

As the Eagles—to their great relief—neared the end of the parade at the Washington Monument, one of the men spotted a little Cub Scout, no more than seven and one of the tiniest on the parade route, waving his own flag. The gray-haired Eagle finally broke ranks and hobbled over to the boy. The Cub and his parents were astonished to see the man.

"Here," said the Eagle, handing the boy his flag, "I'll trade you."

With the briefest hesitation, the Cub Scout made the swap.

"This was in the Parade of Eagles," the man told the boy before he turned to rejoin the march. "Keep it with you. And 10 years from now bring it to your own Eagle Court of Honor. Then pass it on."

NOTES

CHAPTER ONE: THE PHD OF BOYHOOD

1. Calculations in support of this figure can be found in Chapter 7.
2. Boy Scouts of America, *Annual Report 2010*, p. 4.
3. Virtual Boy Scout Museum, Boy Scout Stuff 1910–1919. "The World and Scouting," http://www. virtualscoutmuseum.com/timeline.html; BSA National Archives.

CHAPTER TWO: PATHFINDER

1. David C. Scott, "The Origins of BSA's 1910 Handbook." *International Scouting Collectors Association (ISCA) Journal* 6 (4; 2006): 6–13; BSA National Archives; David C. Scott, *The Scouting Party* (Irving, TX: Red Honor Press, 2010) p. 128.
2. Gary Twite, "BSA's First Eagle Scout," Eagle Scout.org (2005), http://www.eaglescout.org/history/ first_eagle.html.
3. Throughout its early history, the BSA claimed that 2 percent, then 3 percent of all registered Scouts would earn their Eagle. Today the BSA claims that number is 5 percent. The author has averaged these numbers and then weighted the total for the greater number of Eagles post-1960.
4. Approximately 2 million merit badges are currently awarded each year (http://meritbadge.org/wiki/index. php/Merit_Badges_Earned). This means a modern Scout would have to earn an impossible 300,000 merit badges to match Eldred's ratio; Terry Grove, *A Comprehensive Guide to the Eagle Scout Award* (Winter Park, FL: T. Grove, 1991), p. 18.

CHAPTER THREE: SIR KNIGHT

1. National Eagle Scout Association (NESA) archives, www.nesa.org.
2. Much of the Knights of Dunamis material for this chapter comes from three surviving notebook volumes (1925–1942, 1943–1972, and Manuals & Pamphlets of archival history from Knights of Dunamis, 1925 to 1974, including Raymond O. Hanson's correspondence, KD newsletters and flyers, and minutes from annual meetings and conferences. These volumes were provided by the Krelman Company of Pueblo,

Colorado, and were used with the author's deep appreciation.

3. US Scouting Service Project, "Merit Badge History," http://usscouts.org/mb/history.asp.

4. Ward's Book of Days, "February 22," http://www.wardsbookofdays.com/22february.htm.

5. Chuck Wills, *Boy Scouts of America: A Centennial History* (BSA and New York: DK Publishing, 2009), p. 66.

6. J.C. Leyendecker, "Weapons for Liberty," 1917. (Poster and magazine cover), http://en.wikipedia.org/wiki/File:Weapons_for_Liberty.jpg.

7. Boy Scouts of America, "History of the BSA—Highlights" (August 2009), http://www.scouting.org/about/factsheets/bsa_history.aspx; "Effect of World War I on Children in the United States: Boy Scouts," Wikipedia, http://en.wikipedia.org/wiki/Effect_of_World_War_I_on_children_in_the_United_States#Boy_Scouts.

8. History of the BSA, http://www.scouting.org/about/factsheets/bsa_history.aspx; William D. Murray, *History of the Boy Scouts of America* (New York: Boy Scouts of America, 1937), p. 112.

9. For a complete history of the BSA WWI war bond effort, see T.P. McDermott, "USA's Boy Scouts and World War I Liberty Loan Bonds," *SOSSI Journal*, May–June 2002, http://www.sossi.org/journal/scouts-ww1-liberty-bonds.pdf.

10. Boy Scouts of America, "1910," *Decades Fact Sheet*, BSA, 2010, http://scouting.org/100years/100years/SiteFiles/1000/Celebrating100Years/100yearcds/docs/FactSheets/1910.pdf.

11. Murray, *History of the Boy Scouts of America*, pp. 126–127.

12. Boy Scouts of America, "Senior Scouts brochure," 1938.

13. "History and Growth of Dunamis," *Dunamis Doings*, April 1934, p. 1.

14. Ibid., p. 2

15. Raymond O. Hanson, "Knights of Dunamis Manual of Ritual," 1936, p. 20.

16. Robert Peterson, "Gathering of Eagles," *Scouting*, May–June 2000, p. 13.

17. *Knights of Dunamis (1925–1942)*, from contemporary letters and correspondence.

18. "Program Guide of Activities for Local Chapters issued by the Grand Chapter of the Knights of Dunamis," January 1936.

19. "Dunamis Doings," June 1935, p. 7.

20. Boy Scouts of America, *The Guide Book of Senior Scouting* (New York, BSA, 1938), http://www.seniorscoutinghistory.org/archive/NationalDocs/3442.pdf.

21. Peterson, "Gathering of Eagles," p. 13.

22. Indy Nelson, comp. *The History of Camp Royaneh, Operated by the San Francisco Bay Area Council* (2009), p. 10, http://sfbac-history.org/History%20Of%20Royaneh.pdf.

23. Boy Scouts of America, San Francisco Bay Area Council. "Knights of Dunamis, National Eagle Scout Honor Society History," San Francisco Bay Area Council History, http://sfbac-history.org/SFC-KOD.html.

CHAPTER FOUR: FIRE AND ICE

1. The primary source for the Siple section is Patricia Potter Wilson and Roger Leslie, *Eagle on Ice* (New York: Vantage Press, 2008).

2. Those who have read the history of polar exploration will know that there is some question whether Byrd and Bennett really did fly over the North Pole.

3. *Eagle on Ice*, p. 14.

4. *Eagle on Ice*, p. 28.

5. John T. McQuiston, "Milt Caniff, 81, creator of 'Steve Canyon' dies", *New York Times*, April 4, 1988, http://www.nytimes.com/1988/04/04/obituaries/milton-caniff-81-creator-of-steve-canyon-dies.html.

6. West Texas Scouting History, "Eagle Scouts," http://www.westtexasscoutinghistory.net/award_eaglepage.html.

7. National Eagle Scout Association, *Eagle Scout Roll of Honor: National Eagle Scout Registry*, "The History of the Eagle Scout Award," p. xiv, http://www.nesa.org/PDF/58-435.pdf.

8. Wills, *Boy Scouts of America: A Centennial History*, p.106.

9. Christopher Wagner, "Boys' Historic Uniforms: the 1930s," Historic Boy's Uniform Chronology Pages, http://histclo.com/youth/youth/chron/c1930.htm.

10. "The History of the Eagle Scout Award," p. xiv.

11. Wills, *Boy Scouts of America: A Centennial History*, pp. 114–116.

12. "National Geographic Society Presents Hubbard Medal to Dr. Paul A. Siple," *National Geographic*, June 1958, p. 793.

13. Ibid.

CHAPTER FIVE: SHOOTING THE MOON

1. The details of the Apollo 11 moon landing are from the official NASA archives, posted at The History Place, "Apollo 11," http://www.historyplace.com/unitedstates/apollo11/land.htm; orbital data from NASA, "Apollo 11," http://www.nasa.gov/mission_pages/apollo/missions/apollo11.html.

2. Ibid.

3. Wills, *Boy Scouts of America: A Centennial History*, pp. 111–112.

4. "The History of the Eagle Scout Award," p. xvi, http://www.nesa.org/PDF/58-435.pdf.

5. Ibid., p. xviii.

6. Ibid., p. xvii.

7. Wills, *Boy Scouts of America: A Centennial History*, p. 127.

8. Ibid.

9. Ibid., chart, p. 122.

10. "Scouting Quotes," Boy Scouts of America, Orange County Council, http://www.ocbsa.org/category/about-ocbsa/scouting-quotes.

11. "Walmart," Wikipedia, http://en.wikipedia.org/wiki/Walmart.

12 Grand Teton Council, "Boys' Life Magazine," http://www.grandtetoncouncil.org/index.cfm?pageid=506.

13. Wills, *Boy Scouts of America: A Centennial History*, p. 122.

14. Ibid.

15. "National Scout jamboree (Boy Scouts of America)," Wikipedia, http://en.wikipedia.org/wiki/National_Scout_jamboree_(Boy_Scouts_of_America).

16. "The History of the Eagle Scout Award," p. xvi, http://www.nesa.org/PDF/58-435.pdf.

17. Boy Scouts of America, "History of the BSA—Highlights" (August 2009), http://www.scouting.org/about/factsheets/bsa_history.aspx.

18. "The History of the Eagle Scout Award," p. xvi, http://www.nesa.org/PDF/58-435.pdf.

19. "Eagle Scout Requirements," http://www.troop97.net/bseagle.htm.

20. Gerald R. Ford Presidential Library & Museum, "Gerald R. Ford Biography," http://www.ford.utexas.edu/grf/fordbiop.asp.

21. "Leslie Lynch King, Jr.," Wikipedia, http://en.wikipedia.org/wiki/Leslie_Lynch_King,_Sr.

22. Mark Ray, "Eagle Scouts Welcome President Gerald R. Ford Home," *Scouting,* March–April 2007.

23. GoDeke.org, "Brother Gerald R. Ford, Jr., Omicron '35 Remembered," http://www.godeke.org/History/Gerald_Ford_Remembered.htm.

24. "Gerald Ford—Football Player," *Packerville U.S.A.,* October 31, 2007, http://packerville.blogspot.com/2007_10_01_archive.html.

25. Gleaves Whitney, "Model Ford," *National Review Online,* November 14, 2006, http://www.nationalreview.com/articles/219249/model-ford/gleaves-whitney.

26. James Cannon, "Gerald R. Ford," PBS.org, Character Above All, http://www.pbs.org/newshour/character/essays/ford.html.

27. "President Gerald R. Ford Remarks on Taking Office," The History Place, Great Speeches Collection, August 9, 1974, http://www.historyplace.com/speeches/ford-sworn.htm.

28. "Remarks by President Gerald Ford on Taking the Oath of Office as President," watergate.info, August 9, 1974, http://watergate.info/ford/ford-swearing-in.shtml.

29. "Jimmy Carter Remembers Gerald Ford," CNN (Transcript), January 3, 2007, http://www.jimmycarterlibrary.gov/documents/carter_ford.pdf.

30. John R. Fulton, Jr., "Eagle Scouts Welcome Gerald Ford Home," *Scouting,* Mar–Apr 2007, http://www.scoutingmagazine.org/issues/0703/a-ford.html.

31. Bryan Wendell, "Adventure Base 100, Vol. 18 Grand Rapids, Michigan," Bryan on Scouting (blog), May 24, 2010, http://blog.scoutingmagazine.org/category/adventure-base-100/page/2.

32. Phil Gioia, interview by the author, January, 2011.

33. Ibid.

34. Ibid.

35. "National Scout jamboree (Boy Scouts of America)," Wikipedia, http://en.wikipedia.org/wiki/National_Scout_jamboree_(Boy_Scouts_of_America).

36. Wills, *Boy Scouts of America: A Centennial History,* pp. 161, 164.

37. Eric M. Jones, "One Small Step," Apollo 11 Lunar Surface Journal, http://www.hq.nasa.gov/alsj/a11/a11.step.html.

38. Ibid.

CHAPTER SIX: LOST AND FOUND

1. Wills, Boy Scouts of America: A Centennial History, p. 187.

2. Ibid., p. 159.

3. Robert Peterson, "The Perfect Book for a Desert Island," *Scouting,* September 1999, http://www.

scoutingmagazine.org/issues/9909/a-book.html.

4. Wills, *Boy Scouts of America: A Centennial History,* p. 171.

5. Ibid., p. 173.

6. Ibid., p. 171.

7. "The Nation: Windmill Power," *Time*, Dec. 2, 1974, http://www.time.com/time/magazine/article/0,9171,945280,00.html.

8. Steve Henning, comp., "Merit Badges, Past and Present, and Their Evolution," Henning's Scouters' Pages, http://www.scouters.us/homemb.html; Terry Grove, A Comprehensive Guide to the Eagle Scout Award, (Winter Park, FL: T. Grove, 2004) p. 19.

9. Ibid.

10. "Distinguished Eagle Scout Award," Wikipedia, http://en.wikipedia.org/wiki/Distinguished_Eagle_Scout_Award.

11. Wills, Boy Scouts of America: A Centennial History, p. 181.

12. Ibid., p.188.

13. "National Scout jamboree (Boy Scouts of America)," Wikipedia, http://en.wikipedia.org/wiki/National_Scout_jamboree_(Boy_Scouts_of_America).

14. Robert Peterson, "Bill Hillcourt—Still Going Strong on the Scouting Trail," *Scouting*, September 1985, p. 26.

15. Wills, *Boy Scouts of America: A Centennial History*, p. 147.

16. Ibid., p. 147.

17. "National Scout jamboree (Boy Scouts of America)," Wikipedia, http://en.wikipedia.org/wiki/National_Scout_jamboree_(Boy_Scouts_of_America).

18. Wills, *Boy Scouts of America: A Centennial History,* p. 196.

19. Ibid.

20. "William Hillcourt," Wikipedia, http://en.wikipedia.org/wiki/William_Hillcourt.

21. *Scout Handbook,* eighth edition, 1973, pp. 79–81.

22. Wills, *Boy Scouts of America: A Centennial History*, pp. 199–200.

23. Richard H. Truly (Vice Admiral, USN, Ret.), NASA Astronaut (former). Biographical data, National Aeronautics and Space Administration, http://www.jsc.nasa.gov/Bios/htmlbios/truly-rh.html.

24. Peggy Mihelich, "Adventure Defines Steve Fossett" CNN, September 4, 2007, http://articles.cnn.com/2007-09-04/tech/fossett.profile_1_single-engine-turbofan-aircraft-solo-balloon-flight-steve-fossett?_s=PM:TECH.

25. "The History of the Eagle Scout Award," p. xvi, http://www.nesa.org/PDF/58-435.pdf.

26. Boy Scouts of America, "History of the BSA—Highlights" (August 2009), http://www.scouting.org/about/factsheets/bsa_history.aspx.

27. "Nickelodeon Magazine Interviews Steven Spielberg." *Nickelodeon Magazine.* http://www.nick.com/shows/nick_mag/lookInside/index.jhtml?pagenum=8.

CHAPTER SEVEN: GOLDEN EAGLES

1. "Boy Scout Turns 'Mud Pit' into a $60K Playground," September 10, 2009, CNN, http://www.cnn.com/2009/LIVING/wayoflife/09/10/cnnheroes.alex.griffith.index.html?iref=newssearch#cnnSTCVideo.

2. Ibid.

3. Ibid.

4. Ibid.

5. Ibid.

6. Boy Scouts of America, "History of the BSA—Highlights" (August 2009), http://www.scouting.org/about/factsheets/bsa_history.aspx.

7. "Number of Eagles per Year," Boy Scouts of America, NESA; Jon C. Halter, "A Plan and a Vision," Scouting, September 1998, http://www.scoutingmagazine.org/issues/9809/a-plan.html.

8. "Number of Eagle Scouts Year by Year (2000–2005)," College Confidential, Dec. 1, 2006, http://talk.collegeconfidential.com/parents-forum/269133-number-eagle-scouts-year-year.html; "Number of Eagle Scouts by Year (1991–1998)," US Scouting Service Project, http://usscouts.org/usscouts/eagle/numbers.asp.

9. Ibid.

10. Jay Mechling, On My Honor: Boy Scouts and the Making of American Youth" (University of Chicago Press, 2001), web excerpt: http://www.press.uchicago.edu/Misc/Chicago/517047.html.

11. Ibid.

12. "Boy Scouts Kick Out Teen for Not Believing in God," UPI, July 21, 1985, http://articles.sun-sentinel.com/keyword/boy-scouts/featured/5.

13. "Man With Down Syndrome Receives Eagle Scout Honor," WBAL-TV, October 20, 2008, http://www.wbaltv.com/r/17762299/detail.html.

14. "Lawrence Earns Rank of Eagle Scout," Bandon Western World, February 10, 2011, p. 1.

15. "The Coach's Corner," The Varsity Letter, June 2010, p. 4, http://varsity.sdicbsa.org/PDF/newsletter/JuneVarsityLetter.pdf.

16. Mark Ray, "NESA President Steve Fossett: A Tribute," Eagletter, Winter 2007, http://www.nesa.org/eagletter/2007-W.pdf.

17. Peggy Mihelich, "Adventure Defines Steve Fossett," CNN Tech, Sept. 4, 2007, http://articles.cnn.com/2007-09-04/tech/fossett.profile_1_single-engine-turbofan-aircraft-solo-balloon-flight-steve-fossett?_s=PM:TECH.

18. "Steve Fossett quotes," ThinkExist.com, http://thinkexist.com/quotes/steve_fossett.

19. John C. Halter, "Honoring Yesterday, Preparing for Tomorrow," Scouting, Sept. 2005, http://www.scoutingmagazine.org/issues/0509/a-hnor.html.

POSTSCRIPT: A GATHERING OF EAGLES

1. Adapted from Michael S. Malone "A Gathering of Eagles," PJMedia.com, July 2010.

ABOUT THE AUTHOR

Michael S. Malone is one of the world's best-known technology writers. He has covered Silicon Valley and high-tech for more than 25 years, beginning with the San Jose Mercury News as the nation's first daily high-tech reporter, where he was twice nominated for the Pulitzer Prize for investigative reporting. His articles and editorials have appeared in such publications as The Wall Street Journal, The Economist and Fortune, and for two years he was a columnist for The New York Times. He was editor of Forbes ASAP, the world's largest-circulation business-tech magazine, at the height of the dot-com boom. Malone is the author or co-author of nearly twenty award-winning books, notably the best-selling "The Virtual Corporation", "Bill and Dave", and "The Future Arrived Yesterday". Malone has also hosted three nationally syndicated public television interview series and co-produced the Emmy-nominated primetime PBS miniseries on social entrepreneurs, "The New Heroes." As an entrepreneur, Malone was a founding shareholder of eBay, Siebel Systems (sold to Oracle) and Qik (sold to Skype), and is currently co-founder and director of PatientKey Inc. An Eagle Scout, Malone was a chapter commander of the Knights of Dunamis and on the staff of the 1973 National Jamboree. He is currently an assistant Scoutmaster of Troop 466 in Sunnyvale, California, president of the Silicon Valley chapter of NESA, and a member of the Santa Clara County Council board of directors. Malone holds an MBA from Santa Clara University, where he is currently an adjunct professor. He is also an associate fellow of the Said Business School at Oxford University, and is a Distinguished Friend of Oxford.

INDEX

For more information contact:

WindRush Publishers

214-352-7698
www.4percentbook.com

ISBN: 978-0-9859097-0-3